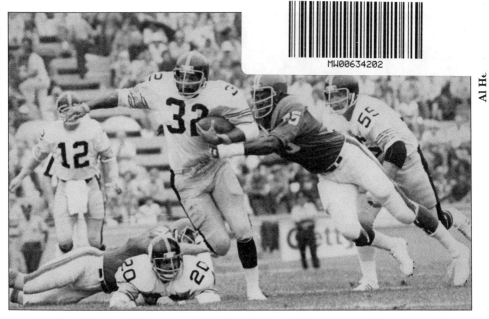

Al He

Rocky Bleier (20) clears way for Franco Harris on 16-yard rush
Aug. 30, 1975

Franco & Rocky

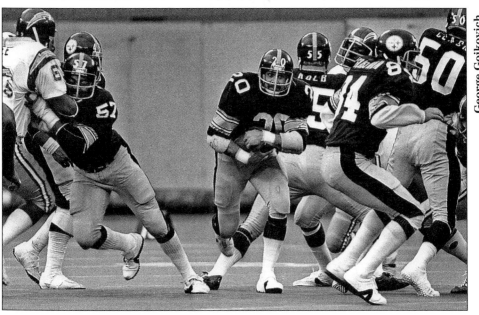

George Gojkovich

Sam Davis (57) delivers block to open hole for Rocky Bleier(20)

1

Jim O'Brien

JIM O'BRIEN

PITTSBURGH STEELERS

Franco, Rocky & Friends

It pays to be a good guy

Artwork by Marty Wolfson

Books By Jim O'Brien

COMPLETE HANDBOOK OF PRO BASKETBALL 1970–71
COMPLETE HANDBOOK OF PRO BASKETBALL 1971–72
ABA ALL-STARS
PITTSBURGH: THE STORY OF THE CITY OF CHAMPIONS
HAIL TO PITT: A SPORTS HISTORY OF
THE UNIVERSITY OF PITTSBURGH
DOING IT RIGHT
WHATEVER IT TAKES
MAZ AND THE '60 BUCS
REMEMBER ROBERTO
PENGUIN PROFILES
DARE TO DREAM
KEEP THE FAITH
WE HAD 'EM ALL THE WAY
HOMETOWN HEROES
GLORY YEARS
THE CHIEF
STEELERS FOREVER
ALWAYS A STEELER
WITH LOVE AND PRIDE
LAMBERT
FANTASY CAMP
STEELER STUFF
PITTSBURGH PROUD
IMMACULATE REFLECTIONS
A WINNING WAY
GOLDEN ARMS
FROM A TO Z
LOOKING UP
FRANCO, ROCKY & FRIENDS

To order copies of these titles directly from the publisher, send $29.95 for each edition. Please send additional $3.75 to cover shipping and handling charges per book. Contact publisher regarding availability and prices of all books in Pittsburgh Proud series, or to request an order form. You can still order the following: Doing It Right, We Had 'Em All The Way, Hometown Heroes, Glory Years, The Chief, Lambert, Fantasy Camp, With Love and Pride, Immaculate Reflections, Golden Arms, From A to Z and Looking Up.

Dedication

To my dad, Dan O'Brien.

After hearing so many stories from Steelers about their fathers punishing them as kids, I realize how fortunate I was to have my dad, who only spanked me twice when he caught me smoking cigarettes at age 10 and 12. He was never in my face. Smoking and drinking helped hurry my dad's demise from emphysema at age 63. I don't smoke and I drink iced tea most of the time.

Dan O'Brien with baby Jim.

Dan, Carole, Jim, Dad and Pal.

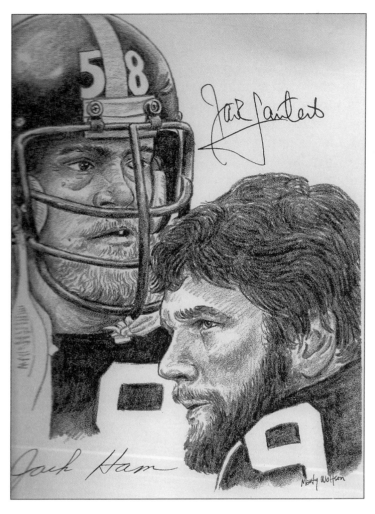

Artwork by Marty Wolfson

Published by James P. O'Brien — Publishing
P.O. Box 12580
Pittsburgh PA 15241
Phone (412) 221-3580

First printing, June 2019
Manufactured in the United States
Printed by R.R. Donnelley Printing Inc.
Pittsburgh, PA 15213
Typography by Cold-Comp
91 Green Glen Drive
Pittsburgh, PA 15227
ISBN 978-1-886348-17-2

All autographs in this
book are reproductions.
Some stories are reprinted
with permission.

Graphic design and
layout by
Cathy Pawlowski

**Cover artwork by
Bob Weaver**

Introduction

By ANDY RUSSELL

Whenever I was organizing any kind of celebrity fund-raiser I could always count on Franco and Rocky to show up. They supported all my efforts and they were always there for me.

It took me awhile to appreciate the way Franco Harris could run with a football. I remember us veterans being critical of him when he first came to camp. He just didn't look that good. One day we were holding a scrimmage and he came out my way on the wing. I was at outside linebacker and I had a clear shot at him. I told myself, "Now I'm going to put a real hit on this rookie." I came at him hard and I hit the ground with nothing in my hands. He just made a move and left me hanging out there. That's when I first realized that Franco was something different, something special.

When you're at linebacker, you're looking into the backfield and trying to figure out what's coming your way. You know the down and yardage situation. You know what they like to do in those situations. You've studied the film and you know their tendencies. It can be quite the cerebral challenge. I thought that was one of my strengths.

Franco was a running back who was doing just as much thinking about what the opposition might do. He was trying to figure out where you might be going. He was unique. Jim Brown didn't do what he did. Brown tried to run over people and he was pretty good at it.

Franco would hit a hole and then back up. He'd stop in the middle of his move. He might dart outside, or move through another hole next door. He had an ability to do that. He had great quickness. He didn't

7

have the speed of a Tony Dorsett, but he was deceptive and could find daylight.

They are always timing football players in the 40-yard dash. I think it's more important how fast you can run five yards, how fast you can explode in five yards. After all, how often does anyone run 40 yards in a football game?

I remember Rocky was selling insurance in the off-season in Chicago after he'd come back from Vietnam and had been with the team a few years. His Notre Dame connections are strong there. He was concerned about his status with the Steelers. Chuck Noll had told him he ought to retire.

Rocky didn't know what to do. He called me during the off-season and told me what was going on. He told me that Noll had essentially told him not to come back. I could feel the pain in his voice. This was before Rocky became a real productive running back for the team. The first year he was with the team when he came back from Vietnam he didn't play. He was just rehabilitating himself. The next year he played on special teams. He was not really playing much in the backfield. It wasn't until 1971 that he really made his move.

I told him he ought to report to camp and make Noll cut him. I told him that the people in front of him could get hurt, or that he could get traded. But I told him he shouldn't just quit.

Rocky started lifting weights in earnest and he built himself up to a rock solid 235 pounds. When he came to camp, he ran the 40 faster than anyone else. It was unreal. He ran a 4.5. Who would have thought he could do that?

The fastest guy on the team, by the way, for five to ten yards, was Jack Ham. He made tackles that Lambert and I could only make if we were stretched out. Ham was the fastest striker. Franco could explode too. He had quickness and vision.

Preston Pearson was ahead of him. He was awesome. He could do everything. Preston got his nose out of joint because he wanted to be the No. 1 runner. Franco was the featured runner. So Preston stopped blocking for Franco. You could see it on the film.

Dick Hoak (the backfield coach) made a comment that when Rocky was in there Franco was picking up first downs. All of a sudden, Preston is on the bench and Rocky is starting. Rocky had this explosiveness for five yards. It came from his weightlifting.

In 1974, Rocky makes a big play in the fourth quarter to score a touchdown against the Vikings in the Super Bowl in New Orleans. Now he's a star.

He and Franco complemented each other in the backfield. Franco has grown as a person. He's the one who calls to set up a dinner with some of our teammates. When some of us are at the Super Bowl on our own, he'll be the one who calls in advance and sets up a luncheon or dinner for us to get together somewhere. He's good at getting everybody together. "Let's have dinner." Or, "Let's have lunch." He wants us to take time out to bond and to stay together. He makes it happen. I don't do it; I don't think about it. He makes a point to get us all together.

I was watching something about Franco on television one day, and it showed him in his football-playing days at Penn State. He wore number 34 then. Of course, when he came to the Steelers he couldn't get 34 because I had it. They wouldn't give a number that a veteran was wearing to a rookie. So, he got 32. I never realized that he had to change numbers when he came here because I had his number. Seems funny now.

Rock has always been very open to relationships. He makes a living speaking about the game and his teammates. What he learned from the experience. He enjoys getting together with the guys. Rock enjoys getting together with anyone.

Looking back, it wasn't all wins. We lost, too. We didn't always win the challenges. Buddy Dial has died at age 71. He was a teammate of mine when I first came to the Steelers. He was a great pass-catcher and a good guy. He was a lot of fun. He was a good teammate. Now he's gone. It makes you think. We lost Ernie Holmes. I lost my closest friend, Ray Mansfield, too many years ago. We experienced so much together, especially off the field. We had the same mindset, the same interests, and a lust for mountains to climb. Steve Furness is gone, and a few guys who weren't here that long are gone as well. It gets you thinking.

I remember when Noll first came to the team in 1969. He denied this story later on, but I remember we had a team meeting and he told us that most of us would be gone in a year. He said it wasn't because we didn't care or didn't try. He told us we just weren't fast enough, that we just weren't good enough.

Only five of us were still on the team when we made the playoffs the first time. That was me, Mansfield, Rocky, Sam Davis and Bobby Walden. Just five survived the coming of Noll.

So we had a special bond. It's important for us, I think, to stay close. That's why I wish Jack Lambert would come around. I have always said that Lambert was the best middle linebacker of our era, better than Butkus and Nitschke. I think Ham was the best linebacker of the bunch on our team.

We missed Jack when we had the 75th anniversary reunion. He would probably tell you he was watching one of his kids' teams playing that day. I know how important that is to him. One time, when he was with us, I said, "Who would have thought Jack Lambert would be the best father among us?" Jack snarled at me and asked, "What do you mean?" You know how he'd say something like that. I said, 'Hey, Jack, it's a compliment.' I hear he mows the grass and lines the fields where his kids play. He umpires. He helps any way he can. And he's home a lot. I respect that. But I wish he would feel as strongly about staying close to his teammates on the Steelers. That's important too. We'd like to see him. We shared a lot together. We achieved a lot together.

Jim O'Brien is clearly the true chronicler of Pittsburgh sports teams and events, safeguarding our so meaningful sports folklore.

Jim has painstakingly worked to preserve our Steelers/Pirates/Penguins/Panthers past. Jim O'Brien is our Pittsburgh sports historian and certainly our Steelers' historian. He has kept alive the glorious past of our great teams and done it with plain old hard work—through research, exhaustive interviews and penetrating insights.

Jim was born and bred in Pittsburgh. During his sophomore year he would have a city-side internship with *The Pittsburgh Press*, having won a *Wall Street Journal* scholarship, and before his senior year a summer internship on the sports staff of *The Philadelphia Evening Bulletin*. During his senior year at the University of Pittsburgh, he and Pitt publicist Beano Cook started *Pittsburgh Weekly Sports* in 1963, which was my rookie season with the Steelers. Later, Jim would write for *The Miami News* and *The New York Post*, experiences that made him uniquely qualified to practice his trade, digging behind the scenes to determine what set those great Steelers and other Pittsburgh sports teams apart from the pack.

Andy Russell

11

THE 56TH

ANNUAL

CALGARY ITALIAN

SPORTSMEN'S DINNER

ASSOCIATION

THURSDAY, MAY 10, 2

Franco Harris

Flying with Franco is the only way to go to Calgary, Canada

Franco Harris held up his right hand, asking an audience of 800 men, most of them Italian-Canadians, to hold on, he'd be right back. His emotions had gotten the best of him when he was talking about his late mother, and trips they'd taken together to her native Italy. He was signaling for a time-out.

He was only two seats to my left at a round-table exchange of stories and reflections, with Al Vento Jr., the son of the man who helped form Franco's Italian Army back in 1972—Franco's rookie season with the Pittsburgh Steelers, and the year of the iconic "Immaculate Reception," sitting in a high chair between us.

Tears formed in the always-luminous dark eyes of Franco, as he tried to compose himself and find his way back to his story, the way he once found daylight when he was carrying a football like few others in the history of the game.

"Hold on," he said twice.

There was no other sound in the gymnasium of Notre Dame High School in Calgary, Alberta Canada. It is a city in the western end of the country, with rivers cutting through it, and it is much like Pittsburgh in that respect, and on this particular night last month it was an extension of Steeler Nation.

Even the fans in the audience who had identified themselves proudly as fans of the Dallas Cowboys were on Franco's side and the Steelers' side.

Franco asked for forgiveness for getting so emotional. But then, after all, it was only four days away from Mother's Day and many of us were thinking about our mothers and even our dads, because one thought led to another.

One of the men in the audience, a high school football coach, told me later, "That was a special moment. For him to share that story, and his tears, before 800 strangers was really something I won't soon forget."

For me, personally, that evening and the three days I spent in Calgary in the company of Franco, Al Vento Jr., Jeffrey Duggan, and our host Frank Mafrica and his friends, is an adventure I won't soon forget. It was truly a once-in-a-lifetime experience.

* * *

Franco, age 68 at the time, and Rocco Mediate, age 57, a well-known and popular pro golfer from Greensburg, Pennsylvania, were the headliners for the program at the 56th annual Calgary Italian Sportsmen's Dinner. The price per ticket was $350, to fund college scholarships for five young men of Italian heritage. It's always a sellout.

I was on the stage to share some stories about the Steelers, the Immaculate Reception, and Franco and to have some fun with all the Italians as one of the few Irishmen in the room. I told them about all the Italian quarterbacks from Western Pennsylvania who played in the Canadian Football League, such as John Congemi, Tommy Clements, Bernie Faloney and Vito "Babe" Parilli, and a few others such as Joe Zuger of Homestead and Ron "The Little General" Lancaster of Clairton, a 5-5 signal-caller who set records in his 16 seasons in the CFL. Yes, he was about the same size as Myron Cope.

Looking about the audience, I said, "This looks like

a casting call for The Sopranos." Most laughed at that line. Some didn't.

Jeffrey Duggan, who drives a Blitzburg bus for Frank Mafrica and Joe Ferraro and their friends when they come to Pittsburgh about five or six times each year to see their beloved Steelers in action at Heinz Field, offered a fan's perspective of the Steelers and Pittsburgh. He's an Irishman from Lawrenceville and, let's just say, has led an interesting life. He's been in and out of jail, on and off the wagon, a recovering alcoholic. He is fun to be with. He talked less than anyone on our sojourn.

Duggan stores this black and gold van in Pittsburgh and drives Mafrica, Ferraro and Co. around Pittsburgh when they come to town. It has images of many Steelers and local media on its yellow interior and exterior, signatures everywhere, and it attracts a lot of attention wherever Duggan drives it.

I first met these men about five or six years earlier when they were shopping for more Steelers stuff and bought many of my books at Hometowne Sports at Station Square, since relocated to the heart of the South Side. They asked me to write my signature with a Sharpie on the interior wall of their Blitzburg Bus. Let's just say my signature was in good company. "You were always so nice to us," said Mafrica when he called to invite me to his dinner in Calgary. Rocky Bleier believes it pays to be nice and this was a great example of that.

* * *

Frank Mafrica has a "man cave" in his spacious home high above Calgary in a community much like our Mt. Washington, only all the homes in his neighborhood cost several million to own. His room is nearly as good as going to any of the sports hall of fame complexes in our country.

There are framed and signed jerseys of some of

the greatest athletes in football, baseball, basketball and soccer, the jerseys of Jim Brown, Johnny Unitas, Joe Montana, Magic Johnson, Jerry West, Pele, Ted Williams, Mickey Mantle. And so many more. There is a replica—a real surprise to Franco—of the statue of the Steelers' star making the "Immaculate Reception" that visitors see when they arrive at Pittsburgh International Airport. It stands next to a statue of George Washington.

Franco shared a photo with me of him standing next to the George Washington statue at the Pittsburgh International Airport that is in his Smartphone.

Mafrica's wife lives in another home nearby. I know my wife would leave me, too, if I had that much sports memorabilia on display. He and his wife still date and go everywhere together. His office at Maf-Worx, a cement and concrete company he owns in Calgary, has more sports memorabilia on display, and so does a small restaurant next door that he added for the convenience of him and his staff, and some workers at nearby companies.

We rode around Calgary in stretch limousines and ate Italian food at the best restaurants in town. I had the best soup of my life. Mr. Mafrica's good friend, Joe Ferraro, sent a seven-passenger private jet airplane to pick us up in Pittsburgh, and take us to Calgary with a fuel stop in Fargo, North Dakota.

If you Google Citation Ultra/CFUBQ you can view images of the airplane. If you watch the TV series "Criminal Minds," and know what the airplane looks like that the police agency uses you will have a good idea of what our transportation looked like.

It's the first time in my life I ever flew in a private jet. For me, it was a big deal. As a sports-minded kid growing up in Glenwood and Hazelwood, I never saw

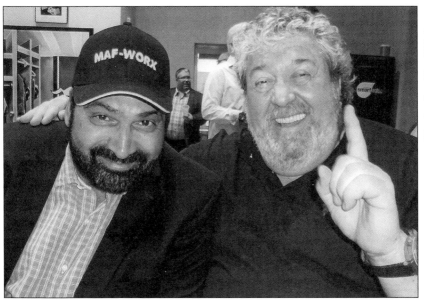

Photos by Jim O'Brien

Franco Harris and his Italian-Canadian friend Frank Mafrica enjoy visit to Frank's office and to his home, which has a mini-museum of sports memorabilia, including a   replica of the statue of Franco's famous "Immaculate Reception" catch in 1972 AFC playoffs.

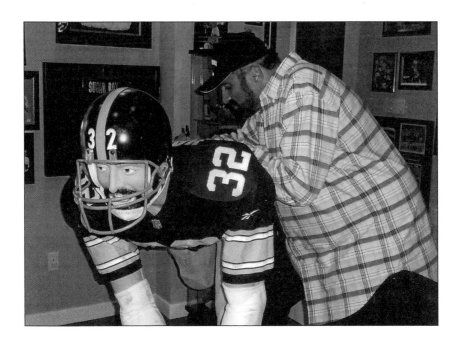

this coming.

Our pilot's name was Felix Nwachukwu, originally from Nigeria, and the co-pilot was Dave Harper, and Dave made sure all of us were comfortable and properly hydrated and fed during the six hours in the air.

Several of us confessed that we had a sense of foreboding about this trip. Al Vento Jr., who lives in West Homestead and operates a popular pizza restaurant in East Liberty, told us he thought about the airplane crash that took the lives of Richie Valens, Buddy Holly and the Big Bopper.

I thought about that, and because we were flying with Franco, I thought about the tragic death in an airplane crash of Roberto Clemente. It didn't help that when I got to my hotel room, there was an excerpt from "The Buddy Holly Story" on the television. I am not fearful of flying, but I had not been keen on flying in small airplanes. I remember flying from Las Vegas to Los Angeles once in a small aircraft and coming back in a rental car as a cautionary move.

As it turned out, the flight with Franco & Co. was uneventful. Most of the time it didn't even feel like the airplane was in motion. The trip was about six hours each way and we were talking the whole time.

It was good to hear that Andrew McCutchen, who came back to PNC Park with the San Francisco Giants for the first time, said he always hated flying from Philadelphia to Pittsburgh because of the turbulent air. It was good to see McCutchen cry, as it was when Marc-Andre Fleury cried when he came back to PPG Paints Arena for the first time.

There is crying in baseball, no matter what Tom Hanks told us in "A League of Their Own." And, thankfully, in football and hockey as well.

I would bet that no member of the media, not even

George Gojkovich

Myron Cope, ever spent six hours in the company of Franco Harris. That was six hours each way on our Canadian adventure. And I felt like I had Franco Harris all to myself.

I have known Franco since 1979 when I came onto the Steelers' beat for *The Pittsburgh Press*, but I know him so much better today. Franco is a fine fellow. He was so friendly and warm with everyone he met. As one of them said, "He's the real deal."

He is so thoughtful and I felt comfortable in his company, sitting just across from me for a total of nine or ten hours, counting limo time. It was like being in a huddle with Harris in his playing days with the Steelers, up close and personal. When I got in and out of tight spaces, like the limo and the airplane, Franco lent a helping hand. I had the feeling he was looking after me.

He is a man in motion. He took a walk in the neighborhood after every meal. He no longer eats meat and he is conscientious about his diet.

When he was telling us about one of his trips to Italy, he boasted that he had been blessed by Pope Francis. "How cool is that?" he asked us with a warm smile.

There was an empty seat or two on the airplane, and I wish you and one of your friends or loved ones could have accompanied us on this once-in-a-lifetime excursion.

Franco was a reluctant interview when he was playing for the Steelers. He lisps on occasion, much like another Penn State alumnus, Jack Ham, who was a teammate on the Steelers. Franco sprinkles "you know" in his conversation like many people do today, and you have to be careful not to follow his lead when he slips into that speech mode.

He was never cooperative with anybody who

wanted to interview him for a book, but he got better about that.

He and Rocky Bleier both had such good stories, and you wanted to get it right. Franco became aware that I was always looking for stories, and did his best to tap dance around my questions.

"I will always cherish and value the special bonds that I formed with my teammates," said Franco. "It was truly an honor for me to take the field with them. I am also appreciative of my entire family and all the coaches who helped me along the way. I want to thank the Steeler Nation, the best fans in the world."

Franco forced a trade to the Seattle Seahawks for his final season in the NFL, but was released in mid-season, something that never would have happened had he stayed in Pittsburgh.

"Yes, I wish I would've finished up with the Steelers."

* * *

Rocco Mediate met us in Calgary. He met us at the Kensington Riverside Inn, a boutique hotel. There were five plush pillows on my king-sized bed and I knew, if anything bad happened, I had gone out in style. The only thing that was missing was my wife Kathie. I didn't sleep well.

Mediate made a point at the dinner that stays with me. "I was ten years old at the time of the Immaculate Reception," said Mediate, when it was his turn at the shared mic. "That's when it all started for the Steelers.

"That's when Franco's Italian Army got under-way and when Steelers' Nation got started. Fans from everywhere, even here in Canada, adopted the Steelers as their favorite football team. All the Steelers have today started at that time."

Joe Greene often said that "the Steelers didn't win

shit until Franco came along."

We returned to Pittsburgh via New Jersey. Franco was meeting his wife, Dana, in New York City. He was among those people who were being honored with a special Statue of Liberty Ellis Island Award, given to achievers whose parent or parents had come to this country through Ellis Island, known as the Gateway to America for over 15 million immigrants.

* * *

I got to know Franco and his friends better on this trip. We were never treated better and now I think that traveling in a private jet is the only way to go. Especially if you fly with Franco and his friends.

We had a lot of time to talk on the trip to and from Fargo and Calgary and back, Franco facing me from three feet away. When my wife Kathie asked Franco what that was like, at a party at Heinz Field on the eve of the Josh Miller UPMC Celebrity Golf Outing, he said, "It was fine, but now I need therapy."

During the flight, I wanted to ask Franco if he felt like he was sitting in an electric chair.

We talked about many topics on the trip. Franco said his first love in sports was playing basketball. "I played basketball and football and ran track in high school," he said. "Sometimes I think that people are forced at a young age to select one sport and they might pick the wrong one."

He thought his kid brother Giuseppe had the skill set to be a big-league baseball player. "But he wanted to be a football player, and it didn't work out that well."

Lots of quarterbacks were good at several sports. The list includes Otto Graham, Dan Marino, Joe Namath, Johnny Lujack, Arnold Galiffa—"The Pope" earned 11 letters in sports at Army—Joe Montana and Terrelle Pryor and Kyler Murray of Oklahoma U., a

No. 1 pick in baseball and football.

Basketball players picked up on tennis in a hurry and I personally watched the early development of Julius Erving, Billy Knight, Connie Hawkins, Billy Cunningham and Rick Barry. "So Barry played tennis," said my wife. "Can you imagine being his doubles partner?"

I knew firsthand that NBA coaches Red Auerbach and Red Holzman were crafty tennis players, and that Kevin Loughery and Rod Thorn could play tennis. So could Earl "The Pearl" Monroe. Doug Smith, who covered the Nets for *Newsday* when I was on the beat, was a fine tennis player and had competed for Hampton Institute, and knew Arthur Ashe well. Smith was later the tennis writer for *USA Today*.

Several members of the New York Islanders were good at tennis, including Lorne Henning, Bobby Nystrom, Clark Gillies and Bert Marshall, and they played often in their spare time at the Baldwin (L.I.) Tennis Club, where I served as the publicity and marketing director while I was a sportswriter for *The New York Post*. Many hockey players were good at golf as well, especially Pierre Larouche, Eddie Westfall, Eddie Johnston and Mario Lemieux. Baseball players such as Dick Groat, Bill Mazeroski and Rick Rhoden were pretty good golfers.

I remember seeing Franco Harris team up at a celebrity tennis tournament in the Pittsburgh eastern suburb of Monroeville with Ethel Kennedy, a terrific athlete who bore 11 children to Bobby Kennedy.

When I asked Franco about his boyhood sports heroes, he came up blank. Franco often worked out and played basketball at Pitt much to my surprise, "I didn't have a favorite," he said. "I really didn't know about anyone in sports. We didn't watch sports on TV. We didn't watch much on TV."

When he was playing for the Steelers, Franco

was a frequent visitor to the Pitt Field House and at Trees Hall across the street with Pitt ballplayers. "We didn't have much of a workout facility at Three Rivers Stadium, so I'd go out to Pitt," said Harris.

My friend Dave Gambridge, a 6-10 front-liner who played basketball at St. Francis of Loretto and St. Vincent, recalled playing basketball with Franco at the Field House. "He'd give you a strong forearm to get open for his jump shot," said Gambridge. "If his team lost he never just sat down. He'd run around the track in the field house until he could get into the next game. So, he was in constant motion for two or two and a half hours."

I remember that when Franco took a handoff in practice, he would just keep running down the field. "No one was allowed to touch me," he said with a smile. "That's why I can still walk without a cane."

"The difference between Try and Triumph is a little umph!"
—Unknown source

Sidebar

Jerome Bettis once met me in the Steelers' clubhouse at Three Rivers Stadium and did a four-hour interview with me, even taking me into a room off the clubhouse that players could use as a retreat, where they could play pool or ping-pong. It was off limits to the media, but Bettis took me there because no one else was in the clubhouse that day.

Chuck Noll invited me to his home in Upper St. Clair. You could see South Hills Village from the deck at the rear of his home. His wife Marianne was there, too. I spent nearly two hours with Noll. Later on, he responded to my request to visit him at his apartment in Sewickley, but didn't invite me into his unit, taking

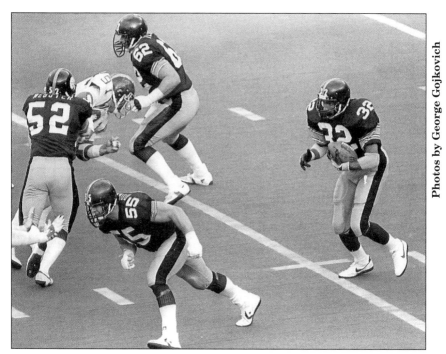

Franco Harris gets blocking from, left to right, Mike Webster (52), Jon Kolb (55) and Tunch Ilkin (62) in the early '80s.

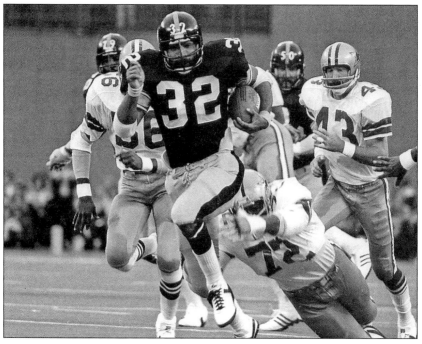

Franco Harris heads for paydirt against Dallas Cowboys.

me instead to a party room down the hall.

Dan Rooney said I had taken advantage of my relationship with the Steelers. When Dan learned that his brother was writing a book about the Rooneys, he rushed his own book into print to beat his brother to the punch, and the bookstores. "He's like that," Art Jr. told me at the time.

Dwight White, one of the brightest of the Steelers, always called me "Book Man." White was the most passionate of the Steelers when he reflected on his time with the team. Ed Kiely, the team publicist prior to Joe Gordon, said that Roy Blount Jr. told him White was his favorite interview when he wrote his wonderful book *About Three Bricks Shy of a Load.*

Dan Rooney

Asked how he got his nickname, Gerry "Moon" Mullins said, "When I was in junior high, we had five Gerrys on our team. Our coach, a former Marine drill sergeant, told me, "This is confusing. We can't have five Gerrys on this team. From now on, you're Moon Mullins.' There was a comic strip character named Moon Mullins back then. And the name stuck."

Moon Mullins

He blocked for Franco and Rocky and for O.J. Simpson at USC

Ispoke to Gerry "Moon" Mullins when he was in mourning for a friend and father-figure. He had learned the day before of the death of Bob Keaney, who had turned his business over to him after Mullins had retired from playing for the Steelers.

Keaney was a next-door neighbor of Pirates' broadcaster Bob Prince, and a board member at the St. Clair Country Club where he and Prince played golf and had a drink or two at the 19th hole.

Keaney was looking for someone to groom at his Industrial Metals and Minerals business in nearby Bridgeville. He asked Prince if he could recommend someone to work with him, and Prince picked Gerry Blaine Mullins for the position. "I wanted something where I could be my own boss," recalls Mullins. Keaney tutored Mullins for 14 years and turned the company over to him in 1995 and moved to Del Ray Beach, Florida.

One of Bob Keaney's daughters, Ann, and her husband Dr. Dave Stapor, share tickets with me for Pitt basketball, mostly so they can catch the ACC game with Duke, Dave's beloved alma mater. "I'm glad Moon knows about my dad's death," Ann told me by e-mail. "I didn't know how to get hold of him. Thank you."

That business had been in decline along with many manufacturing and industrial plants for some time and Mullins closed shop in November of 2018 to retire to his home in Saxonburg, just over 40 miles or an hour's drive north of Pittsburgh. He said his wife Joan wishes he was still working. "I guess I get in the way," he confessed. He does his best to keep busy and help their son get established in business.

Mullins is always fun to talk to. He may live in Western Pennsylvania, but he still has a lot of California in the laid-back way he talks. He was a handsome young man when he came to the Steelers in 1971 after playing tight end at Southern California. He enjoyed life and ignored camp curfews and on-the-road hotel curfews. Chuck Noll told him when he called on draft day, "You don't have to practice catching passes. You're playing on the line for us."

Mullins was one of those undersized linemen Noll liked who could pull out of the line and lead end sweeps. He had quick feet and could execute trap plays well. He weighed 225 at the end of one season. He was a right guard, playing next to Ray Mansfield and then Mike Webster (1971-1979). Mullins remembers he was the first of the starters from the '70s to be cut by Chuck Noll. "The Browns wanted me and the Redskins wanted me," he said, "but I didn't want to leave Pittsburgh. I'd had enough of football."

When he retired from football he retired from football. He hardly watched a full game of the Steelers, and he soon surrendered his two season tickets. "I enjoyed playing football, not watching football," he explained. "I just wasn't into it."

He shows up for player reunions and golf outings and he likes getting together with his former teammates. He always adds to the laughs, things he says, his smile and laughter. It bothers him that so many of his teammates have died. He's always been willing to talk to me, and for that I am most grateful.

I saw Moon and his wife Joanie at the memorial service for Bob Keaney on Saturday, March 30, 2019 at Westminister Presbyterian Church in Upper St. Clair. Art Rooney Sr. told everyone they had to show up for funerals.

When I mentioned Franco Harris to him, Mullins immediately said, "He's a great guy." I knew right away we were on the same wave length.

I remembered a few years earlier when I was having breakfast on a patio at the Allegheny County Club for Andy Russell's celebrity golf outing to raise money for prostate cancer research at UPMC that Mullins was mulling over seeing Rocky Bleier in "The Play" at Heinz Hall. "How did he remember all those lines?" said Mullins, standing up like he was on stage.

"Hey, it's his life story," said Randy Grossman. "If he forgot a line or two, he could fill in something else. He knows his story."

They also spoke about Lynn Swann landing the job as athletic director at his alma mater, the University of Southern California, which was also Moon's school.

"Some guys are born under the right star," interjected Grossman.

Mullins might have been one of them. At USC, he blocked for O.J. Simpson for one season, and with the Steelers he blocked even more for Franco Harris and Rocky Bleier.

"Those two teamed up to become one of the best running duos in the NFL," said Mullins.

"I was a freshman when O.J. was a junior. Freshmen were not eligible to play varsity then, but I practiced with him, and I played with him for one year. He was good with us; he was king from Day One."

* * *

Then the subject switched from O.J. back to Franco. Remember O.J. running through an airport in those TV ads for Hertz Rent-A-Car?

"Franco has always been good at getting the guys together. In our playing days, he hosted card games at his home on the North Side.

29

"I don't have any contact with the current guys, so I don't know what their world is like. I've seen some of them at reunions, but I don't really know them. A kid who has been a ballboy with them told me they don't really have parties together much these days; they tend to go their own way. Everyone is looking out for No. 1."

That led, naturally, to us talking about Antonio Brown and Le'Veon Bell, two outstanding players who had been at odds with management the past year. Brown would be traded a few days later to the Oakland Raiders, and Bell's status was still up in the air, but everyone figured he'd soon be gone, too. Within the week, Bell would be traded to the New York Jets. I figured that would be an interesting development in his life. If he thought the sportswriters in Pittsburgh were punitive wait until he lives with the Manhattan madness.

"You can't keep a team together now the way we did," said Mullins. "We didn't have free agency and we had over 20 (22 in fact) of the same guys on our four Super Bowl champions. I don't think Chuck Noll would want to coach under the current conditions.

"They're like soldiers of fortune," said Mullins. "They're looking for what's best for them even though they may not know what's best for them. Bell and Brown were both so successful here but that doesn't mean they'll be successful where they go next. I think A.B. will miss Ben Roethlisberger. If he goes to a bad team, he won't be happy. He shouldn't have any financial problems. I think A.B. has always had a me-me attitude. I'm not a student of the current game, but everybody is out for No. 1. The guys who speak for the old team remain closer together. Antonio Brown may be the best at his position, but he outlived his welcome here. I don't know what sent him over the edge. I think it was time they parted ways.

I asked Mullins who played cards regularly, and he mentioned Ralph "The Plumber" Berlin, the team's trainer from Bethel Park, L.C. Greenwood, Joe Greene, Frenchy Fuqua and Mullins.

"Franco liked to build the team up, make us closer," said Mullins. "He still hosts parties at the Super Bowl each year with his Penn State teammate Lydell Mitchell, and he's hosted holiday parties, and parties on the anniversary of his Immaculate Reception. It's always a good time."

Mullins, who would turn 70 on August 14, 2019, said he felt good with a few aches and pains that old football players still experience. They know when they get out of bed in the morning that they were once football players. Moon is OK with that as long as he keeps getting up in the morning.

Harry Homa/Steelers

Returning home from successful road game are, left to right, Franco Harris, Terry Bradshaw and Moon Mullins.

"I've seen Ju Ju Smith-Schuster and he can be sensational, but they will double up on him now instead of Brown. I think the Steelers will survive.

"They could all learn a lot from Franco and Rocky. They were smart and they were team guys. They were definitely team guys. Franco was never loud or boisterous, but he had a mind of his own. If something was bothering him, he'd speak up. Joe Greene was the most visible and audible team leader, but Franco was right up there. He had some strong feelings about some things.

"I had lunch with him last month with my oldest son. Franco has a good mind for business, and I'm trying to help my son get started, and make some connections. Franco and his son Dok are involved in so many things. He's got a lot on his plate. One of his business partners just passed away, and that's been difficult for Franco.

"Rocky was a straight-ahead runner. Franco was different; he had his own style. Franco had more finesse. Rocky was a power runner. They liked each other and they complemented each other. Rocky did a lot of blocking for Franco. I'm not sure Franco returned the favor in that regard. Jerome Bettis came after us, but he was a team player, too.

"I remember the season (1976) that Rocky ran for 1,000 yards and so did Franco. The whole team was rooting for Rocky to reach that plateau. That was a great moment; everybody rooted for Rocky.

"I don't think Rocky would have done well at the combine where they evaluate college players. It's a business, but you can't evaluate somebody's heart."

Bleier rushed for 122 yards in the final game at Houston to top 1,000 yards. They were only the second duo to do that in NFL history. Four years earlier, Larry Csonka and Mercury Morris of the Miami Dolphins were the first to do that. I had covered the Dolphins

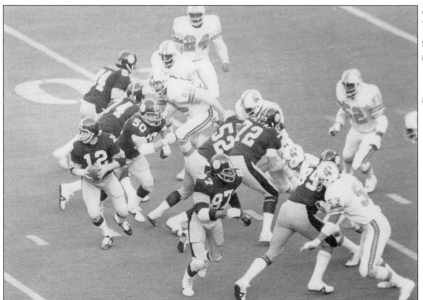

Moon Mullins (72) is in the middle of madness that precedes Terry Bradshaw (12) getting ready to hand off the football. Below, Moon Mullins in whites listens in on conversation with, left to right, Billy Conn "The Pittsburgh Kid" and former light-heavyweight champion of the world, his good friend Art Rooney Sr. and Sam Davis, a Steelers' guard in his days as a sales rep for the H.J. Heinz Company. Sam's jersey number was 57 and Heinz boasted it had 57 varieties of food offerings.

for *The Miami News* when Morris, who grew up in the same neighborhood where Three Rivers Stadium was built, and starred at Avonworth High School, broke in as a rookie. We combined forces on a "Dairy of a Rookie" feature three days a week in the afternoon newspaper.

"One of my other fond memories," added Mullins, "was when NFL Commissioner Pete Rozelle presented The Old Man with the Lombardi Trophy after we won our first Super Bowl in New Orleans. Mr. Rooney had tears in his eyes, and so did some of us. We were so happy for him. After all those losing seasons, the Steelers were finally winners in the biggest way.

"I can still remember when Rocky returned after sitting out a year rehabbing from his injuries in battle in Vietnam. He was a war hero and he was walking with a crutch and then a cane. We were so proud to have him, but we weren't sure he'd be able to play and to contribute. It didn't look good; it wasn't that promising. That was big when he and Franco both rushed for 1,000 yards.

"We had a photo taken of our offensive line, guys like Jimmy Clack, Gordon Gravelle, Ray Mansfield, Sam Davis, Larry Brown, Mike Webster, Rich Druschel, Dave Reavis. I still have that picture in my den. It was taken in Houston after that last game. Somehow Lynn Swann snuck into that picture."

He has gone from being a California beach boy to a Pennsylvania outdoorsman. He was one of the Steelers who used to shoot clay pigeons at the Millvale Sportsmen's Club and he continues to shoot and to hunt and has trophies to prove it. He has Steelers' memorabilia. There are moose heads and elk heads and antlers on the walls.

"It was cold and gray the first day I got to Pittsburgh, and I wondered what I had gotten myself into," he said. "But it's turned out fine and I am at home here.

"Noll knew the kind of players he wanted on his team and I'm glad I was one of them. He let go of some talented players because they didn't fit into what he wanted. I was crazy and everybody thought I was a real whack job. But I was smart and I learned the play book in a hurry. Noll would forgive physical mistakes, but not mental mistakes. Football came natural to me. I knew what I was supposed to do and I usually did it. I was able to get assimilated with the Steelers right away. Ray Mansfield and Bruce Van Dyke liked me, and they showed me the way.

"There was a 15-year stretch when 20 percent of the fatalities in the NFL were former Steelers. That gets you thinking. How could I complain."

Moon Mullins signs autograph at Steelers' Alumni golf outing at Diamond Run in Indiana Township. Assistant coach Paul Uram of Butler is in background

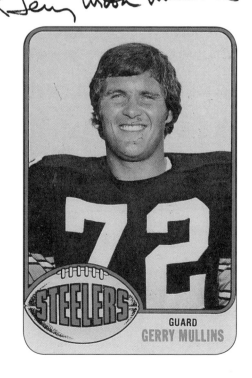

GUARD
GERRY MULLINS

Mel Blount

Says books help to keep Steelers of the '70s alive

Mel Blount grew up on a large farm in Vidalia, Toombs County, Georgia, a region best known for producing sweet onions as well as one of the sweetest defensive backs in Steelers' and National Football League history.

As a youngster, Melvin Cornell Blount became aware of workers on nearby farms, hired hands, share croppers, and he noticed that when they got older and were no longer as strong and efficient as field workers that they were cut loose and turned away from the farm. One day they were just gone. Life in the sports world is like that, too.

I recall riding in a chartered bus with the Steelers when they played an exhibition game in Knoxville, Tennessee and we passed a handsome pale-yellow landmark home behind a white picket fence that had a big sign in the yard that read THE BLOUNT MANSION.

"That was probably owned by some slave master who gave me my name," said Blount for all to hear, and smiled at his own observation. Actually, the home on Hill Avenue was owned by William Blount, the only territorial governor in the Southwest Territory.

When he joined the Steelers in 1970, the same season quarterback Terry Bradshaw came on board, Mel Blount saw how the coach, Chuck Noll, cut veteran standouts that simply didn't fit into his plans to build a championship team. They just weren't up to speed. They didn't fit into his plans.

One of those Noll sent packing was the team's star receiver, Roy Jefferson. "I had no problem with that," Blount says now. "I like Roy, but he was disruptive in the locker room. He was sending out the wrong messages to young players like Joe Greene and myself. The player I wasn't happy about him getting rid of was Ron Shanklin."

When I saw Jefferson at one of Andy Russell's celebrity golf outings, after we had not seen each other for 30 years, he smiled and said, "You're old, but I can still see your face." Jefferson told me he had made peace with Chuck Noll and admitted he had not conducted himself properly, leading to his dismissal.

Blount later ran into a difficult situation with the Steelers and Coach Noll, and he even sued the team and its coach, but both sides came to their senses and straightened out the situation. But Blount could have been discarded as well.

Antonio Brown and Le'Veon Bell were two of the best players on the team in 2018 and 2019, but they turned out to be disposable as well.

Jim O'Brien

Joe Greene, Mel Blount and Roy Jefferson are reunited at Andy Russell's Celebrity Golf Outing.

Blount made it his business to make sure he learned what he needed to learn to stay in the NFL and wanted to be in a position to some day call it quits on his own terms. He played 14 seasons and 200 regular season games and holds the team record with 57 interceptions. He retired after the 1983 season. He was inducted into the Pro Football Hall of Fame in 1989.

His size, speed, strength and bump-and-run tactics restricted receivers so much that the National Football League changed the rules on what defensive backs were permitted to do in order to give receivers a fairer chance to catch the ball.

While he was playing for the Steelers, Blount got involved with business and corporate types in town and offered his services where needed. He still advises young players to get to know the right people in Pittsburgh. He convinced former teammate Louis Lipps, for instance, that he'd fare better career-wise in Pittsburgh, Pennsylvania than in his hometown of Reserve, Louisiana.

When Blount retired from the Steelers, team owner Art Rooney Sr. recommended him to then NFL Commissioner Pete Rozelle to serve the league office as Director of Player Relations, a position he held for seven years.

Blount developed a ranch and boys' home in Vidalia in 1983 to help troubled youngsters get straightened out so they could have productive and rewarding lives. Then in 1989 he did the same in Claysville, on a 300-acre spread out in Washington County in Western Pennsylvania.

He's been at it ever since. He and his wife, TiAnda and the staff work with the kids in a Christian-driven environment out in what Blount terms "God's country." He likes to share their success stories.

As a youngster in Vidalia, Blount enjoyed cowboy

TiAnda and Mel Blount manage boys' home in Claysville. Mel, at right below, misses his dear friend L.C. Greenwood.

movies and loved the likes of Gene Autry, Roy Rogers, Joel McCrea, Tom Mix and Tex Ritter. Tom Mix, by the way, grew up in DuBois and became one of the first cowboy movie idols. Mel Blount has become a cowboy at home on his own range. His trademark is a large white cowboy hat and he wears cowboy boots, which makes him loom even larger than the 6-3, 220-pound man that he is.

People are always telling Blount, a formidable figure at any gathering and still in great shape at age 70—he would turn 71 on April 18, 2019—that he looks like he could still play for the Steelers. He's familiar with the dozen books I have authored about the Steelers and he often says, "You keep us alive!"

When we spoke in March of 2019, I told him I wished that were true. His teammate and dear friend, defensive end L.C. Greenwood had died at the age of 67 from kidney failure following his 16th back surgery. Dwight White had died in 2008, at 58, following back surgery. Ernie Holmes died the same year in an auto accident at age 59. There were 13 Steelers from the first four Super Bowl teams of the '70s who had died before they were 60 years of age.

Blount was aboard one of his horses at his ranch in Claysville, talking to me on a cell phone as he practiced for competition in the National Cutting Horse Association (NCHA), a circuit in which he still excels and picks up some paychecks. I told him it was the first time I had ever interviewed anybody when they were on a horse.

I had covered a little horse racing in my early years, but never interviewed a jockey aboard a horse.

"You have to guide boys and steer them straight," he said of his efforts at his boys' home.

It has been my honor to write about Blount and so

many former Steelers who have moved on into what Noll termed "their life's work."

I wrote a book about Noll—*A Winning Way*—and the Steelers of the '70s and I believe it is "the definitive work on the head coach and his Steelers."

I had an opportunity after Noll retired to spend several hours with him and his wife, Marianne, at their home in Upper Saint Clair and one in Sewickley. I didn't realize when I started on the project just how many notes, newspaper clippings, and legal pads worth of interviews and photos that I had in my files. I felt that as far as members of the media were concerned, only the late Myron Cope enjoyed a closer relationship with Noll.

In researching the book, I visited many of the Steelers in their homes such as Rocky Bleier and Andy Russell, and in the offices of Randy Grossman, Jack Ham, Mike Wagner, Tunch Ilkin, Craig Wolfley, Judge Dwayne Woodruff, Art Rooney Jr., Moon Mullins, Franco Harris and in Manhattan with Terry Hanratty, at golf outings with Mel Blount, Lynn Swann, Frenchy Fuqua, Glen Edwards, and over the telephone with Ted Petersen, J.T. Thomas, John Stallworth, Larry Brown, Jon Kolb, Cliff Stoudt and Coach Paul Uram, Coach Dick LeBeau and trainer Ralph Berlin.

I did earlier interviews with Dwight White, Ernie Holmes, Joe Greene, Jack Lambert, Mike Webster, Bill Cowher, Sam Davis, Art Rooney Sr. and Dan Rooney.

I was struck by how profound their thoughts were about their experiences with Noll and the Steelers.

Theirs is a legacy worth keeping alive.

> ### *"You only get what you demand."*
> ### —Chuck Noll

Mel Blount

Talks about Franco Harris, Rocky Bleier and team-mates, and offers opinions about Le'Veon Bell and Antonio Brown

There was a gray glaze covering the water in the Boone Reservoir near the entryway of Waterdam Farms where we had been living for nearly three years. This was in North Strabane in Washington County just over the border that separates it from Allegheny County. There were families named McMurray, Boone and Donaldson in this area.

I can see cows on a farm from the deck of our home, and even Ireland, I swear, on the green hills beyond the pasture. Two huge pigs—black and white and gray walked across my lawn in April 2019.

"I'm glad to know you are smart enough to have come out to God's country," Mel Blount had told me.

The Mel Blount Youth Home, which helps challenged kids from the city get their acts together, is located in Claysville, just south on Washington Road or Route 19. It was 22 degrees out. It had been much colder a week or so earlier, and the reservoir which I prefer to call Waterdam Lake or Crystal Lake, had been frozen over. My wife Kathie asked me if she could come along. She wanted to meet Mel Blount and she said she'd do some shopping while we talked.

I remembered seeing a racial slur burned into a fence rail at the entrance of the Youth Home, and I had heard about a Klu Klux Klan element that burned a cross on the property soon after Mel moved in. Steeler Nation was not always that neighborly, after all. "I've gone through a lot out here," he told me. "I need to write my own book about it."

43

Melvin Cornell Blount, the pride of Vidalia, Georgia where they grow those sweet onions, and Pittsburgh, where Mel was an MVP defensive cornerback for four Super Bowl championship teams in the '70s when the Steelers were named the NFL's Team of the Decade and Pittsburgh was proclaimed The City of Champions.

Mel had suggested we meet at North Strabane Square, at Panera's, which was about midway between Claysville and Waterdam Farms. It was a 20-minute ride for a 3 o'clock meeting. We listened to a mix of Willie Nelson and Elvis Presley on Sirius Radio along the way, a mix of country and gospel music, a perfect blend to set the mood for a meeting with Mel Blount. I should say I listened to Willie Nelson and Elvis Presley, not Kathie's kind of music.

Mel told me he still rides his horses every day on his ranch which I have visited several times through the years. "You're out here in redneck country with a black man," Mel told me when he was leaving after two hours of warm conversation.

Mel normally wears a white cowboy hat which looks right on him, but this time he was wearing a white Football Hall of Fame ballcap with blue and red trim on the HOF logo. He stood tall on his cowboy boots as he came through the front door of Panera's at 3:03.

"Here he comes," called out Kathie as he came through the front door. Several customers stared at him as he moved past several tables. Mel remains one of the region's most recognized figures. Some would later be all smiles when we left, and shake his hand, saying "Mr. Blount, it's great to see you." And he returned their greeting with a great smile of his own.

Mel, at a ramrod straight 6-3, is an inch shorter than Mario Lemieux, the Penguins' great player and owner, in Pittsburgh's pantheon of great athletes. Lemieux was even taller when he stood on ice skates. They are living statues.

During our conversation, Blount said that Ben Roethlisberger, the star Steelers' quarterback, had addressed him as "Mr. Blount," when they met at a Steelers' reunion. It was a term of respect for an earlier Steelers' icon. "It makes you feel old," said Blount, who said he was 71. He was getting ahead of himself because this was March 5, 2019 and he wouldn't be 71 for another month, not until his birth date of April 10.

Mel had a big hug for me—I disappeared into his black varsity jacket—and he had a big hug for Kathie. The salt and pepper short whiskers on his cheeks met her cheek. "So good to see you."

* * *

It wasn't long before he said he would put both of our names on his "guest list" for the annual Mel Blount Celebrity Roast, set for April 5 at Heinz Field on Pittsburgh's North Side, which the Steelers called home. Joe Greene and his new wife were also attending.

Agnes, his sweetheart during their days at North Texas University, had died of breast cancer in 2015 after 47 years of marriage, and Joe established a scholarship in her name at their alma mater. Joe and Mel were roommates at camp and on the road during their days with the Steelers.

Blount and Greene were among the first inductees into the team's Hall of Honor in that same sports venue two years earlier.

Blount had been a Pro Bowl selection five times, stretching from 1975 to 1981, had been a first-team All-Pro selection four times, a member of the NFL's 75th anniversary all-time team, a 1980s All-Decade

Team, and the NFL's Defensive Player of the Year in 1975.

After his playing career was concluded, Mel became the Director of Player Relations for the NFL, serving from 1983 to 1990. He founded the Mel Blount Youth Home, a shelter and Christian mission for victims of child abuse and neglect, in his hometown of Vidalia in 1983. In 1989, he opened a second youth home in Claysville, Pennsylvania, about 50 miles from Pittsburgh via I-79 south and I-70 west.

"We don't house these kids anymore," he told us. "I'm getting too old. We have them come out on weekends and we have a summer camp for them. Sometimes, when it seems a little too much for me and my wife Tia, I think about closing it down. But then I think that these kids need me, and too many people left them alone. I can't abandon them."

I knew that Franco Harris had helped him physically and financially with his mission. "I don't want to get into numbers but Franco sends me a substantial check every year," said Blount. "So does Art Rooney Jr. He and Bill Nunn both belong in the Football Hall of Fame for the players they drafted for the Steelers. Art Jr. knew the black coaches in the South almost as much as Bill Nunn. I know he talked to Ron Brown, who was my defensive backfield coach at Southern U."

A mutual friend of ours, the late Elsie Hillman, once the chairwoman of the Republican Committee in Allegheny County, and a financial contributor, along with her husband, Henry Hillman, to many charities, had been a big booster of the Mel Blount Youth Home. "We all miss her financial help," Kathie chimed in.

Blount smiled at the mention of Mrs. Hillman. "Once, when the older President George Bush flew in from Houston to see her, she invited me to bring some of our kids to the airport to meet him. He invited some of the kids to get on the airplane when it was parked. It was a big deal for black kids from the inner-city to meet the President of the United States."

I told him that Mrs. Hillman used to buy ten of my Pittsburgh Proud books each year and that she had sent one of them to President Bush as a Christmas gift. He sent me a hand-written "thank you" card with a personal message that I have kept in my writing desk as a treasured memento.

George H. W. Bush, our 41st President, created a "thousand points of light" during his 1988 campaign, and Blount proudly told me he was No. 218 on that listing that acknowledged the virtue of service and volunteerism.

Mel and I sat in a booth in the middle of the dining area at Panera's and talked about his teammates, especially Franco Harris and Rocky Bleier, both personal favorites of Blount, and Le'Veon Bell and Antonio Brown, two highly-talented Steelers who had abandoned the ship, and had been bringing negative publicity to Pittsburgh and its pro football franchise the previous two years.

When I told Mel that his former teammate John Banaszak had branded Brown "a spoiled brat," he said, "I'll go along with that. We're losing two of the greatest talents in the league these days, and it's all because of selfish interests. It's all about the money.

"Ben Roethlisberger asked me to talk to Antonio Brown, and I did, but I don't think it had any impact on his behavior. I told him he had to respect the Rooney legacy, the franchise and his teammates. He couldn't be showing up late for practice, or arguing with teammates and coaches on the sideline. I've been looking after kids with problems for many years and I know how this stuff starts. Antonio listened but I don't know

47

if he actually heard what I had to say.

"The guys who are in the NFL and NBA these days often come from difficult backgrounds. They don't have the same kind of parental influence that most of the players of my generation had. We might not have had much money, in a lot of cases, but we had concerned parents who offered proper guidance and discipline. There are too many kids being raised by their grandmothers, or one parent, usually the mother, and they often get into trouble of one kind or another, or into drugs.

"I see young versions of Antonio Brown and Le'Veon Bell, and it's not easy to straighten them out, or keep them on course. Many of today's players would not have been accepted in our locker room. You couldn't be just out for yourself. You had to care about your teammates. The team came first. Team goals were more important than individual goals. We were competitive with other teams and among ourselves, but we didn't talk down our teammates the way these guys do today."

* * *

I brought about a dozen photos from my Mel Blount file to give to Mel, and two books, one on basketball and one on boxing. "I have most of your books about the Steelers," he said. As for the photos, I liked the way he was looking at them. He especially liked the ones showing him with Willie Stargell of the Pirates and one of him with the late L.C. Greenwood—"I'll treasure these," he said with a warm smile—and one of him with one of his sons, Akil, now 24, sitting on his lap when he was about half that age at Legends of the North Shore, a neighborhood restaurant on East North Avenue next door to Allegheny General Hospital. It was often frequented by the late Dan Rooney and his wife, Pat. Jim Sacco of Heinz Field was a regular diner.

When he saw the photo with his son, he said, "He's

getting his master's degree in business administration at Florida A&M soon. I'm so proud of our kids."

His stay with the Steelers wasn't all roses and honey. After the 1975 season, in which he won so many awards, including the MVP Award in the Super Bowl, Blount had a salary holdout of 56 days, and it got so bad that Blount sued the Steelers. "No one ever did that back then," he told me at Panera's.

"I was trying to get a new contract for a hundred thousand dollars. I was making about $60,000 at the time. Dan Rooney had spoken to me at the start of the season and he said he would take care of me when I needed a new contract. Nowadays, these guys get so much money right out of the gate."

The minimum salary for first-year NFL players is now $480,000, and it goes up to $630,000 the second year, and $700,000 the third year.

"When it came contract time, Dan Rooney didn't see me. He sent Jim Boston, who handled most player contracts, to see me. He flew to New Orleans to meet with me at the Marriott Hotel. He offered me a $5,000 raise, which I promptly rejected. His response to that was to tell me, 'You'll starve to death if you don't sign this contract.' That was the worst thing he could have said. He was telling me that if I didn't sign with the Steelers, I couldn't do anything else—even play in another league or Canada if I had to. I was pretty certain I could make a living. To me, it was worse than if he had called me a dirty nigger."

Blount pointed out that many of the players who made up the Steelers of the '70s had come from the South and they weren't far removed from the civil rights movement, the death of Dr. Martin Luther King and Malcolm X, segregation and even slavery.

"My mother lived till she was 103," he said. "And

her mother was the daughter of a slave. In some ways, segregation was worse than slavery. If you were a slave you had a home and food and a job, and the master looked after you. During segregation you were often denied housing and a good job.

"Chuck Noll was upset with George Atkinson of the Raiders for hitting Lynn Swann so hard he knocked him out. He said Atkinson was part of a 'criminal element' in the league and should be kicked out of the NFL. Atkinson sued Noll for $5 million dollars. Somehow an Oakland lawyer coerced Noll into including me in the 'criminal element' category and I sued Noll for $5 million for defamation of character. I later dropped the law suit."

There was a court case in Oakland and among the witnesses who testified were Raiders' owner Al Davis and coach John Madden, Atkinson and Swann, of course, and Terry Bradshaw, Franco Harris and Rocky Bleier as character witnesses. It was a difficult time for the Steelers, however, and team didn't fare as well as expected in the 1977 season.

Blount seemed taken off guard when I introduced the story of what Jim Boston had said to him about 'you'll starve to death.' I never spoke about that incident at any press conference I ever did," said Blount. "But I'll talk to you about it now. I trust you to get it right. I don't know how you heard about that, but I'll talk about it now."

* * *

Around this same time, national sports commentator Stephen A. Smith blamed Ben Roethlisberger for chasing away Antonio Brown and Le'Veon Bell. "You would think a star quarterback would want to keep the best running back and the best receiver," said Smith.

J. T. Thomas

The man from Macon, Georgia takes you behind the Steel Curtain

James T. Thomas, better known as J.T. Thomas, or just T to his beloved teammates from the Steelers of the '70s—the most glorious period of pro football in Pittsburgh—is still special. He was a valued and under-valued member of what many sports historians believe was the greatest football team ever.

Now that Dwight White has died, Thomas may be the most passionate and eloquent spokesman for the Steelers from three of their first four Super Bowl title teams. Thomas was ill with a rare disease known as Boeck's Syndrome, a tuberculosis-like ailment in the chest, and had to sit out the 1978 season and the third Super Bowl triumph by the Steelers.

White called me "Bookman" and did his best to terrorize me when we were doing an interview about the Steelers. Jack Lambert liked to do that as well.

Once, I dropped my notebook at Lambert's shoes when I was speaking to him. "You still make me nervous," I said. To which Lambert said, "Good, let's keep it that way."

Thomas entertains me with a constant smile and enlightening stories. There is something about the rhythm of his words, like he is composing a spiritual song, that is enchanting.

"I smoked a pipe in college," said Thomas, "but I stopped smoking a pipe when I was 29. I found I had what was thought to be the flu, at first, after the Super Bowl in 1978.

"I was going to camp the following season and I went in for a routine physical. Dr. (David) Huber saw something he didn't like on an x-ray. Then they took a biopsy. No one knew what was wrong with me. I was in a hospital for three days. My wife was pregnant with our first kid. I was 24. I had a Super Bowl ring. I had the check and hadn't spent it yet. People weren't sure I could survive this."

Dr. Huber and Dr. Tony Yates, two of the physicians on the Steelers' medical staff, were both mentioned in a law suit brought by former NFL players, including Glen Edwards of the Steelers, for dispensing pain-killers to players well above the NFL average. In the pioneer days of the Steelers, they had some team doctors and dentists of questionable ability.

Things had improved a great deal by the late '70s. Players on those great teams were routinely using steroids before their use was banned by the National Football League. This may have contributed to so many Steelers dying in their 50s.

The NFL began testing for steroid use in 1987 and started issuing suspensions for substance abuse in 1989.

A 2012 study shows that former NFL players die at an extremely low age—53 to 59 years—depending upon the position played. The average life expectancy for men in America is just over 68 years.

Thomas was on a comeback when I was covering the Steelers for *The Pittsburgh Press* from 1979 to 1983. Danny Marino was playing quarterback for the nationally-ranked Pitt Panthers during that same span. Jackie Sherrill was their coach, perhaps the most under-rated coach in Pitt history.

A lot was going on in the world in 1979. It snowed for 30 minutes in the Sahara Desert, our embassy in Pakistan was destroyed in a mob attack, tornadoes

Necrology

This is a list of Steelers who played at times from the 1970 to the 2018 season who have died that was compiled by John Bennett, a football and baseball researcher and historian from Shelburne, Vermont.

Name	Date died	Age	Name	Date died	Age
Bobby Maples	2/16/1991	48	Terry Cole	11/11/2005	60
John Bruno	4/13/1992	27	Dave Brown	1/10/2006	52
John Rodgers	1/2/1995	59	Bernard Dafney	1/11/2006	37
Ray Mansfield	11/3/1996	55	Jim Clack	4/7/2006	58
Willie Fry	7/10/1998	43	Theo Bell	6/21/2006	52
Chuck Hinton	1/30/1999	59	Lloyd Voss	3/1/2007	65
Fred Bohannon	2/8/1999	40	George Webster	4/19/2007	61
Steve Furness	2/10/2000	49	Ernie Holmes	1/17/2008	59
Henry Davis	6/11/2000	57	Dwight White	6/6/2008	58
Tyrone McGriff	12/9/2000	42	Marquis Cooper	3/1/2009	26
Dan Turk	12/23/2000	38	Jim Mandich	4/26/2011	62
Joe Gilliam	12/25/2000	49	Derek Hill	1/21/2012	44
Ron Shanklin	4/17/2003	55	Ralph Wentzel	6/18/2012	69
Mike Webster	9/24/2002	50	Tom Keating	8/31/2012	69
Mike Haggerty	11/28/2002	73	L.C. Greenwood	9/29/2013	67
David Woodley	5/4/2003	44	Ocie Austin	7/22/2014	67
Fred Small	6/24/2003	40	Mel Holmes	12/24/2015	65
Jim Wolf	12/17/2003	67	Lorenzo Freeman	10/10/2016	52
Scoop Gillespie	5/24/2004	42	Chuck Allen	12/15/2016	77
James Parrish	3/10/2004	35	Bennie Cunningham	4/23/2018	63
Justin Strzelcyzk	9/30/2004	36	Rolland Putzier	4/25/2018	52
David Little	3/17/2005	46	Ron Johnson	7/10/2018	62
Terry Long	6/7/2005	45	Gabe Rivera	7/16/2018	57
Ray Oldham	7/23/2005	54	Bobby Walden	8/27/2018	80
Steve Courson	11/10/2005	50	Glen Ray Hines	2/1/2019	75

Necrology definition:
An obituary notice;
a list of deaths.

53

were leveling homes in Texas and Oklahoma, Saddam Hussein was in the news in Iraq and Pope John Paul II was holding forth at The Vatican. The Pope got reports of priests preying on young people. That's preying, not praying.

I came back to Pittsburgh after ten years away, one in Miami and nine in New York, and was in time to see the Pirates win the World Series and the Steelers win their fourth Super Bowl in six seasons. That's good timing and good luck.

J.T. Thomas signs autographs for young fans at Steelers' training camp.

* * *

And then there was J.T. Thomas. I love to talk to Thomas. He always has some new tales to tell, and refines old tales, but never tires of talking about the good old days. He is both informative and funny. We both chuckled as he continued from one story to another story, seamless in what he chose to share. Like they say about Terry Bradshaw, J.T. is a real hoot. He holds your attention with his "he say" stories.

J.T. is a sharp dresser, walks with great confidence and talks in a fashion where you better be able to take notes fast and be able to read those scribbles later. He is a salesman to the core, like Rocky Bleier, always selling hope.

I have noticed that the farther we get from those glory days, and with so many such as White gone to heaven, J.T. assures you, the old Steelers have loosened a once-secure vault with inside stories. They are more willing and freer to take you behind the Steel Curtain. It's like a journey to Oz with Dorothy and her dog Toto, and Steelers' versions of the Tinman, Scarecrow and Cowardly Lion.

There are stories in this book that you won't find in *About Three Bricks Shy of a Load,* once thought to be the best book about the Steelers. That book was written in 1973 before the Steelers landed Lambert and Swann—Lambert said he should have been the Steelers first draft pick, not Swann, in 1974, and John Stallworth and Mike Webster, so it's missing some of the most amazing Steelers of all. The above-mentioned four are all in the Pro Football Hall of Fame. I get credit from some uninformed readers that I wrote that book, but it was by a southern gentleman named Roy Blount, Jr., no relation to Mel Blount, but a great story-teller

From Myron Cope

Myron Cope keeps company with another great writer, Roy Blount Jr. of *Sports Illustrated*, who authored *About Three Bricks Shy of a Load.*

55

of real merit. I also get credit for Rocky Bleier's book, *Fighting Back,* but that was authored by Terry O'Neill, whom I got to know when he was working at ABC-TV Sports. I used to get called O'Neill in my New York days by a sportswriter named Bob Waters, who was especially adept at writing about boxing for *Newsday,* the Long Island daily, and by Dick Young of *The New York Daily News*, the best baseball writer ever for a daily newspaper.

There have been some terrific books about the Steelers and I suggest you read as many of them as possible if you truly want to know the Steelers story. My book *The Chief: Art Rooney and His Pittsburgh Steelers i*s presently being offered on Amazon in pristine condition for $972.54. A real bargain. Don't smile, I know for a fact that a used copy of my book *Remember Roberto* sold for $240 at the Half-Price Book Store in North Fayette, Pennsylvania.

J.T. plays the piano well, his former teammate Mike Wagner told me, has a strong spiritual side and comes off as a self-assured bit of an intellectual and Biblical scholar. He had his share of struggles and successes with the Steelers, and the same can be said of his ventures in the restaurant business.

He and teammate Larry Brown once owned a string of successful Applebee's in western Pennsylvania, but they had disagreements and went their separate ways. Thomas can now be found at Crazy Mocha, a national coffee shop outlet in a strip near the Hill House in Pittsburgh's Hill District. The Hill House was in financial distress when I talked to Thomas in mid-February, 2019, and its endangered status was raising doubts about the future of J.T.'s attractive coffee venture. He had previously owned and operated Red Hot & Blue, a barbecue restaurant in The Waterfront in West Homestead, on the site of the former U.S. Steel Works.

Former teammates and former partners Larry Brown and J.T. Thomas at Applebee's headquarters.

I told J.T. I owned stock in Starbucks and several other national restaurant chains and that this was a lot easier way to make money than opening and closing restaurants on a daily basis. My daughter Rebecca O'Brien has been in the restaurant business the past 25 years and I know how challenging that can be.

J.T. offered interesting reflections on Franco Harris and Rocky Bleier, but so much more. He loves and respects them both in a Pro Bowl manner, but he also shared stories about Sister Josepha, Joe Greene, L.C. Greenwood, Dwight White, Ernie Holmes. The latter trio have all died, much too soon, and that gives Thomas an opportunity to share some rare reflections about religion and his spiritual side. He'll also tell us about Sister Josepha. Thomas tells you he is a deacon at his church with the same pride he once spoke about being a Pro Bowl performer following the 1976 season. He used to play the piano and the organ at Ebenezer Baptist Church on Wylie Avenue in The Hill before that church was leveled by a fire.

Now he worships at the Macedonia Baptist Church on Bedford Avenue. "It's the place to be on Sunday morning," reads one review. "I don't play in church these days," said Thomas. "I play for myself, to relax and meditate on my own."

The Steelers of the '70s were different from the Steelers of recent vintage. They were more team-oriented, less about "me" and more about "us," and driven to succeed in life and death.

"I don't worry about the first death," Thomas told me. "I worry about the second death. I look at death differently. I don't look at it as terminal. The first death should open the door to heaven and eternal bliss. The second death, if you're not careful, can lead to hell and eternal damnation. It's the first time you're not going to be with Christ. It's the first time you're in a place where God isn't."

I asked J.T. if he knew anyone who went to hell. I was certain Adolph Hitler had made the list, but didn't say anything about that to Thomas. I didn't want to put words in his mouth.

"If there's a hell," he said, almost on an ESP level, "I'm pretty certain Hitler is there. But a rabbi once told me that might not be so, that he might have been forgiven."

If Hitler is there, he might be joined someday by Robert Bowers, the madman from Baldwin who shot and killed 11 and wounded seven others with a rapid-fire rifle at the Tree of Life synagogue on October 27, 2018 in what has become known as "The Squirrel Hill Massacre." I was familiar with the synagogue. I was the guest speaker for a Little League awards banquet there, at the behest of Barbara Cloud of *The Pittsburgh Press,* in late October, 1982, two days after the death of my brother Dan. Thomas resided in Squirrel Hill for two years before moving to Monroeville in the 1970s.

That's where he and Larry Brown opened their first Applebee's and where J.T.'s wife has been a librarian at Gateway High School.

"I knew some people from that neighborhood in Squirrel Hill and that hit home with me. I have a friend who knew some of those people. It's happened at black churches in the South. It keeps you on alert. There is still hate in this world. That hatred does not go away. When you think of the evolution of this city it makes you wonder how far we've actually come. Why do we still have such hatred?"

*   *   *

Thomas told me he got a phone call from Joe Greene soon after Dwight White had died. White's nickname was "Mad Dog" or just "Dog," but I remember Dwight telling me in his latter years that he embraced the nickname and all that went with it in his playing days, but that he'd outgrown that moniker.

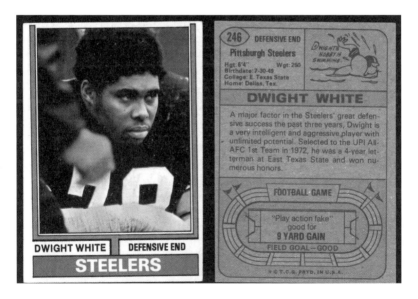

Even so, Greene began the conversation with Thomas by asking, "T, do you think Dog is up there?"

"By up there, do you mean heaven?"

"Yeah, I do."

"I think so. I know Ernie is up there because he was an ordained minister when he died. He found The Lord before it was too late. L.C. has to be up there too. He lived a good life."

* * *

When Thomas was with the Steelers he and Lynn Swann always sat in the last row of seats on the left side on the chartered airplanes. They had a seat open between them that they told people was for Elmer. It turned out Elmer was a figment of their imagination. "He was our imaginary friend," said Thomas. Art Rooney and Chuck Noll sat in the front row.

Tony Parisi, the team's equipment manager, once asked Swann and Thomas what they saw when an airplane crash was pictured. "You always see the tail end intact," pointed out Parisi.

"An airplane never backed into the side of a mountain," said Thomas. "I was in college when the football team at Marshall University perished in a plane crash. So, we always sat back there. We figured our chances for survival were greater there.

"Swann sat next to me because the media sat in the back of the plane and Lynn liked the media."

* * *

Here's what Thomas had to say about Rocky Bleier and Franco Harris:

"I think Rocky's really concerned about others. He's concerned about people and their family's welfare. He's been really giving of his time to this and that project, especially about anything involving veterans.

Steelers' equipment manager Tony Parisi in his workshop at Three Rivers Stadium.

"He's always gracious. A lot of players don't do well in dealing with people who invade their time and space. Some guys tolerate it, but Rocky embraces it. His transformation from being wounded in Vietnam to starring for the Steelers was impressive stuff.

"Chuck Noll drafted character. They always said he drafted the best possible athlete, but I think he wanted to know who had the best character. That included their spiritual side.

"Donnie Shell was strong in that area. Donnie came to the team when the veteran players were on strike. He'd been a linebacker for a small school in

"I joined the Steelers in 1980, and liked Franco Harris from the start. My boys were little then, but they followed me to the training camp and they always told me how nice Franco treated them. I was the assistant equipment manager and field manager who replaced Jackie Hart, but Franco couldn't have treated me any better. After he retired from playing, he would also stop in to say hello to Tony Parisi and me."
—Rodgers Freyvogel, Steelers equipment manager

South Carolina. Mel Blount and I were watching the Steelers in a pre-season game, and we had to laugh watching Donnie try to backpedal. We said, "What the hell is that? It was funny. We felt our jobs were secure. He can't backpedal.

"Donnie was a demon on our special teams, at the start, and he worked on his footwork and became a good defensive back, and in time a great strong safety. Donnie ended up saving Mel and I. Football changed and they, at first, wanted Mel and I to switch sides depending on the set the other team was in. But we were so used to playing the ball on our inside and just weren't as good from the other side. Bud Carson, our defensive coordinator, permitted us to play the way we had because Donnie could deal with it either way. So, he saved us. Donnie Shell made it possible for us to stay home. That was one of the elements for our success, but not much was made of it. Donnie deserves credit for that."

Carson, who could be demanding, said, "Stay on your side."

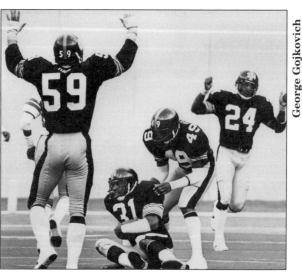

Steelers' secondary from left to right Jack Ham (59), Donnie Shell(31), Dwayne Woodruff (49) and J.T. Thomas (24).

* * *

"Sister Josepha told me I should sign up to be a student in a newly-integrated school. She was a nun and she always looked after me. She was an influential person in my life. Her and my mother helped me.

"I told the school officials I wanted to play football. Now here's a black kid coming into a previously all-white school and telling them what he wanted to do. Seventeen of us black kids integrated the school.

"I had a speech impediment and I couldn't say friend. I couldn't figure out whether it was an 'i' or and 'e' that came first. I'm talking but I'm not talking like I should. This one teacher, Margaret Tatum was her name. She came from New York and didn't speak like a southerner. Miss Tatum told me that a friend was a friend to the *end*, and that is how I learned to write and say 'friend' properly.

* * *

"I was prepared when I was the first black football player at Florida State. I was a sprinter on our relay team. I was interested in going to the University of Georgia in my home state but Vince Dooley, the head football coach, said his program wasn't ready for a black to be on the team. Bill Peterson, the coach at Florida State, read a newspaper story about that and he called me and said Florida State was ready.

"Glen Edwards came from a town near the Okeechobee Lake in Florida. We called our linebackers and defensive backs 'Chobees.' Even Jack Lambert. Dwight White also called Lambert 'a damn racist' from time to time. We liked to give everyone a hard time.

"We had a Chobee party and Lambert said that blacks were not invited. He didn't care what he said. We got used to it. Dwight didn't ever get used to it.

Glen Edwards and Bobby Bell at Andy Russell's Celebrity Golf Outing at the Club at Nevillewood.

"We got after each other on and off the field. One time, in a game at Denver, Haven Moses caught a touchdown pass on me; he went up high and pulled it in, jumping above me and catching it one-handed in the end zone. They were at the five-yard line and we were jammed pretty tight. Greene got upset, and came back and got in my face. He screamed in my face. 'What the hell's wrong with you? You can't defend against a pass like that?' Dwight came in and defended me. He hollored at Greene, 'if they hadn't been trapping your big ass one play after another, they wouldn't have been on the five-yard line in the first place.' Dwight and Greene are going at it in the huddle. It was unreal.

"Chuck picked up on it and at halftime he comes to me and asks, 'T, what is going on out there? Are they pointing fingers out there?' I told him that was exactly what was going on. You wouldn't believe some of the stuff that went on."

OF FAMER

CO HARRIS

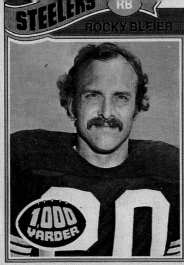

STEELERS
RB
ROCKY BLEIER

1,000 YARDER

Steelers

32

ROCKY BLEIER
STEELERS

20

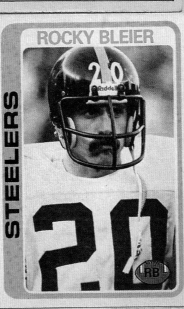

ROCKY BLEIER

STEELERS

20

RB

FRANCO HARRIS

STEELERS

RB

OCKY BLEIER
RB

AFC ★★★ ALL-PRO

STEELERS
FRANCO HARRIS
RB

Topps

STEELERS   FRANCO HARR

DeBlasio's
Restaurant

HOURS:
MON Thru THURS 11 a.m
FRI & SAT 11 a.m. 1a.m

Photo by George Gojkovich

Lara Logan
The woman in the red suit

Kathleen Churchman O'Brien

Lara Logan is a lovely lady, a woman of worthwhile substance, smart, courageous, daring, who enjoys challenges and proudly speaks her mind. This cost her dearly in February of 2019 when she and CBS News had "a parting of the ways" because she was critical of the liberal media on a conservative podcast. "This interview is professional suicide for me," she told conservative host Mike Ritland.

It was, indeed. This break-up occurred two weeks after I had seen and heard Lara Logan when she appeared Tuesday, February 5 in the Town Hall South Speakers Series in the auditorium of Upper St. Clair High School in Pittsburgh's South Hills.

Logan is an attractive woman, to begin with, and she was especially eye-catching in a vibrant red suit. It was a snug-fitting suit, and she kept tugging at it to straighten its line, and she frequently twirled her brown hair. Many women were critical of her performance.

This is a fearless woman who gained fame mostly as a war correspondent for CBS. She is the mother of a boy and a girl and she was pregnant with each of them in a Mideast war zone. She covered assignments in Afghanistan and Iraq. She was attacked and sexually assaulted by a mob of men in Egypt.

She had great stories to share. She shocked some when she said, "I'm the woman with the big boobs, and I can live with that."

I told my wife Kathie, who was sitting next to me, that Lara Logan looked sumptuous in that red suit. I had read somewhere in a John Grisham book the week before that "you can't ignore a woman in a red dress." The same can be said for a red suit.

Lara Logan was even more appealing at a lunch and Q. and A. session at the St. Clair County Club that followed her speaking appearance. She was even looser with her comments. More informative and funnier.

I had a chance to speak to her one-on-one for a few minutes. She is 5–6 so I could look her in her vibrant eyes. She is South African, born in Durban. I told her she has to write a book about her experiences. Not many people have survived her experiences.

I told her I was working on my 30th book, this book. "Maybe you can help me," she said.

I gave her my business card with my phone number and address. She had shared a story earlier in which she had given a Russian official a false phone number in exchange for a visa to visit Russia on one of her assignments. "This is my real phone number," I said, "not like the one you used to get into Russia."

She smiled. Our eyes met. "I can help you," I said. "I lead one writers' group for seniors and another for elementary school kids at an after-school program. I know how to do it."

She smiled once more. "Are we still talking about the book?" she said innocently.

Is it any wonder I fell in love with Lara Logan?

"Who are you writing a book about?" she asked.

"It's about Franco Harris and Rocky Bleier?"

"Who are they?" she said.

It's a question one does not expect to hear in Pittsburgh. But she's from South Africa and not the South Hills.

Photo by George Gojkovich

Photo by Jim O'Brien

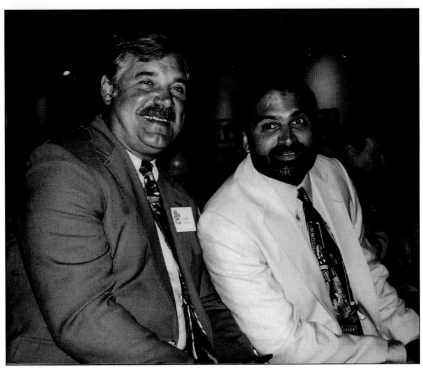

Larry Csonka of Miami Dolphins and Franco Harris of Steelers meet at Pro Football Hall of Fame in Canton, Ohio and, below, Dante Lavelli of the Cleveland Browns meets Rocky Bleier at the same site.

Rocky Bleier and Mike Wagner enjoy reunion at Andy Russell's Celebrity Golf Tournament at The Club at Nevillewood. Bleier, left to right, with John Paul and Mel Blount at same outing.

Photos by Jim O'Brien

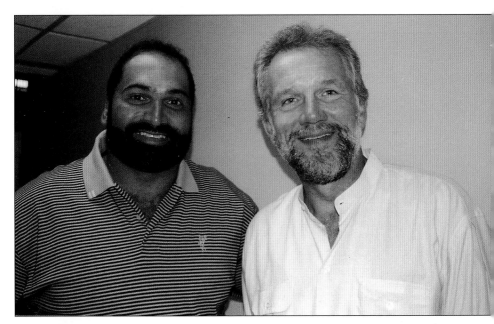

PENN STATE STARS—Franco Harris and Jack Ham in press box at Heinz Field. Franco and Lenny Moore when Franco was inducted into Pro Football Hall of Fame in 1990.

Franco Harris, Joe Paterno and Ralph Papa of Citizens Bank at Heinz History Center awards program.

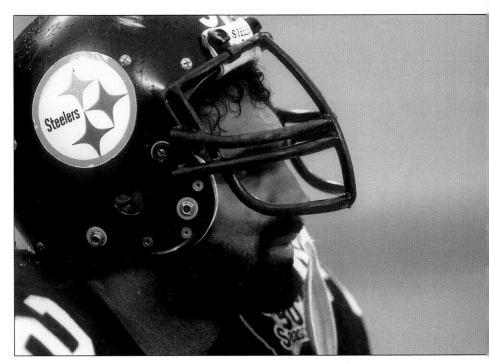

Franco Harris follows pulling guard Sam Davis (No. 57) on end sweep.

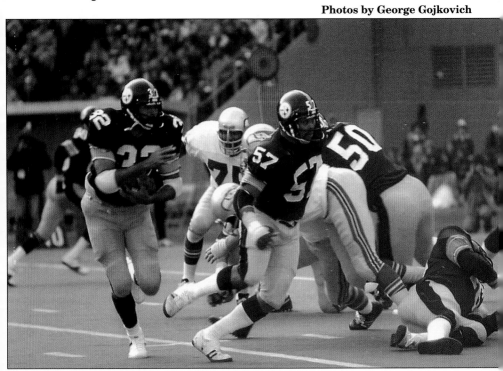

Thomas said that on-the-field episode, the players hollering at each other, prompted Ernie "Fats" Holmes to bring a handgun to the next practice. Joe Greene and Dwight forgot about it, but not Fats.

"Linda Washington from Homestead was the receptionist at the time and she saw that Ernie had a gun with him. She reported this to Dan Rooney, the team president.

"You know who took the gun away from Fats? It wasn't Joe Greene. It was Dan."

* * *

"Franco was a true friend from Day One," said Thomas.

"Most guys of his stature protect themselves from the public. Franco goes to so many places. Franco will be the last guy to leave when we get together. He's walking out with the janitor.

"His wife Dana is delightful. And so funny. She'll say, 'I guess I'm going to take off my shoes. He's going to turn the lights off.' He has such a great heart. I've seen guys who won't mix with the fans. They don't give a shit; it's that simple. You want your picture taken with him, Franco poses with you until you like the photo. I was with him once at a signing at Shop'n Save. They didn't know me until they heard my name. Franco they recognized right away. He'd tell me to get in the picture. I've seen him pose four times with someone.

"You could call Franco at three in the morning. He'd say, 'You got a problem? What can I do?' That's Franco Harris. He's very compassionate. He's very concerned about everyone's welfare, just like Rocky.

"Joe Greene has been a good friend to me. Most people don't know what he's really like. He's not Mean Joe Greene. He's so big and intimidating. They don't see the soft part. We saw that side of him.

Dwayne Woodruff, J.T. Thomas and Joe Greene.

"You know our team came out of a tough time in this country's life. We're talking about segregation, segregated schools, hotels, restaurants, bath rooms, drinking fountains, the civil rights movement, the protests, the back of the bus business, killing of Dr. Martin Luther King, and somehow we all came together in Pittsburgh. How did we come together?

"How did we get such a fine focus on what we needed to be winners in the NFL? How did it happen? I had a seat in the balcony and I saw what happened. That's what I'm going to call my book, *From the Balcony.*"

I told him when I was a teenager, back in the mid to late '50s, that I used to sit on the left side of the balcony as you faced the movie screen, and all the blacks sat high up on the right side of the balcony. There were no signs. No restrictions. Yet, by choice, we were segregated. It's just the way it was.

Among Steelers' alumni at Mel Blount Dinner are, left to right, Blount, Terry Bradshaw, Donnie Shell and Randy Grossman.

                              *   *   *

One time in the late '60s, I was in Toronto with people associated with the Pittsburgh Penguins, the new
team in town. As I approached the Royal York Hotel
in downtown Toronto, I recognized Errol Garner, the
great jazz pianist from Pittsburgh.

I had never seen him in person before, just pho-
tos. I introduced myself and had a question for him.
There had been so many great jazz musicians from
Pittsburgh.

"Mr. Garner, I just
wanted to say hello. My
name is Jim O'Brien, and
I'm a reporter for *The
Pittsburgh Press*. How
do you account for the
fact that so many great
jazz musicians are from
Pittsburgh?"

Mr. Garner stroked
that little so-black goa-
tee of his for a moment in
thought. "I guess," he said
through shining coal-black
eyes, "because they were
born there."

Jazz pianist Errol Garner

I think I was looking
for something deeper, but
maybe that's all there was to it. Why were the Steelers
so good in the '70s? They signed the best ballplayers.
The stars were in their favor. They got lucky. It was
that simple, nothing deeper.

"I was a big fan of the Green Bay Packers in the '60s," said Thomas. "I liked Herb Adderly, who was a defensive back and wore number 24, and Willie Wood, a defensive back who wore number 26, and I always wore those numbers.

"I looked up the players who came before me. There was respect for the older guys.

"The colleges provide a minor league for pro football. It's a great business model. What's different today is that the players are so selfish. When they act like Antonio Brown and Le'Veon Bell they make it appear that Mike Tomlin can't control the team.

"They make the Steelers look bad, Pittsburgh look bad and Mike Tomlin look bad. They say he can't control the team. Worse yet, they say he can't control *his own people*.

"Antonio Brown is on a journey, in a boat, out in the ocean, and he doesn't care about anyone else. You'd think that out of respect for his own coach he'd behave better. His problem is that it's all about me. You're spittin' in the face of folks who made you a millionaire many times over.

George Gojkovich

Antonio Brown is now with Raiders

"I remember how Chuck Noll and Bud Carson pulled Mel Blount out of a game because they didn't think he was getting the job done. Carson told me, 'I hear you're complaining to the press about it. If you fuck up again in the Super Bowl like you did against Oakland, your ass will be back on the bench.' They didn't mince words to get your attention."

Chuck Noll lines up with Franco Harris, Dermonti Dawson, Lynn Swann, Mel Blount, Louie Lipps and Mike Wagner at Heinz Field reunion.

ROCKY

Special day at Pro Football Hall of Fame

I was excited and eager for the day to get underway in late March, 2002. I was going to the Pro Football Hall of Fame and I was going with Rocky Bleier. That's a special day.

Bleier, one of the best comeback stories in sports, owns a Purple Heart from the Vietnam War and four Super Bowl rings from his days as a running back with the Steelers. He had been asked to speak at a ceremony in Canton, Ohio to open a new exhibit at the Hall of Fame called "Football and America: The NFL Responds During Times of National Crises."

Bleier obliged when I asked him if I could go along for the ride. I met him at 8:30 a.m. at his beautiful home in the Virginia Manor section of Mt. Lebanon. I was greeted at the door by his wife, Jan. She had Rosie, who was 3, in her arms. They were soon joined by Elly, who was 4. The former Jan Gyurina was an investment broker from West Mifflin when they met.

Bleier played in the Homestead Lions' golf outing that July at the Duquesne Golf Club (now Westwood) for the first time, and had been invited back. He said he would return when his schedule permitted.

The Bleiers had been married for six years. It's a second marriage for Rocky. They lived the first three years nearby in Scott Township and then moved to Mt. Lebanon. Rosie and Elly were giving their Dad hugs and kisses as he was about to leave, and Rocky was smiling like he'd just scored another touchdown. Bleier looked great.

Jan and Rocky Bleier

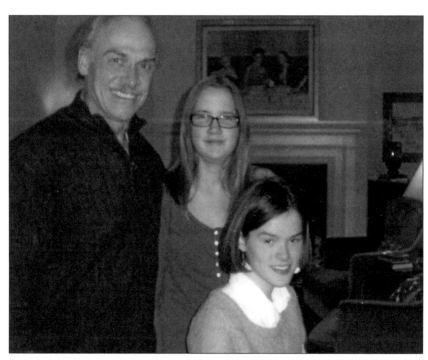

Rocky, Rosie and Elly Bleier at their home in Mt. Lebanon.

It was supposed to be a 2 1/2 hour drive, but Rocky missed the turnoff on the interstate highway in both directions. I didn't mind. We were so busy talking we weren't paying attention to the road signs. An extra hour with Rocky Bleier was a bonus.

"They don't call him Rocky for nothing," cracked Craig Wolfley, a former Steelers' lineman who once blocked for Bleier, and now owned a martial arts studio in Bridgeville, when I told him about our Hall of Fame odyssey.

Bleier said he averaged about 110 speaking engagements a year. He still attracts handsome fees for motivational talks. Following a brief stint as a TV sportscaster, that's how Bleier has been making a living for nearly 40 years since retiring from pro football. He remains one of the most popular of the Steelers. His comeback after being wounded in Vietnam to star with the Steelers, to rush for 1,000 yards in a season alongside Franco Harris, is quite a tale.

He still frets about what he's going to say, and how he will be received. I understood what he was saying. He wants to make a positive impression.

He succeeded and then some at a luncheon program that preceded a ribbon cutting ceremony. Bleier is featured in one of the display segments. It's a display that was inspired by the events of September 11, the terrorism that sparked a renewed patriotic spirit in America. It's an impressive display showing NFL players involvement in America's war and national crises. It was put together by the NFL and the Hall of Fame.

One of the displays showed the New York Giants in full football gear marching with faux rifles on their shoulders, something they did for an hour each day at practice during World War II. There's a listing of all NFL and pro football players who saw military service. It's compelling stuff.

"My dad used to tell me, "Son, someday you'll be in the Pro Football Hall of Fame,' " Bleier said for beginners, "and here I am, so to speak. I hope this counts, too."

* * *

Bleier is a busy man. I told him I could ride shotgun and take notes as he was driving to and from Canton. I learned a lesson in journalism from none other than Bill Bradley, the Princeton-educated basketball star of the New York Knicks and later a U.S. Senator from New Jersey.

One day I met Bradley after the Knicks had practiced at the gym of the School for the Deaf on Long Island—the Knicks almost never practiced at Madison Square Garden. Bradley lived in Manhattan and didn't have a car. I had a Volkswagen Bug.

Dollar Bill, as he was known because his dad was a banker back in Crystal City, Missouri, and Bill was making what was considered big money in the early '80s, told me to give him my keys. "We can save time," he said, "if I drive and you write while we're talking."

I've been doing that sort of thing ever since. Plus, Rocky Bleier was driving a large black Mercedes-Benz, and you couldn't have asked for a better chauffeur.

Bill Bradley of New York Knicks

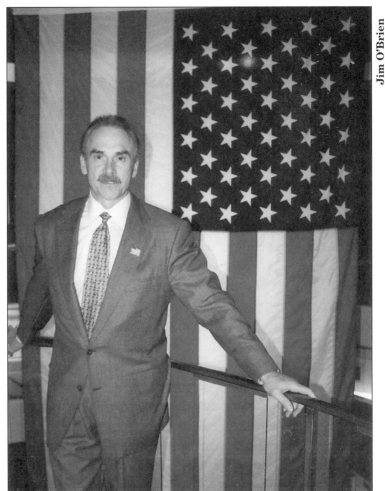

Jim O'Brien

Bleier stands by American flag at Pro Football Hall of Fame in Canton, Ohio.

End Of Prayer Rocky Would Say Before a Game:

"One more thing, Lord. Please allow me to play the way I am capable of playing. Let me have a good game, so I don't embarrass what I stand for—my religion, my school, my family, or myself. You've given me the grace to be out here. Now give me a little more so I can do a good job. Thanks, Lord."

—From *"Fighting Back,"* Bleier's biography

Jack Ham

Franco wasn't the greatest practice player; everyone roots for Rocky

Jack Ham has been in the Pro Football Hall of Fame since 1988, the first year he was eligible for induction. More importantly, Andy Russell regards Ham as the greatest linebacker in Steelers' history. Ham is happy to have Russell's respect and regard. Jack Lambert won't tell me how he feels about that.

The 1974 draft class of the Steelers might have been the best draft class in NFL history, but the 1971 class that included Ham as the No. 2 choice ranks high on the list. Thirteen of the 22 selections made the team.

It's been 17 years since I last interviewed Jack Ham in his office at the Airside Business Park in Moon Township—I still am reminded of that day when I see snow dripping like glaze on a bundt cake when I drive through a certain passage on the Parkway West—but his thoughts about Franco Harris and Rocky Bleier remain intact and valid.

"I remember when Franco Harris came to the team that year after I did. I had played with Franco at Penn State and I knew how good he was. We had Lydell Mitchell in the same backfield as Franco at Penn State, so we were loaded there.

"The Steelers had a bad experience with a Penn State back before we got there. Bob Campbell didn't pan out for them. He dropped punts and fumbled the ball. Some of the veteran players were down on Franco from the start with the Steelers.

"When he came into camp some of the veterans and press guys were ready to put him in the same grouping as Bob Ferguson and Dick Leftridge, two running backs from Ohio State and West Virginia who had failed miserably with the Steelers.

"Franco wasn't the greatest practice player and that only added to the doubts about his ability. Then we played in an exhibition game in Atlanta and Franco ran about 80 yards for a touchdown and that's when everyone knew he'd be fine.

"Franco just had his own schedule. He and L.C. might have been the worst practice players in the team's history. They moved to the beat of their own drums. Franco saved himself for the real stuff. He walks better than most old running backs these days.

"We had a great set of running backs in Franco Harris and Rocky Bleier. I met Rocky in 1971, and I thought he had a tough situation. But he made it. In '76, when he got the thousand yards, I never saw 44 guys pulling so hard for one guy to get an individual goal like that. Everyone roots for Rocky. He's that kind of guy."

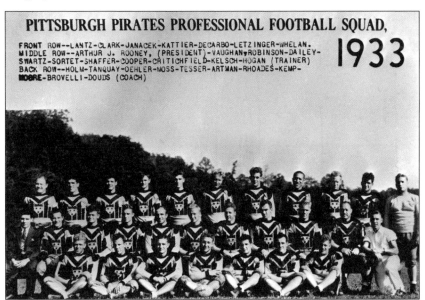

PITTSBURGH PIRATES PROFESSIONAL FOOTBALL SQUAD,

FRONT ROW--LANTZ-CLARK-JANACEK-KATTIER-DECARBO-LETZINGER-WHELAN. MIDDLE ROW--ARTHUR J. ROONEY, (PRESIDENT)-VAUGHAN-ROBINSON-DAILEY-SWARTZ-SORTET-SHAFFER-COOPER-CRITICHFIELD-KELSCH-HOGAN (TRAINER) BACK ROW--HOLM-TANQUAY-OEHLER-MOSS-TESSER-ARTMAN-RHOADES-KEMP-MOORE-BROVELLI-DOUDS (COACH)

1933

Jack Ham and Joe Paterno at Pro Football Hall of Fame induction ceremonies in 1988.

Mike Fabus/Pittsburgh Steelers

STEELERS LINEUP—Mike Wagner and Ray Mansfield in foreground, second row left to right, Pete Rostosky, Bill Hurley, Tony Parisi, Frank Sciulli, J.T. Thomas;back row,Steve Furness, Ted Petersen, Craig Wolfley, Emil Boures, Robin Cole, Craig Bingham, John Banaszak, Bill Cowher, Jack Lambert, Rodgers Freyvogel, Rocky Bleier, Moon Mullins and Andy Russell.

Mel Blount in white hat hosts, from left to right, Andy Russell, Dan Rooney, Terry Bradshaw, Chuck Noll and Donnie Shell at his annual celebrity dinner.

Joe Greene

The first building block of dynasty

"Joe Greene is a great man."
—Art Rooney

Some say that it all began with Joe Greene. When the Steelers selected Joe Greene out of North Texas State with their first pick in the 1969 college draft a headline in the next day's Pittsburgh daily screamed **"JOE WHO?"**

But Steelers' fans and the National Football League found out fast that Joe Greene was one of the greatest defensive linemen ever to come along. "Mean Joe Greene" was the first building block of Chuck Noll's dream team of the '70s.

It all began when Noll said, "OK, we'll go after Greene in the draft."

Then came L.C. Greenwood and Terry Bradshaw and Mel Blount and Franco Harris. Greene argues that it all began with Franco. "Before Franco, the Steelers didn't win shit," said Mean Joe one day when he was feeling particularly feisty.

Before Joe Greene came along, the Steelers were known as S.O.S.—the same old Steelers. They had never won a championship in the first 40 years of the franchise and seldom posted winning records.

The first time I ever laid eyes on Joe Greene he was coming through a door behind Mel Blount into a dark stairway at the Steelers' summer training camp in July of 1979, and I was so glad they were good guys. Otherwise, to be honest, they'd have appeared ominous, the way opposing teams saw them.

97

George Gojkovich

Terry Bradshaw and Joe Greene were the building blocks for the offense and defense of the Steelers' four title teams. Below Roy Jefferson and Joe Greene.

Jim O'Brien

When I attended the Mel Blount Celebrity Dinner on April 5, 2019, I was not surprised to see Blount and Greene sitting next to each other. They were roommates in their playing days and they have remained close friends.

*   *   *

Greene was the leader of the Steelers' "Steel Curtain" defensive line during the 1970s. He dominated the line and helped lead the Steelers to four Super Bowl titles when they were tabbed the NFL's "Team of the Decade."

He was named the NFL's Rookie of the Year in 1969 even though the Steelers posted a 1-13 record and he received the first of his 10 Pro Bowl invitations. He was all-NFL five times and was twice the league's Defensive Player of the Year.

He came up big in the biggest games. He was credited for making big plays in the Steelers' Super Bowl IX victory over the Minnesota Vikings when he had a pass interception and a fumble recovery at Tulane Stadium in New Orleans.

Chuck Noll said Greene was the greatest defensive lineman in the league.

During a players' strike in 1974, Joe Greene stayed home in Denton, Texas. "I didn't want to carry a picket sign against the Rooneys," he explained. "They're the nicest people I know. If the other owners were like the Rooneys, there wouldn't be a strike."

After the Steelers had won four Super Bowls, an independent promotion was launched featuring Greene, showing him wearing four Super Bowl rings on the fingers of his right hand, and a bare thumb thrust upward, with the theme "One For The Thumb in '81" emblazoned across T-shirts and such.

By JIM O'BRIEN

Franco Harris has a sense of history, ev
doesn't always reveal it. Then, too, maybe the
outstanding runner is, at age 29, simply too you
preciate the greatness of the old pros he is pass
record books.

Today at Three Rivers Stadium, when the
play the Cincinnati Bengals, Harris can bec
fourth greatest ground-gainer in National
League history.

The former Penn State star needs only 67
pass San Francisco's Joe P—— ho, with 8,3
is fourth amon—————— hing leade
compil———————————————————

Vets

Franco In A Reco

(A feature on how Franco's fortunes changed this
season appears in today's Roto.)

Franco Harris has a sense of history that gives him
special pride in his present-day performance in pro
football.

Harris stuck his head into the kitchen at the Steelers'
office complex at Three Rivers Stadium the other day
and caught the eye of Art
Rooney Sr., who was eating a
bowl of lima bean soup.

X's & O's

"Hey, Franco," said the
Steeler owner, "do you know
who Bronko Nagurski is?"

"Sure, I do," responded
Franco. "He was some fullback."

Rooney smiled at Franco's
fast reply. "Well, good," said
Rooney. "The other day I told
Sidney Thornton that he was
running more and more like
Bronko Nagurski and he said,
'Who's he?'"

By Jim O'Brien

"I'll straighten him out on that," offered Franco with
a wink.

Harris has his heroes and Thornton has his, listing
Jim Brown and Jim Taylor as his all-time favorites.

Going into today's game with the Washington
Redskins at Three Rivers Stadium, Harris and Thornton
form the hottest running tandem in the American Football Conference.

With three 100-yard plus efforts in the last four
weeks, Harris has moved into second place among the
leading rushers, right behind Earl Campbell of the
Houston Oilers. Campbell has compiled 812 yards to 610
for Harris. But Harris has a higher average, 4.8 yards
per carry to Campbell's 4.5. On the other hand, Campbell has 12 touchdowns to his credit while Harris has
six.

Thornton, with 521 yards in 102 carries for a 3.9 average, ranks seventh. Thornton has scored five
touchdowns by running and four on receptions to rank
behind Campbell in the AFC touchdown-scoring chart
with nine.

Franco is now fifth on the career touchdown list for
National Football League running backs with 67, two
behind Steve Van Buren of the Philadelphia Eagles.

Harris is just 13
player in NFL h
eight years. Only
that honor.

Among the all-t

HARRIS
with Walter Payton of the
move into the top 10.

All-Time Lead

	Name	Team	Yr
1.	Jim Brown, Cleveland		
2.	*O.J. Simpson, Buffalo-San Fran.		
3.	Jim Taylor, Green Bay-N.O.		
4.	Joe Perry, San Francisco		
5.	*Franco Harris, Pittsburgh		1
6.	*Larry Csonka, Miami-N.Y.-Miami		
7.	Leroy Kelly, Cleveland		
8.	J.H. Johnson, S.F.-Det.-Pgh-Hou.		10
9.	*Lydell Mitchell,Balt.-S.Diego		
10.	Floyd Little, Denver		9
11.	*Walter Payton, Chicago		5
12.	John Riggins, N.Y.-Jets-Wash.		9
13.	Don Perkins, Dallas		8
14.	Ken Willard, S.F.-St. Louis		1
15.	Lawrence McCutcheon, Los. Ang.		8
	*Still active.		

It didn't get Greene as much attention as his famous Coca-Cola TV commercial, where he tossed his soiled game jersey to a young boy in the runway, but it played well in Pittsburgh.

Art and Dan Rooney were both present for the "One for the Thumb" promotion at the Downtown Hyatt. "Joe Greene is a great player," said Art Rooney, a man of few words. "Joe Greene is a great man."

When Greene got up, he said, "Why do I play? The organization, that's why. Mr. Rooney gave me a job, and I enjoy working for him. Then there's Dan. He's not only an outstanding boss, but a friend.

"There's Chuck Noll. This is a guy who's created an environment for us football players to use our talent in the proper way. There are two sides to everyone's personality, a positive side and a negative side. He's created an environment for us to bring out the positive side.

"Any type of losing is something we as players don't accept. So when our backs are to the wall, and we're losing, we know we can turn it around. Everything is positive. It's all because of the tutelage of Chuck Noll. He's always the same, win or lose. You have to take first things first. Chuck Noll says it all the time.

"You have to start at the top with the decision-making process. Chuck Noll and Dan Rooney sit in the same seat. I've seen them form this championship team. I've been here when it wasn't so good. We're going to be championship caliber material as long as Dan Rooney and Chuck Noll are together."

As Greene approached his 33rd birthday and his 11th season with the Steelers, he knew there'd be questions about how long he could continue to play for the team. It would be the same for Rocky Bleier.

"Basically, we're the same age," said Greene. "We've both been beaten up. But I know what Chuck wants from me on defense, and Rocky Bleier knows what Chuck wants from him on offense. Some kid might come in who can make us both look bad in the 40-yard dash. But he won't know what Chuck Noll wants."

Joe Greene was the guy you wanted to talk to after a Steelers' game, win or lose. No one captured the spirit of the competition or what it all meant better than he did. He was so expansive in his explanations. It didn't play well on radio and TV, however. Jack Ham was the last guy you wanted to talk to after a game. He was boring. But Ham is great on the air. He sees what is happening, and he can analyze it more succinctly than Greene or most other former players.

But when you wanted an in-depth story on the Steelers you said thank God for Joe Greene. On Monday, May 6, 2013, Greene announced that he was retiring for the third and final time from the Steelers—as a special assistant to GM Kevin Colbert in the pro and college personnel scouting area. Greene previously retired from the Steelers after 12 seasons as a player (ten-time Pro Bowl performer) after the 1981 season, and later after a five-year stint as defensive line coach after the 1995 season. He helped Chuck Noll finish his 23-year tenure as head coach.

"Joe has been an inspiration in this organization is so many capacities over so many years," said team president Art Rooney II.

Joe Greene sat down to talk about his days with the Steelers during one of his visits to Pittsburgh to participate in a sports card show in Monroeville and Andy Russell's golf outing at The Club at Nevillewood:

"I'm not young anymore. I see the gray in my whiskers"

When I sit down with the guys I played with, I am back at Three Rivers Stadium and at summer training camp at St. Vincent College. It comes back so quickly. We are young again. Those were the good ol' days.

Yes, it's more meaningful now, much more meaningful. I know I'm not young anymore. I see the gray in my whiskers and in the hair on my head. I can't kid myself about that. The mirror tells me every morning that I've gotten older. My children are as old as I was when I was wrapping up my playing career with the Steelers. My wife Agnes, dear Agnes, has died and that was a wake-up call.

Sitting there, with the guys at Andy Russell's golf outing, I had a little melancholy moment. I was looking at L.C. Greenwood, Glen Edwards, Andy and Moon Mullins, Gordon Gravelle and Mike Wagner. We started reminiscing. When I got sad, I looked at all the years that have gone by. I'm one of the old people now.

I'm glad to have those kinds of memories.

As a coach with other teams, seeking that Holy Grail, I've got a better idea of how difficult it can be to win a championship in this league. What we did—winning four Super Bowls in six seasons—was a tremendous accomplishment. I realize that more than ever now. The enormity of our accomplishment has been validated.

Joe Greene carries Lynn Swann off the field.

We were in a good place at the right time. We had outstanding leadership. I was with an outstanding group of guys. Chuck Noll's leadership made it all mesh.

I knew nobody like him before I met him and I've never met anybody like him since. There's no hyperbole about him. None at all.

He masked his emotions. I remember one time, I was watching him and John Stallworth made one of those fantastic one-handed catches, and I was looking at him and he was smiling. He wasn't smiling with his mouth; he was smiling with his eyes.

I was headstrong when I first came to the Steelers, and thought I knew everything. He got rid of players I liked, and I wondered what he was doing. I was in my second year when he traded away Roy Jefferson, for instance, and that upset me. What did I know? At the time Chuck was building. When a team is in a building process, sometimes it's difficult to comprehend what's happening and why. You don't see the big picture.

The things he was teaching us, I hadn't seen a lot of evidence that it was working (the Steelers' record was 1-13 his first year).

I thought Terry Bradshaw was quite a quarterback when we were teammates. That's been verified, too. I've talked to Terry from time to time and I know he cherishes his Steelers' experience. I remember what Terry told us, "You can lose with me, but you can't win without me." He said it mostly in jest, but he was right.

He was there when we needed him. He was a big game player. I've seen other teams with championship quality, but they couldn't win again and again as we did. You look at the Chicago Bears (of Mike Ditka in the mid-80s) and they just had an outstanding team for five years. But they won one Super Bowl. They didn't always have the same quarterback. Jim

Joe Greene wasn't so mean in his portrayal in this award-winning 1979 Coca-Cola ad where he tossed his jersey to a kid for giving him a Coke.

McMahon wasn't always the quarterback the way Terry Bradshaw was always our quarterback. Terry was there for us...all the time.

That's the incredible thing. You mention guys like Swann and Stallworth, and they were always there, too. You never mentioned dropped balls when you talked about those guys. They pulled in everything, especially in the clutch. They were champion receivers.

Terry struggled at the start, as we all did. He had some rough times. Outside of Pittsburgh, there was talk that Terry wasn't real bright. Terry threw a lot of interceptions for awhile. But it wasn't true that he wasn't bright. Terry had so much confidence in his arm, sometimes he did things that came back to haunt him.

People in Pittsburgh know what he meant to our team. That's why I was glad that he got the reception he got when he came back to Pittsburgh as an honorary captain (in 2002). He deserved that.

I talked to Brad about that, and he said, "I was amazed. I didn't know they liked me so much."

It's the same everywhere. When things don't go well, the quarterback is an easy target. Terry had a rocky start in Pittsburgh. The day he got hurt and they cheered as he was coming off the field stuck with him. I know that hurt him badly, and he never really got over it. He never forgot it, anyhow. That had to be painful.

I always liked to say that no man knows another man's pain. That's why we shouldn't be too quick to judge other people when they're having problems.

What I understand better today, as a coach and consultant, is how difficult it is to make decisions. Maybe what you think is right goes against the tides. No one may know it's the right decision but you. But you have to do the things you believe in.

Chuck Noll being a young guy—he was 33 to 40 years old—when he first had us. He lived an awful lot in a short time. He made some great decisions. If I could say there was one failure—and I use that word guardedly—we were slow to change once we fielded the finest team in the league. None of us wanted to leave. No one was happy when they were cut or traded away. Some guys were kept one year too long. I might have been one of them.

But look at the good decisions he made. He picked Terry Bradshaw over Terry Hanratty and Joe Gilliam. Believe me...that was not an easy decision when it was made.

Look at how he traded away Bruce Van Dyke to open a position for a young Gerry Mullins. Mullins was a college tight end, yet Noll took him to play guard. What about moving Larry Brown from tight end to tackle? How about taking a college center and turning him into the outstanding offensive tackle of his era?

George Gojkovich

I'm talking, of course, about Jon Kolb.

I know now how difficult it is to get 45 to 50 guys to work in unison. But Chuck Noll did this. That's why we're still being remembered.

"Love yourself and realize that whatever you attempt to achieve in life is a direct reflection of you."
—**Joe Greene**

An unknown soldier saves Rocky's life

"I had collapsed on the ground when my arms and shoulders gave out. Now a guy said he'd carry me fireman-style, over his shoulder. I never knew his name, and I don't think he ever knew mine. I didn't know anything but nicknames for most of the guys. But the Army had a beautiful way of making names seem unimportant...and race, and color, and creed, and social status. We never looked for that in each other. The Army is a great equalizer.

"I was white, this guy was black. We had each traveled thousands of miles to meet in a jungle. After this night, I would never see him again. We both knew that. Yet here he was, offering to pick me up bodily and help save my life. That's a special kind of love."

Excerpt from Fighting Back,
Rocky Bleier biography

War and Peace

Some stories from sources, not to be attributed

Vito Stellino covered the Steelers for the *Pittsburgh Post-Gazette* in the '70s and he wrote a story suggesting the team was getting lax in following Chuck Noll's curfew rules.

His story reported that players, coaches and even members of the media were staying out late, past their bedtime, drinking and carrying on at bars on Route 30 near the St. Vincent College campus. Bobby Dale's and The Touchdown Club were hot spots.

Noll was upset when he read this story and called a team meeting to read the riot act to one and all. He wanted this to stop. Noll never went out at night, but his assistants did. Stellino never went out at night, either, but Norm Vargo and Myron Cope and I did and we got the inside scoop on a lot of issues. We'd mention a name of someone we thought would be cut and the coaches would nod or wag their head but not say anything. We knew who was going to be cut before it was announced. This gave us a head-start on stories.

That same night, after Noll had chewed out the players about their behavior, one of those stay-out-late offenders recalls "one of my teammates is dancing on top of the bar under a ceiling mirror, like John Travolta in 'Saturday Night Fever.' It was funny as hell." So much for discipline.

"I think Noll stuffed cotton in his ears when he went to bed, hoping Ralph Berlin wouldn't be knocking on his door with any bad news," said a source. Berlin, known affectionally as "the Plumber," was responsible

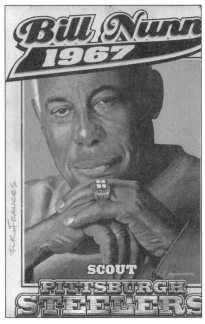

Courtesy of Art Rooney Jr.

for checking the rooms at night to make sure the Steelers were tucked in their beds.

The late Bill Nunn, Jr., a Steelers' scout and the camp director, once related to me that Noll did not want to know some things. "He picked his battles carefully," said Nunn. "He knew who was staying out late, but with some of the guys he didn't want to make a big deal of it. He didn't want to win a battle but lose the war."

* * *

Another former Steelers star thinks that the term "team leader" is often over-rated. He said some of the quieter Steelers often set the standard for everyone in the locker room.

He remembered the day Ernie "Fats" Holmes, a defensive tackle who was a legendary member of the "Steel Curtain" defense—that banner originally referred only to the front four—brought a handgun to practice.

Ernie was a volatile sort, and had gotten annoyed with some teammates over stormy encounters at practice. Ray "The Ol' Ranger" Mansfield, for instance, hated to go against Holmes in practice. Mansfield, a center and team leader, complained that Holmes practiced with the same ferocity that he played in actual games. He never took a down off.

Ernie let everyone know he brought his "piece" to practice, and he was going to use it if someone agitated him. Ernie was easily agitated.

"You know who took the gun away?" asked my Deep Throat. "It wasn't Joe Greene."

I had no idea.

"It was Dan," said the former Steeler.

"You mean Dan Rooney?"

"Yes, Dan Rooney."

Now there was a real leader.

None of this, by the way, appears anywhere in *About Three Bricks Shy of a Load*, the wonderful book by Roy Blount Jr., after he hung around the Steelers during the 1973 season. That was the year before they had the greatest draft in NFL history, and the year before they won their first Super Bowl.

It's a classic, but there are more stories. The stories never end.

* * *

On March 16, 1973, Ernie had an emotional breakdown while driving on the Ohio Turnpike. He was firing shots at a police helicopter that was pursuing him after seeing him driving erratically.

He abandoned his car alongside the highway and ran through a field. Finally, he tossed his gun and threw up his hands. Ernie knew the routine. He was depressed, having some marital problems, and was feuding with his teammates.

"Can you imagine the kind of exposure something like that would get today with all the social media?" asked another former Steeler.

Holmes was taken to Western Psychiatric Hospital in Pittsburgh where he was diagnosed with acute paranoid psychosis, depressed mental problems.

Art Rooney dispatched L.C. Greenwood to Western Psych to check in on Ernie Holmes.

Greenwood told me during an interview that Ernie screamed at him, "You gotta get me out of here! These people are all crazy!"

The Rooneys came to the rescue and somehow got Holmes off without any jail time. They exercised that kind of influence in those days.

Despite this behavior, most of his teammates will tell you, "Down deep, Ernie was a good guy." He dressed up as Santa Claus for team family celebrations at Christmas time.

Noll said Holmes was the best defensive player over a two-year stretch, "but he ate and drank himself out of the league. Ernie was a man of great excesses."

After he retired, Holmes came back to Pittsburgh for reunions and golf outings and usually ran up big bills for telephone and room service.

He always had weight problems. He wore a rubber suit to practice one day at St. Vincent, hoping to sweat and shed some pounds. "He started stinking so bad you didn't want to be near him," recalls one former Steeler. "Noll was a hands-on coach and he liked to get in the huddle with his players. But that huddle kept getting bigger and bigger as Noll and the players were backing away from Fats."

Holmes had a tragic ending. He had been an actor and a wrestler —is there a difference?—and he became an ordained

Jim O'Brien

Ernie Holmes

minister in a small town in Texas. He was driving one day, without a seat belt, and his car left the road and rolled over several times. He was found dead on the scene near Beaumont.

Holmes, Dwight White and L.C. Greenwood have all died and people offer condolences to Joe Greene, the only remaining figure from that famous and infamous front four. Steve Furness also died.

Staggering Statistics: The average age for NFL players dying is between 53 and 59 years, depending on position played. And 78 percent of NFL players either go bankrupt or are under financial stress within two years of retirement, according to May 2019 issue of *Money* magazine.

George Gojkovich

L.C. Greenwood, Mel Blount and Joe Greene at Steelers' reunion at Heinz Field.

ROCKY

On the Road to Canton

Here's what Rocky Bleier had to say on our trip to and from Canton, Ohio on March 27, 2002. It's hard to believe it was that long ago. He could have been saying the same thing yesterday. None of this was in "The Play," the story of Rocky Bleier on stage. I never used a tape recorder; I just took notes. I don't think I missed too many words. And, after all, this was not Lincoln's Gettysburg Address. Rocky reflects:

Some people criticized Franco for running out of bounds and avoiding collisions, or going down without fighting for more yardage if we didn't absolutely need it. Franco missed seven games in his career. So ultimately it was for the good of the team, not proving how tough you are. I might have done that myself, but I couldn't get that far. I was out of breath by the time I got near the sidelines. I wasn't fast enough to run out of bounds before I got tackled.

Along the way, we always see things from our own perspective. We worked out together, but sometimes you didn't get to see the other sides of people and get to know them as well. When you try to put into perspective life's accomplishments, you're always thinking how to make it better, more outstanding. People want to know why you did this or that. "Why were you so successful?" they ask. At the time, you didn't know. Maybe now you know.

It's part of what I talk about. Before you become aware of what's happening, you have to reach a certain sense of security about yourself.

Will I know the plays? Are they going to holler at me?

That's truer of guys like Randy Grossman, Donnie Shell and me—they were free agents and I was a real late pick—than the majority of guys who make the team.

And your insecurities that you have—that you bring with you. Are you able to compete at that level? Certain insecurities can make you afraid to do things. When I think about it now, I know that I have experiences to fall back on. Now I know I can do certain things and do them well. Because I've done it before. That doesn't mean you don't go over it in your mind, and worry about what you'll do, but you have your past experience to assure you that you'll get through it. The more you do, the more comfortable you become, just like playing football. Part of that is aging.

I always saw myself as the kid struggling to make the team. Part of that was a driving force. I wanted to excel. That driving force will always be there. I'm older now, but that kid is still there. That kid always resurfaces.

Yes, in a sense, as you put it, I guess I am still fighting back, like in the title of my autobiography.

I was talking to my high school coach, Torchy Clark, the other night. I had called him after learning that one of my high school teammates, a kid on our basketball team, had died, in his mid-50s. His name was Bobby Rammer. A classmate of mine in Appleton sent me the information by e-mail. He thought I would want to know, and I wanted to make sure Torchy knew. Torchy coached me in basketball and in football in high school.

Bobby Rammer died a few days earlier, on a Saturday night. He had cancer. He was a year older than me. Torchy had him from third grade through high school. He was a little rotund guy, a pretty good shooter from the corner.

Ultimately, Torchy and I got into a conversation about influences in our lives. He's 72 now (in 2002) and he teaches some classes at the University of Central Florida. He started the basketball program there when it was called Florida Tech, before it was Central Florida. He has a great recall for names and events from our days in Appleton. He remembers the players he coached. He was saying that sometimes he wondered whether he was too tough on certain people. One never knows. When he was talking about influences, he said he remembered asking me about that when I was at Notre Dame. He asked me who my greatest influence had been. He said, "In the back of my mind, I was thinking it was me." I told him he was certainly one of the biggest influences in my young life.

But I mentioned an event that had stuck in my mind that gave me great inspiration and resolve. Our family lived upstairs of my dad's bar and restaurant. From my bedroom, I could see St. Joe's Church, about a block away on the left side of the street. On Sundays as I sat in my room, when I was 8 or 9, before or after we'd gone to church, I could see the people going to church. There was a football player who had played high school ball in Appleton. I happened to see him going to church. I knew he'd gone to the University of Wisconsin to play football. I remember wondering what he was doing home. He should have been at school playing ball. So, I asked someone about that. I was told he had quit college and come home because he was homesick for his girlfriend. I thought to myself how stupid that was. I thought that I'd never give it up. I thought he blew it. At that moment in time it became clear to me that I'd never do something like that. You pick up stuff like that along the way.

One of the great things The Chief did; he always dropped the note or postcard. He took the time to show he cared about people.

The needs are simple. I picked them up in a management book. They're so important. One of the things that has been drilled into us—from coaches and teachers and parents—is that there is no "I" in TEAM. You have to work together as a unit. Do things for the good of the whole. But if you move the letters around a little in TEAM you can come up with ME in what we do when we're on a team, whether it's in sports or in a work situation. You have to buy into opportunities.

There are six basic needs: 1) expectations; 2) you need materials to be able to do your job; 3) you need a chance to be the best you can be; 4) you need a pat on the back now and then to make you feel wanted and appreciated; 5) hopefully, you can find friendships within the team; 6) a sense that people are interested in you, that they will give you help when you need it.

I have a speaking engagement in Blacksburg, Virginia. I am going to be speaking to two groups that total 5,000 students—6th through 12th grades—and then I'm speaking to 650 student-athletes and students at Virginia Tech. The theme is "Winning Choices." It's a program in character building, as part of the school curricula. They started it last year. I've been thinking about it since I got the call. How do you relate to those students?

I was doing some rehab at Joey David's clinic in Mt. Lebanon. Nellie King was there. He was talking to me about how ballplayers are so different today. He said when he was playing ball the players used to talk to each other for hours during bus trips, that they even sang some songs. They talked to one another and they really got to know one another. He said that today the ballplayers put on their earphones as soon as they're on the bus or airplane, and they're listening to their CDs. (This was before Smartphones, of course) Nobody talks to anybody anymore. They're all in their own little world. They want their own rooms on the road, even suites. Roommates used to be important people in your life. You loafed together, lunched together, went window-shopping together, went out together.

I've averaged about 110 talks a year over the last 15 years. It comes out to a couple a week.

You know you're getting older. How things are different now. All those things you hear about as a young man in your formative years are things you're telling others to do. You don't put any relevance or importance to it at the time, but you were absorbing it. All the books, and things we read, the talks our parents gave us when we were kids. It might not come to the forefront till later on, but it's always there, providing you with a sound foundation for what you do and how you approach things.

I have empathy for players who are down on their luck. Some of them have encountered real difficulties. Things happen that put you in that situation. Some of them, though, are not doing what needs to be done. Sometimes you have to swallow your pride and just go out and get a job. It's harder the older you get to find a place in the job market.

Doing motivational talks is my business. Other people do it as an adjunct to their regular jobs or business careers. They're not depending on it. This is my bread and butter.

"The lessons I learned in Vietnam and in the NFL reinforced one another: teamwork, sacrifice, responsibility, accountability and leadership."
—Rocky Bleier

119

"I wasn't really living what I was talking about."
—Rocky Bleier

After I got out of Notre Dame, I was selling insurance in the off-season in Chicago. I was doing what you do when you start out in the insurance business. You call family and friends to get going. I called a college teammate of mine. He was selling motivational tapes. I called and asked him if I could come and talk to him about his insurance needs. It was a difficult call. Selling was not a part of my personality.

Two things happened at that meeting. I sat in on a meeting my friend was conducting. Part of that meeting was a 20-minute motivational film. It was Rev. Bob Richards, the minister who was an Olympic pole-vaulter. Now I knew who Bob Richards was because he was pictured on the side of the Wheaties cereal box that was on my breakfast table as a kid. In the early morning in grade school, as I'd be eating my bowl of Wheaties, I'd be reading about Rev. Bob Richards on the side of the box.

As I watched the tape at my friend's office, I was mesmerized by the positive talk Rev. Richards gave. His body language and his voice inflection were great. He could really command your attention. I remember thinking that some day I'd like to do that. Then we talked about my friend's insurance needs. Ultimately, I ended up buying one of his motivational kits. It cost me $740. It proved to me that he was a better salesman than I was. I looked at the tapes and I remembered what I learned from them.

One of the points that were made was to be sure to pay yourself first. Don't wait till you've paid everyone else to set some aside for yourself, or you could end up with nothing. I was 23 years old and I had no reference to that kind of thinking. It wasn't that way with my parents. We always had enough to provide for our family's immediate needs. We didn't want for anything. But there was no money being set aside for the future, or for my parents' retirement. That was something I learned. Time goes so quickly; you'd better be prepared for tomorrow.

There was also something about making choices. The clearer the vision you have the better choices you can make. I can relate to that in my football life. But not in my personal life. To some degree, you lead your life the way you've been raised. My dad worked hard and had a business. My mother worked hard and she was always there for us kids. My father did the work and my mother paid the bills. She took care of the money. As you go along, those things kind of happen. You have an idea of how you want to live your life.

You make some choices. One of the things is that if you don't know an answer or where you want to go, you go with your gut instinct. Don't be talked out of something. You need to know what is happening in the world today. What do you want? How many children do you want? What are your feelings about alternative lifestyles? How do you feel about abortions? I think you have to talk those things through.

It's a thought process. How are you going to live your life? It's more difficult if you have no direction.

You are made up of three kinds of people: how others see you, how you see yourself and what you really are.

You have to be true to yourself. I found myself giving speeches about motivation, and I felt fraudulent, like I wasn't living my own life the way I wanted to. I was just reciting words. It sounded good. I wanted people to think well of me. But I wasn't really living what I was talking about.

When I confronted the truth, as I did, you say you have to do something about it. I had to admit I was living a lie. Ultimately, I came to that epiphany. What the hell am I doing? If I wanted to live the way I speak about I had to change my life. I had to be true to myself.

So, I have a lot of thoughts running through my mind right now. What am I thinking about as we're coming here today? You've been telling me about what L.C. Greenwood said and what Randy Grossman said and how good Dwight White was. Well, the competitor in me wants to be better than they were. I want to be more quotable than they were. I'm smiling as I say this, but I'm serious, too. I want to come off well in your book. How do I want people to perceive me? I want to be witty, charismatic, and insightful. That's just part of my competitive nature.

"It's tough to say never."

I don't know whether the Steelers will ever repeat what we did in the '70s. It's tough to say never. I've been raised never to say never. I don't think so, though. The economic situation of the game has made it impossible to keep a team together like we did.

They certainly have a great running back in Jerome Bettis, another Notre Dame guy. He is one of those surprising running backs. He runs with power. He runs straight ahead, yet it's tough to get a shot at him once he gets his momentum going. He has big legs and he's always pumping them. It's tough to wrap your arms around him. He's very effective and he can take a beating. Even when he was hurt, he was effective.

He hits that hole and there's nothing there and he can move outside. You can't compare him with Franco Harris. They have different running styles. The times are different, the offenses are different. Franco had great acceleration. Me, I hit the holes. I couldn't shift speeds. I was a one-speed guy.

I played with Dick Hoak my first year and then he was a coach when I came back to the team after my Army stint. Dick played the game on a pro level and that gained him a good deal of respect from the players. As a runner, consistency was his strong point. He was reliable. He's very knowledgeable about the game. His goals are different from most assistant coaches. He's not there to move up; he's not there to rock the boat. He's an organization man.

He respects his players. He doesn't yell at you or scream at you. He corrects mistakes. He teaches you what needs to be done. He complemented Chuck Noll very well, and I assume he does the same for Bill Cowher.

There was a magic, indeed. The magic was created because of the continuity we had. And we had it for a long time. Teams can have a magic for one year, but let's see what they can do over a long period of time. We had 22 players who won four Super Bowl rings. That's a strong nucleus. We had a lot of guys who had three and two Super Bowl rings. There are only 29 players in the history of the NFL who have four Super Bowl rings. (As of 2019, there were 38 players with four Super Bowl rings, and Tom Brady had six Super Bowl rings. Charles Haley of the 49ers and Cowboys had five Super Bowl rings.) If there was one characteristic about team it was that we were always ready to play. We came to play. I hope people remember that.

I go to most of the get-togethers involving our team. I see Andy Russell and Mike Wagner more often than most of them. I've been seeing more of Franco in recent years. We get caught up on each other's lives. This past fall Jan and I had three couples at our home for dinner. Dwight White and Karen came, and Franco and Dana, and Andy and Cindy.

I always worked hard to make a good impression. It was a matter of wanting to be accepted and liked.

I'm happy to be in Pittsburgh. I could live elsewhere now and do what I do. Chicago might make more sense because I travel and do what I do (the temperature as I write this at my computer desk today (January 30, 2019) in Chicago is -12 degrees). But I like Pittsburgh. My fame and fortune are here. You get entrenched. If you marry a Pittsburgh girl you'll never leave.

Roots are important in Pittsburgh. People don't leave Pittsburgh. People who leave would like to come back. Jan has a close-knit family so I'm sure we'll stay here. We had 21 people for dinner at our place recently.

I've felt so comfortable in Pittsburgh right from the beginning. I go back to the days when the Steelers hung out at Dante's in Brentwood (as did I). I remember the Wednesday night buffets there. Players don't do that anymore. The writers and sportscasters were there, too, right alongside the Steelers. That's never going to happen again. I met people like Billy Conn and Joey Diven, real Pittsburgh characters and great guys. They were friends of Mr. Rooney. They liked Notre Dame, so they were good to me. We hit if off. So, I know a little about the history of our city.

Art Rooney and boxing champion Billy Conn.

ROCKY

Bleier was back at Dad's bar, only in a South Hills setting

Rocky remembers it all so vividly. His boyhood in Appleton, Wisconsin, where he grew up over his parents' bar and restaurant, his Notre Dame days when he played on a national championship football team as a junior in 1966, and was the captain as a senior in 1967, his stutter start with the Steelers when Art Rooney made sure he had an honest chance to stick with the team, his Vietnam combat experience, his comeback from bullet and shrapnel wounds in his upper legs and backside, when he couldn't run and required a cane just to walk when he returned home and resumed his career as a running back with the Steelers.

Three of his toes are still deformed and he wears different sized shoes, and there are still shrapnel pieces in his body. Can he pass without a problem through the metal detector at the airport?

He wore four Super Bowl rings as he shared his story, with some excerpts from "The Play," written so well by Gene Collier, once a colleague of mine at *The Pittsburgh Press*. There were plans to create a portable setting so "The Play" could be produced at area venues other than the O'Reilly Theatre in downtown Pittsburgh. I had seen it twice and it was a good evening on his memory lane.

He did that and more for the enjoyment of 57 men and two women filling a club room at our Good Guys Luncheon at Atria's Restaurant & Tavern in McMurray on a Thursday afternoon, March 22, 2018. He did it mostly as a favor to me, and because our group sponsors service dogs for veterans who require their calming effects from problems they have as a result of their own harrowing military experience in Vietnam or in the Middle East.

Rocky turned 73 on March 5, 2019. He has a Purple Heart and Bronze Star in addition to his four Super Bowl rings. He sat on a bar stool with an old-fashioned bar front behind him, so it was a perfect stage setting.

* * *

Robert Patrick Bleier has been a poster boy for Vietnam soldiers ever since he came home, safely if scarred. I rode shot-gun with him once as he drove a black Mercedes-Benz to Canton, Ohio and the Pro Football Hall of Fame when they did a special program to recognize all the former NFL players who had been in the military. Rocky represented all NFL players who were veterans at this event.

The New York Giants Football Team, for instance, followed practice each day with military marching drills and faux rifles over their shoulders to be ready in case they were called up during World War II. Because

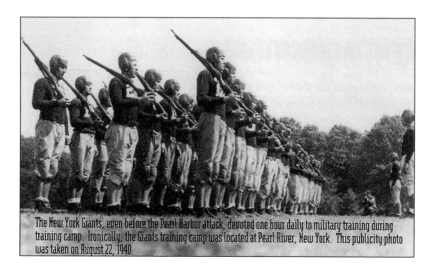

The New York Giants, even before the Pearl Harbor attack, devoted one hour daily to military training during training camp. Ironically, the Giants training camp was located at Pearl River, New York. This publicity photo was taken on August 22, 1940.

of the shortage of men, the Steelers and Philadelphia Eagles merged teams at that time for the Steagles, and then the Steelers with the Chicago Cardinals for the Pitt-Cards.

I took notes on the way to and from Canton that day so I know his story well, too, and could pinch-hit for him if it were ever necessary for his stand-alone performance. I've spent time in the company of his beautiful wife, the former Jan Gyurina, who is from West Mifflin.

Rocky was at Atria's for a total of four hours and he never stopped smiling, staying late to have a chance to eat salad with salmon and enjoy an Arnold Palmer drink. He engaged everyone in the room and, after his talk, he signed drawings of himself by the artist Bob Weaver, a former art teacher and athletic coach at Yough High School. Everyone in the room received a signed likeness of Rocky Bleier.

"We loved him. He was so patient with everyone, not rushing anyone who wanted to talk to him, or get his autograph, or to pose for a picture," said Christina Doperak, who tends bar at Atria's and looks after diners in that lounge area.

The young women on the wait staff at Atria's all wanted to be in a photo with Rocky, so I dubbed them the Rockettes.

Artwork by Bob Weaver

"We love waiting on the Good Guys," said Beth Swart. "They are all real gentlemen. And they are so kind to us." Rocky posed for pictures with her son, Easton, a special needs young man who buses tables for his mom after school, and Rocky had Easton put the four Super Bowl rings on his own fingers.

*   *   *

"I finally broke into the starting lineup because I could block better than any of our other backs," Rocky related. "I wasn't bigger or faster than any of them, but I could block better. It took me five years to break into the starting lineup with the Steelers.

"Franco had to get hurt, and someone else had to get hurt, and I went from being a backup to a backup, the fifth running back in a four-back system, to get to play regularly. Chuck Noll asked our backfield coach, Dick Hoak, who was his best blocker, and Hoak said I was. 'Well, then get him in the starting lineup,' Noll instructed him.

"I could block. I had a talent that served me well, and we all have a talent. And we have to use it as best we can. I salute you men for supporting the Guardian Angel Service Dog program and other worthy non-profits in the area."

*   *   *

Andy Russell, who was once a guest speaker for the same group and then became a regular at the monthly luncheon sessions, couldn't be there this time. He and his wife Cindy were at their ranch in Basalt, Colorado, but Andy sent me an e-mail to read as an introduction for Rocky at the luncheon.

Andy's message, sent on March 8, 2018, read like this:

"Best wishes on your upcoming Good Guys Luncheon. I know those fellows will really enjoy your speech. You always worked harder than any other Steelers and you blocked for Franco and other Steelers, until, when Noll decided to let you run the ball, you had your own 1,000-yard year.

"When people ask me if I was a veteran, I hesitate in answering because I believe real veterans, like you, were in combat. The only dangerous thing I did during a two-year experience as a lieutenant in Germany was to drive my Porsche on the Autobahn.

"I will always honor your Vietnam experience. Have fun with your speech!!"

*   *   *

Franco and Rocky both rushed for over 1,000 yards in the 1976 season. I was in Cleveland Stadium during the 1979 season when Rocky and Franco both had 100-yard rushing efforts in a victory over the Browns.

Rocky only carried the ball ten times total in his first four seasons, and saw action mostly on special teams, and was so frustrated he thought of quitting the team. It was Russell who talked him into returning. "Don't make the decision for them," he told Bleier. "You make them make that decision."

The rest is history, all captured in a book by Terry O'Neil, a Notre Dame classmate, called *Fighting Back*.

*   *   *

Tom Atkins, who has attended every Good Guys Luncheon meeting over the previous four years, asked Bleier how he got the nickname of Rocky. For the record, this is not the same Tom Atkins who portrayed Art Rooney Sr. in a one-man play called "The Chief."

"I was a chunky baby," he said with a smile. "My Dad was so proud of me and when the guys who came into the bar asked about his newborn son, he'd say, 'Oh, you should see him. He's all muscles and looks like a little rock sitting up in his crib.' And then when the guys came back to the bar, they'd ask my dad, 'How's your little Rock?' And soon I was just Rocky. Bob Bleier's pride and joy."

He shared stories about the regulars in the bar, all characters, and some who slept in rooms next to the bedrooms of Rocky and his two brothers and a sister upstairs, and how you always knew when the one wasn't feeling well because he boiled garlic in his room, and the fumes stunk up the whole house.

"My sister wondered what else he might be doing in his room, and she had nightmares about it for three years," related Rocky.

That got a laugh. So did so many of his anecdotes. Several of the men remarked aloud that they admired him for his service, and for what he accomplished with the Steelers. I think those good reviews made Rocky feel good. My friend, Bill Priatko, and I have both visited that bar in Appleton on different occasions so we could picture the scene.

Appleton was also the home town of the magician Harry Houdini, the author Edna Ferber, controversial U.S. Senator Robert McCarthy, the actor Willem Dafoe, and TV commentator Greta van Susteren.

"I have a street named after me in Appleton, and none of them do," said Bleier. "Jim begged me to include the names of the other famous people from Appleton, and I did when he came to see the show just to appease him. That street named after me, by the way, is a short dead-end street. If my name were Aaron

Rogers or Brett Favre or Vince Lombardi, they would have named the main street after me; it's still Packers country. My father owned a bar in Appleton, so everyone knew me. My father said that the only thing you have is your reputation. I never forgot that."

Rocky has always been one of my favorites. He and Russell and Mike Wagner and Tunch Ilkin, along with Pirates' manager Chuck Tanner, all were featured stars at different fund-raising dinners I emceed at Asbury Heights, a senior care complex in Mt. Lebanon. They raised about $150,000 that director John Zanardelli used to pay for care for those whose personal funds were exhausted.

Rocky Bleier spent time with my mother, Mary O'Brien, who was in residence there, and with staff members and was a big hit. Rocky has told me that it's what you do before and after you speak that makes it work, and it's a valuable lesson.

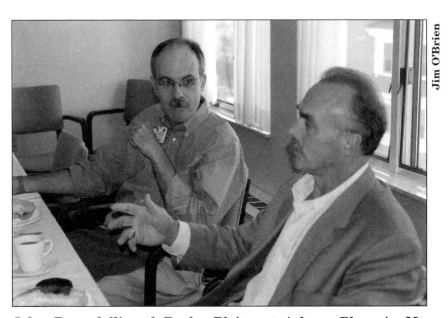

Jim O'Brien

John Zanardelli and Rocky Bleier at Asbury Place in Mt. Lebanon, a senior care facility now under UPMC umbrella.

Photos by Jim O'Brien

Rocky Bleier and "the Rockettes" of Atria's Restaurant & Tavern in McMurray, from left to right, Kelly McGrail, Rachel Miles, Christina Doperak, Rebecca Stevens and Beth Swart in foreground.

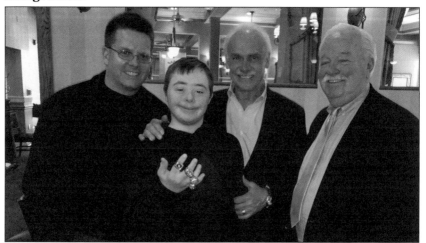

Four Super Bowl Rings – Easton Swart smiles about wearing championship rings of Rocky Bleier, who is flanked here by Scott Colombo and Jim O'Brien.

Friends

I was so pleased that Rocky Bleier obliged me by agreeing to appear at my Good Guys Luncheon series at Atria's in McMurray on Thursday, March 22, 2018.

As I was introducing him, however, he interrupted me, and started saying some unflattering stuff about me—trash talk or jagging me, as we said when we were kids. I felt awkward. I felt badly; he was embarrassing me in front of my friends. Or so I thought.

I wanted to be somewhere else. It was so unlike the Rocky Bleier I always enjoyed and admired. When I asked him later why he had said the things he did—it wasn't a roast after all—he smiled and patted me on the shoulder and said, "That's what friends do."

A few weeks later, I told Randy Grossman about the exchange with Bleier. Grossman agreed with Bleier. "That's what friends do," he said.

Jim O'Brien

I told my buddy Alex Pociask what had happened. He agreed with Bleier and Grossman. "Yeah," he said, "that's what friends do." I don't know...

ROCKY BLEIER

Larry Brown

Franco watched Larry Brown of Redskins to see how he did it

Steelers Coach Chuck Noll was talking about some of the great running backs in the history of the National Football League, and he reflected on Franco Harris and Larry Brown in the same breath.

Both Brown and Harris had Pittsburgh connections. Brown had come out of Schenley High School in Pittsburgh to star at Kansas State and with the Washington Redskins, and, of course, Harris was a star running back at Penn State and even more so with the Pittsburgh Steelers.

Harris had been Noll's No. 1 running back for eight seasons, at this time, or since the Steelers made him their No. 1 draft pick in 1972. Brown was the best running back, along with John Riggins, in the history of the Washington Redskins.

At the onset of the season, Harris ranked fifth on the NFL's all-time rushing list, trailing only Jim Brown, O.J. Simpson, Joe Perry and Jim Taylor. Close on the heels of Harris was Larry Csonka, who had made a strong comeback for the Miami Dolphins since returning from the World Football League.

Brown ranked 14th at the start of the season, right above Steve Van Buren of the Philadelphia Eagles.

Brown retired after the 1976 season, after eight years with the Redskins. He was really effective in only five of those campaigns. He was banged up; his knees were no good, and it was over all too soon. Brown was working for E. F. Hutton, an investment firm, in Washington, D.C.

Ed Vereb: Another Pittsburgher to rush for Redskins

Larry Brown, by the way, was the second running back from an Oakland school to play for the Redskins. Back in 1956, the Redskins' No. 1 draft choice was running back Ed Vereb, an All-America at the University of Maryland. Vereb came out of my hometown of Hazelwood, a Pittsburgh inner-city community, to star at Central Catholic High School. He opted to sign instead with the British Columbia Lions and was a star in the Canadian Football League. He did a stint in the U.S. Army and joined the Redskins for one season in 1960 before returning to the CFL. He became a dentist when his playing days were done. He died in Bowie, Maryland at age 80 in 2014 from complications from Alzheimer's Disease.

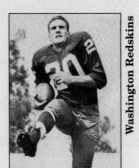

Washington Redskins

Ed Vereb

Harris took pride in the fact that he was still a starter for the three-time Super Bowl champion Steelers.

"When Franco first came up," recalled Noll, "we finished our exhibition season with a game against the Redskins at Three Rivers Stadium. Franco couldn't get over Larry Brown. He just sat there and watched him in awe. It really had an effect on him."

Asked what the effect was, Noll went no further. "You'll have to ask Franco about that," he responded. "I'm sure he'll remember."

Harris might have been the most private member of the Steelers, just as cautious as his coach when talking to the media. His handsome theatrical face took on a frown, or he appeared puzzled whenever anybody probed into his life or thoughts. He did not volunteer thoughts on anything, and he was often difficult to interview after a game because he was so soft-spoken.

Now that he's turned 60 he is much more conversational, much more at ease, once you get him started.

The mention of Larry Brown brightened his eyes, however, and Harris recalled his reaction to seeing the Redskins' great runner for the first time. It was late in the summer of 1972 at Three Rivers Stadium, Franco's first year with the Steelers.

"Here was a guy who played with so much intensity and desire," Harris said of Brown. "I couldn't believe how much he wanted it. With every inch they could get...he just wanted it very badly. Yes, it did have a big impact on me.

"It kind of made me realize that to be effective in the pros I would have to play differently than I did in college. In college, you have a certain ability, and you can go through the motions and get by. You can't do that up here. It gave me some insight for what you have to do here. Not only play after play, but year after year."

When I read a story I wrote for *The Washington (D.C.) Star,* it makes me realize that Franco was more forthcoming with me when I covered the Steelers for *The Pittsburgh Press* than I had realized. I drew this assignment from Dave Smith, the sports editor of *The Star*, who had held a similar post at *The Miami News* when I worked there in 1969.

Hold on now. Harris certainly did not run the way Brown did. Maybe Earl Campbell of the Houston Oilers did and Jim Taylor played that way, too, but Harris was a dancer. He didn't just lower his head and power into the line. That definitely was not his style. Then again, maybe fans just haven't appreciated that Harris fought for yards his own way.

Talking about Earl Campbell earlier this season, Harris said, "He seems like he's an easy-going guy

Larry Brown
Schenley High star

off the field, but he unleashes everything on the field. We're different. Our styles are different. He's a halfback who runs like a fullback and I'm a fullback who tries to be a halfback."

Larry Brown's style, somewhere between the battering-ram method of Campbell and the finesse Franco displays may have had a two-fold impact on Franco.

Three years after Franco's first season in the league, Brown retired. "If Larry had nowhere to go, he'd still take the punishment," offered Franco. "It takes its toll. I guess that's where we kind of differ. Sometimes you have to know when it's time to go in there and take all those bumps, and when it's best not to fight it and go down or out of bounds."

Franco even spoke about his policy at practice sessions, where he insists that no one tackles him or hit him unnecessarily. "The other guys joke about that," he said, "but, frankly, I feel that I take enough punishment during the season, and I don't want to get hurt when we're playing among ourselves. It makes no sense to me."

When Franco got off to his usual slow start, the fans were on him in a hurry. A caller on one of the sports-talk shows screamed on the air. "I want to see Franco Harris go from goal line to goal line, not from sideline to sideline!"

Harris realized the fans were critical of him. "That's all a part of it," he said after the team had its first loss of the season, a frustrating 17-14 setback to the Eagles in Philadelphia. He had been playing in a regular season game for the first time in his home area—he was born in Fort Dix, New Jersey, and his family was residing in Mt. Holly—and he'd been the goat of the game, fumbling at the goal line instead of going in for a touchdown in the final period.

His ankle was still bothering him, but Franco wasn't looking for excuses. He never did. It was not his style. "I felt pretty good," he said. "I was looking forward to it myself. The way things worked out, well. I have to be sharper. I have to be sharper."

Harris had played in four of the first five games but he hadn't gained much ground. He had 189 yards to his credit on 64 carries, an average of 3-yards per carry. Sidney Thornton was leading the team in rushing—with 309 yards on 55 carries for a 5.6 yard average—and Rocky Bleier had 102 yards on 26 carries for a 3.9 average, while leading the backs in the receiving category.

Questions regarding Harris' poor start continued to surface. Had he lost a step? Was he nearing the end of his career? Couldn't he get outside anymore? An unidentified Steelers' assistant leaked to the press that he had lost a step and that he couldn't cut the corner anymore.

Noll came to Harris' defense, as he always did when one of his players was criticized. "When he gets well, he'll be fine," said Noll. "We haven't noticed him slowing down. There's nothing wrong with Franco, and he's running as well as he ever has.

"One thing you learn about football is it's a team game and mistakes by other people have led to Franco's statistics. Everybody has contributed to the problem.

While Noll would not be critical of Franco's performance, he did rave about Rocky Bleier and a rookie back named Anthony Anderson.

Dick Hoak, the backfield coach, felt that Harris would rebound from the slow start, as he always had. Hoak had supported Franco from the start.

"I think it bothers him," said Hoak. "That might be part of the problem. He's pressing a bit, trying to break the big one."

Only the previous January, just before the Steelers won their unprecedented third Super Bowl, when Harris was being spoken about in a much different manner.

D.D. Lewis, a linebacker for the Dallas Cowboys, had this to say about Harris: "He's 230 pounds, but he can stop and accelerate better than anyone I know outside of Tony Dorsett. He can run east and west, stop on a dime and then cut north and south."

Ernie Stautner, the Cowboys' defensive coordinator, Hall of Famer and former tackle with the Steelers of the Bobby Layne era, stated: "He can be running toward the hole he's supposed to go to and if the hole is closed, he'll stop, change direction very quickly, find another hole and get through it."

Added Hoak: "He has a great sense of where he is on the field and where everybody else is."

139

Franco Harris and Larry Brown were both pictured already in the Pro Football Hall of Fame, but they had to wait until they were retired five years to be eligible for entry. It was only a matter of time.

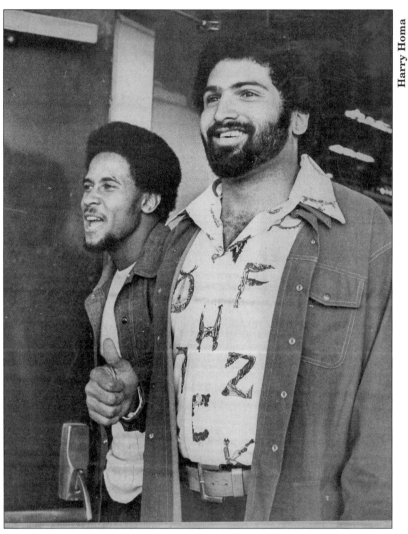

Harry Homa

Lynn Swann and Franco give "thumbs up" salute.

ROCKY

What makes Rocky run?

Robert Patrick Bleier, or Rocky Bleier as he's better known, might have been the runningest back in pro football. And this is a guy who was told that he might never walk again, let alone run.

His comeback story still resonates with audiences across America. He runs more than Mitt Romney.

He won't make anyone forget "Bullet Bill" Dudley or Red Grange or Jim Brown or Tony Dorsett, and he wasn't as feared as Franco Harris or Earl Campbell in his day, but Bleier might be in motion more than any of them on a year-round basis. Campbell can hardly walk these days because his knees are so shot.

Most fans are familiar with Rocky's heroics on the football field for the Steelers. He was inducted in 2018 into the second class for the Steelers' Hall of Honor at Heinz Field. The class included Alan Faneca, Buddy Dial, Art Rooney Jr. and Bill Nunn Jr. "It's truly a great honor," said Bleier.

Rocky was recognized for what he had accomplished in 12 seasons as a running back for the Black& Gold, as a member of four Super Bowl champion teams. He has also served as the NFL's poster boy for veterans who saw fire in Vietnam and lived to talk about it. He still has some bits of shrapnel in the back of his legs.

He was a star and the team captain of the Notre Dame football team under Ara Parseghian, but he was undersized and not particularly speedy, yet he overcame war wounds and some physical limitations to contribute in a big way to the Steelers' success.

Rocky Bleier and Notre Dame Coach Ara Parseghian

Less chronicled is his hectic—more like frantic off-the-field ambassador of goodwill for the athletic world, God, apple pie, his hometown of Appleton, Wisconsin, motherhood, non-hot dogs, the oft-ignored Vietnam veteran, the Steelers, the Rooney family, the American family, all things bright and beautiful. And, of course, Rocky Bleier.

Gene Collier chronicled most of this in "The Play," a beautiful stage reminiscence by Rocky himself. After I saw its premier, I wanted to run up on the stage from my second-row seat on the aisle at Heinz Hall and hug him. I was so happy for how well he had remembered and delivered his lines.

One of his teammates, Gerry "Moon" Mullins, was amazed by Rocky's recollection and shared his enthusiasm with Randy Grossman, John Banaszak, Mike Wagner, Robin Cole and myself at a patio breakfast at the Allegheny Club at Andy Russell's Celebrity Golf Outing soon afterward.

"Well, it's his life story!" said Grossman. "If he forgot a line, he could certainly fill in whatever he needed to move the show along."

Plans were for Rocky to do a one-night stand, but his friends urged him to do it again. I suggested a more intimate venue, such as the O'Reilly Theatre, and Rocky ended up doing a one-week stand during the Christmas holidays in 2017. It was a big hit and he is hopeful of a reprise at other showcases.

Before I saw the show for a second time, I urged Rocky to add a line or two about the other famous folks from Appleton, and he obliged me.

After all, Appleton has some pretty special sons and daughters, besides Bleier.

Appleton's other luminaries include the author Edna Ferber, the magician Harry Houdini, actor Willem Defoe, political commentator Greta Van Susteren. And the political firestorm Senator Joseph McCarthy, who grew up on a farm in Chute, near Appleton.

The prior success of "The Chief," a one-person stage show by Pittsburgh actor Tom Atkins, helped pave the way for "The Play." The Art Rooney production was the most successful stage show in the history of the O'Reilly Theatre.

I suggested they add an opening line to that production and the show's producer, Ted Pappas, had a hissy fit over my temerity. I had known and written often about Art Rooney and Pappas had never met the man.

I wanted Atkins to come out on the stage, for openers, look over the audience, and ask one of the people, "Where you from?"

And no matter what the person said...Garfield...Greenfield...McKeesport...he would respond by saying, "I knew a guy there...he was a bookie!"

Bleier failed, as did Olympic wrestling gold medalist Kurt Angle later on, as a sports broadcaster at WPXI-TV, but given a script Rocky was a real success and in-demand performer simply telling his own feel-good story. He's been at it ever since, running here and there with a schedule that would shame even Marco Polo.

His furious public speaking schedule would have shamed Oral Roberts, Joel Osteen, Billy Graham, Reverend Moon, Little Richard, George Jessel, Norman Vincent Peale and Cyril Wecht.

Former Steelers quarterback Terry Hanratty, who has a good sense of humor, referred to Rocky as "Audie," as in Audie Murphy, a war hero who became a popular movie star. He'd address him as Audie when he wanted to hear Rocky's war stories.

"If Rocky's not speaking tonight at the VFW" Hanratty remarked, "he'll be at the American Legion or the Daughters of the American Revolution."

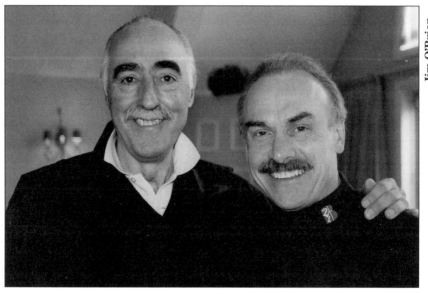

Jim O'Brien

Terry Hanratty and Rocky Bleier

Like his father, who owned a bar back home, Rocky's in "the people business."

When he was still playing, Rocky ran through more airports than O.J. Simpson. Those who raved about Rocky's leaping catch for a touchdown against the Dallas Cowboys in the 1979 Super Bowl should be at Greater Pittsburgh Airport to see a late-arriving Rocky catch an airplane to Atlanta, or Oklahoma City, or Chicago, or wherever his appointments secretary, Gloria Ashcroft, sends him.

On a Pittsburgh basis, he was involved in a meaningful manner, and not just in an honorary role, with the Allegheny Chapter of the Multiple Sclerosis Society, the Pennsylvania Association for Retarded Children through the Bike Hike, United Way, the Veterans Administration, and he participated in many of The Pittsburgh Press Old Newsboys fund-raising activities for the benefit of Children's Hospital.

Jim O'Brien

Rocky Bleier and Ray Mansfield

In his spare time, he was a partner in the investment banking firm of Russell, Rea, Bleier & Zappala at the Downtown Roosevelt Arms, where the Steelers offices were located when it was the Roosevelt Hotel.

I first met Rocky Bleier at his office prior to the opening of the Steelers' summer training camp in July of 1979. So, we have known each other for 40 years.

Rocky was 33 at the time, which he referred to as "the twilight zone," in a reference in his book to a former teammate, Ray Mansfield when "The Olé' Ranger" was that age. Bleier was then one of the oldest running backs in the NFL, but was looking forward with great enthusiasm to his next training camp.

"I have my priorities," he said. "Rocky Bleier will be there giving 100 percent, as I have to."

A guy can get out of breath just listing Bleier's activities on a computer.

Why, though? The question persists.

Budd Schulberg wrote a novel I loved when I was a student at Taylor Allderdice High School in the late '50s. It was called "What Makes Sammy Run?" I still have that copy, plus a less-tattered copy I have purchased in more recent days.

Sammy Glick started out as a newspaper copy boy and ran over a lot of people before becoming a Hollywood playwright. Rocky Bleier is no Sammy Glick, but one has to wonder what makes him tick. A good place to start to find the answer was the biography, "Fighting Back," a book about Bleier written by a Notre Dame classmate Terry O'Neil, later an ABC-TV executive who was a contemporary of my friend Beano Cook.

Some of the findings follow:
- The mortgage on his house.
- Humble but solid beginnings.
- To cover up for an inferiority complex.

- His gratefulness over surviving Vietnam.
- He'd rather run than limp.
- Fear of God
- He thinks his grade school nuns are still chasing after him.
- He's a throwback to a simpler era. In short, he's just a genuinely good guy.
- Some or none of the above.

Take your pick. "I was very concerned with my image," he said of his earlier schooldays. "I wanted everybody to think highly of me. To this day, in fact, I place a high premium on making a good impression."

Alex Pociask

Author visits College Football Hall of Fame where Pitt's Tony Dorsett is on display at front doors.

Early Days

Everyone is just a kid from somewhere

I can relate to Rocky Bleier and Franco Harris on several levels and on others I cannot. We played all sports when we were kids. Football, basketball and baseball took up much of our time. We did what we had to do in school, mostly good grades but not as good as they should have been.

Bleier and Harris were head and shoulders above their classmates when it came to sports. I could hold my own in most sports, but I wasn't an all-star in any of them. I never aspired to be a pro athlete. I wanted to be a writer.

One of the fellows I played basketball with as a kid, Richard Portis, who went on to play at Point Park College, told some friends of mine, "Jimmy wasn't a very good athlete, but he was always there. There were several of us who were good enough to play college ball, and you wondered what Jim was doing there with us. But he was always there!"

From Franco's family album

Franco drives to hoop in his high school days.

148

That says something about my true grit. A woman I know named Carole Shields has a husband Bill who was a good ballplayer. One time, during a platform tennis match, she told me, "You're the most competitive person I know." I think it was offered more in the mode of a complaint rather than a compliment.

I always thought Dick Groat, who was great at basketball and baseball, was the most competitive person I ever met. I always thought it was a wonder that Groat didn't grind his teeth to dust.

*   *   *

Franco told me he hardly went anywhere as a kid. His father was stationed at Fort Dix, in southern New Jersey. "We didn't stray too far from home. We hardly watched any TV, and I didn't know many sports stars. I didn't idolize any sports stars. We didn't go to many movies."

I had sports magazines on my nightstand, especially *Sport* magazine. It was a thrill when I wrote stories for *Sport* when I was a young writer. I knew the stories and stats of the stars in every sport. I collected bubble-gum cards of sports stars.

Franco said his family's couch was covered in plastic—remember those covers?—and his mom was all about "keeping the house clean and raising her kids."

Franco said his family didn't go to restaurants. Not many did in those days, not like they do now. My mother worked a swing shift at The State Store—where they sold liquor and wine—one day early, the next day late. So, one day I'd go to lunch with my mother at a restaurant—there were several to choose from—near The State Store. I'd have lunch at home the next day.

My family didn't have a car. My mom had a driver's license and my father didn't know how to drive.

They lived in adjoining wings of a duplex house in their late teen years, and that's where they met and got to know one another. My father had been born on a couch in a home at 5413 Sunnyside Street. Our family moved into that home and we lived there till I was five years old. Then we moved across the street to 5410 Sunnyside Street after two families had moved out of a three-story row house.

We only traveled to two distant places. One of those was East Brady, Pennsylvania—later the hometown of Hall of Fame quarterback Jim Kelly—where my father had relatives. The other travel destination was Bridgeport, Ohio, just across the Ohio River from Wheeling. My mother was born in Bridgeport. My older brother Dick lived there all his life. He came along during the Great Depression and my parents thought he was better off living with his Uncle Jim, who had money, or so we were told.

Dick was a big sports fan and a favorite coach of many kids in Bridgeport, including Joseph Maroon, who grew up to become one of the Steelers' team doctors and a neurosurgeon at Allegheny General Hospital and now UPMC. Dick bought five out-of-town newspapers on Sunday just to read the sports sections. My brother was a big fan of John Havlicek and the Niekro and Groza brothers, all from the Ohio Valley. Havlicek died at age 79 in late April, 2019.

Everyone who shared my boyhood home is buried in Mt. Calvary Cemetery, a Catholic cemetery in Wheeling: my mom and dad, my brothers Dan and Robert, my sister Carole and her husband, Dick Cook, my nephews Dickie Cook and Dan O'Brien, my grandparents on the Burns side of the family. The plot belonged to the Burns family, so my dad is identified on the back of his tombstone as Son-in-Law. The final indignity. My wife Kathie has told me she's going to do the same thing for me when I die.

I first got to travel when I enrolled as a student at Pitt in 1960. I went to New York with the cross-country team as a freshman to report on an IC4A championship meet. As a sophomore, I became the first underclassman to be the sports editor of *The Pitt News*, and I traveled with the football team to Seattle, Washington, to Notre Dame in South Bend, Indiana; Waco, Texas and Miami, Florida. That's when I made up my mind that I wanted to be a sports writer.

When I told Randy Grossman that I never dreamed of being a big-league ballplayer in any sport, he said, "I doubt that Rocky Bleier or Franco Harris ever dreamed of being a sportswriter."

* * *

Rocky Bleier's dad, Bob Bleier, and my dad spent a lot of time in bars. They worked different sides of the bar. Bob Bleier owned a bar and restaurant and his family lived upstairs with some roomers in Appleton, Wisconsin. My dad sat on a stool, with a brass bar at his shoe-tops, and ordered "another round for the bar." He and my brother Dick were both big spenders. There were also brass spittoons along the bottom of the bar.

I visited the Bleier bar in late June of 2002 with my pal, Alex Pociask. We went on an eight-day sports odyssey from Chicago to Milwaukee and Detroit, and surrounding places, checking out old and new ballparks, hangouts for stars in all sports, Notre Dame, the Green Bay Packers' Hall of Fame, a memorial to George Gipp in Laurium, Michigan, the hometown of Notre Dame's first All-America football player.

We saw some photos and framed newspaper clippings about Bleier in that bar, now owned by someone else, and we felt like Rocky was taking us on our tour.

Mom and Dad in a frivolous embrace in our backyard.

Rear of O'Brien home at 5410 Sunnyside Street in late '40s. It was my job to keep it neat.

1931 Graham-Paige that belonged to my mother. The Burns and O'Brien families shared a duplex home on Almeda Street in Glenwood section of Pittsburgh.

I was back there again in my mind, anyhow, when Rocky did his one-man show about his life called "The Play." It was staged in a replica of Bob Bleier's bar. It made the show more personal. I'd been there. I thought I was the only guy in Pittsburgh still living who'd been to the Bleier bar besides Rocky, but I learned that another pal of mine, Bill Priatko, who had spent time in the training camp of the Packers in the late '50s, had visited the Bleier bar as well.

The old Bleier bar was known at the time of our visit as TrimB's Restaurant & Pub and was owned by Bob and Tina Packwood. The Bleiers hadn't owned the place for nearly 20 years. It's located at the corner of Lawrence & Walnut. A gracious woman who was tending bar identified herself as Donna. In answer to a question, she said, "Lots of people stop by and ask if this was Rocky Bleier's place. His family lived over the bar. Every other day, somebody asks about him."

Jim O'Brien

View of Bleier's boyhood church, St. Joseph's Catholic, from Bob Bleier's Bar in Appleton, Wisconsin.

From where I was standing, I could see through a window and view St. Joseph's Catholic Church on the other corner of the street. That was the church Rocky's family attended. It was a view Rocky Bleier had told me about in an interview. That's what he could see from his bedroom window. It made his story-telling that much more vivid. There was a police station directly across the street from the front door of TrimB's. I felt funny knowing I was standing where Rocky used to hang out, helping his parents take care of the patrons.

That's where he learned to be Rocky Bleier.

*   *   *

There were 37 bars along a one-mile stretch of the main street—Second Avenue—of my hometown of Hazelwood and Glenwood. There were seven of those bars within easy walking distance of our home. I delivered newspapers to all of them. I knew them well and can still see their interiors. There was a large framed artwork of Custer's Last Stand from Budweiser on the wall of Capri's, the closest to our home. Adolphus Busch, the owner of Budweiser, had commissioned an artist named Otto Becker to paint the original. Capri's—named for the Isle of Capri in Italy—had a dumb waiter to bring food from the kitchen upstairs in the dining area. It was owned by Emil Bersani and his son Mario often served as the bartender.

I was assigned the task of going to these bars to bring my dad home for dinner. He worked from 11 to 7 on the graveyard shift or overnight shift and started drinking early in the day. He always made it to work.

Franco's father was more disciplined, and also disciplined his children. He had to. They were more than his wife Gina Parenti could parent on her own. There were nine of them, Piero or "Pete," Luana,

154

Alvara, Marisa, Daniela, Albert, Mario, Giuseppe and, of course, Franco. "My mother named all the children; my dad didn't get a vote," says Franco with a smile.

I served nearly two years (1965-1966) in the U.S. Army and I had drill sergeants who looked just like Franco's father. I found it fascinating that Franco's father was named Cadillac. He was called Cad by his friends. I'd have insisted on being called Cadillac. When I drove a Cadillac in 2009 and 2010, Joe Gordon, the publicist of the Steelers often referred to me as "Cadillac Jim."

Franco resisted buying a Cadillac or any kind of fancy car when he signed with the Steelers in 1972. Blacks and Italians are known to enjoy driving Cadillacs—Franco was a bit of both—but he didn't do it because he didn't want to have that kind of image.

"People asked me, 'where's your Cadillac?' I didn't want to be like that," said Franco. "I didn't have a car."

He had a modest apartment in the East Liberty section of Pittsburgh and he often walked several miles to get to work at Three Rivers Stadium, or he took the bus and even hitch-hiked if he was running late. "I still come across people who tell me they picked me up and gave me a ride to the stadium when they saw me with my thumb out," said Franco.

His favorite restaurant near his apartment was Vento's Pizza, and that is how Franco's "Italian Army" got started, with Al Vento and his friend, Tony Stagno, who owned a bakery nearby, found a unique way to show their support of Franco and the Steelers.

*   *   *

After Franco finishes a meal these days, he likes to take a walk around the neighborhood, even when he travels out of town. As a boy, he liked to run. "I was always running," he says now.

Franco Harris pays his respects at viewing of Al Vento Sr. at McCabe Brothers Funeral Home on Walnut Street in Shadyside in late June 2018.

Franco with Al Vento Jr. and their friend Frank Mafrica of Calgary, Canada at funeral repast at South Hills Country Club in Whitehall, where Al Sr. and his wife Rita resided in retirement.

Franco lettered in three sports at Rancocus Valley Regional High School. He didn't think about college or even consider the possibility until he started winning honors for playing football, and when his older brother Mario got a sports scholarship to Glassboro State College, he realized that he might be able to do that as well. His high school coach thinks Franco could have been a big-league baseball player if he had chosen to concentrate on that sport. Franco felt the same way about his brother Guiseppe. Their brother Pete was an All-America safety for Joe Paterno at Penn State.

"When you're young, you might pick the wrong sport," said Franco. He said he was a shy kid and that he was way behind when he entered first grade. "I had to work hard to catch up," he said.

I recall the first time I ever heard of Franco Harris. The Pitt football coach in the late '60s was Dave Hart. "I thought I had a chance to get this kid from Mt. Holly, New Jersey named Frank O'Harris," said Hart, or at least that was the way I heard it. "He's a good one, but he's going to Penn State."

I thought it would be great to have an Irish back at Pitt. I have learned that others thought his name was Frank O'Harris, so I don't feel so stupid. Dave Hart might have had some success at Pitt if Harris had come to play in Pittsburgh.

Joe Paterno, the coach at Penn State, could talk a little Italian from his boyhood days in Brooklyn, and he charmed Franco's mother when he brought her a bouquet of roses. Joe knew how to speak to a woman from Italy. Hart had no chance.

Harris might have done for Hart and Pitt what Tony Dorsett would later do for Johnny Majors and Pitt, when Tony D led the Panthers to a national title in 1976. Hart went 1-9 three straight seasons and was fired. All of his young assistant coaches became head coaches at other colleges and, in the case of Leman Bennett, the head coach of the Atlanta Falcons.

Harris had no love in his heart for Pittsburgh. He didn't want to play pro ball in Green Bay—too cold—or Pittsburgh, too gray. And the Steelers had never been that successful.

* * *

There's a picture in the Harris home showing the statues at Pittsburgh Airport of Franco flanking George Washington, and Franco is proud to be keeping that kind of company. "Those statues were supposed to be at the airport only for a short while," said Franco, "but I'm flattered that they decided to keep them there this long. I might have missed the big money but I wouldn't take the money over playing for the team and the guys I played with. I'm sorry I said what I said about not wanting to play for the Steelers when I was coming out of Penn State, and for saying I didn't want to play in Pittsburgh. It's turned out pretty good for me."

Penn State Football Coach Joe Paterno is honored with Lifetime Achievement Award at Heinz History Makers Dinner in spring of 2006, flanked by Franco Harris, left, and Ralph Papa of Citizens Bank. Hazelwood's Herb Douglas, a 1948 Olympic medalist in the long jump, was honored with Leadership Award at the same dinner.

Rocky Bleier

You have to deliver the paper on time

Rocky Bleier took pride in being a paperboy in his youth. He delivered the evening newspaper, the *Appleton (Wisconsin) Post-Crescent,* and recalls his first business endeavor in a fond manner.

"Me and another fellow had a route with 120 papers, and I remember that I thought I was pretty good at folding them real neatly, and I took pride in my throwing ability. Heck, I could throw the paper at least halfway to most of the houses."

Bleier's bit of humor brought a smile to the faces of the 12 *Pittsburgh Press* paperboys who were honored at a recognition luncheon for outstanding sales and service. They couldn't call them paperboys or newsboys any longer, not with Theresa Di Perna of McKees Rocks in the ranks. She was one of the dozen selected from more than 6,500 news-carriers for top performance.

That number of news-carriers seems remarkable today. There are fewer and fewer dailies in this country now, and most of the papers are delivered by adults driving around in the dead of the night. No one collects money anymore. That's done by checks and credit cards.

I was writing for *The Press* back in December of 1980, a week before Christmas, and represented the newspaper at this awards event. I did everything I could to make myself more valuable when I worked at newspapers, and often provided stories for the business section, the radio-TV section, the op-ed page and the Sunday magazines with no extra compensation.

I felt comfortable in the company of Bleier and the

Scene from Broadway stage show "Newsies."

news-carriers because I credit my success to my beginnings as a newsboy. I learned everything I needed to know from that experience to succeed in life. We are all salesmen. "We are all offering hope," Bleier has told me in reference to his public speaking efforts.

I started out, at age eight, helping my older brother Dan with his *Post-Gazette* morning route in the Glenwood and Hazelwood sections of inner-city Pittsburgh. You had to get up earlier than your classmates, you had to go out, just like the mailmen, in all kinds of weather—I hated it when there was lightning in the sky—and get the papers delivered before you went off to school. You had to go out and knock on doors to collect money. You had to pay for the papers whether or not you had collected all the money. You had to be responsible for handling that money. The paper was five cents per copy so that was 30 cents for six days of delivery. The *P-G* offered an insurance policy for an extra two cents a week. How that worked, I have no idea. But you had a card for each customer with chits half the size of mail stamps to be pulled off as receipts when they paid their bill. A fourth of my customers were black, others from different ethnic groups, and you learned how to get along with everyone.

We'd come home and my mother would have breakfast ready for us, sometimes just cereal, sometimes hot oatmeal, sometimes eggs and bacon or ham, and buttered toast. We'd have a little time to scan the sports section of the newspaper, and I am certain that is where I developed my early interest in writing for a newspaper. It seemed like a great gig, traveling to cities with sports teams, and interviewing the star players.

The program for the *Press* news-carriers was held on the eve of Rocky's final game with the Steelers at Three Rivers Stadium. His wife had surprised Rocky by inviting his parents and other relatives and friends to their home in Fox Chapel so they could celebrate the occasion. Even so, Rocky took time from his schedule to salute the award-winning *Press* carriers.

That tells you all you need to know about Rocky Bleier, and why he has always been one of my favorite pro athletes.

Bleier has an inspirational message to suit all occasions, and he didn't disappoint this time, either.

"It's an experience," he told the youngsters, "that will always serve you in good stead. You get a chance to meet and impress people and to sell them a product— yourself and the paper. You have to learn how to handle money and to be responsible for it. The paper has to be delivered every day, and this instills discipline."

Rocky's hometown of Appleton, one learns from his book *Fighting Back*, has an average snowfall of 47 inches each winter, and the average January temperature is 15 degrees, with a wind-chill factor of plus 2.

So, it wasn't easy delivering papers there, just 20 miles from Green Bay. Remember "The Ice Bowl" game between the Dallas Cowboys and the Packers in Green Bay for the NFL championship?

"It doesn't matter when it rains or snows, though," Bleier told his young audience at the Hilton (now Wyndham) by Point State Park. "You have to get the paper delivered on time. People don't care what the weather is like; they just want their paper."

This may have also prepared Rocky for running the ball for championship teams on a high school, college and pro level. Fans don't care what the weather is like, either.

Rocky had come through the previous Sunday with the game-winning touchdown against the Kansas City Chiefs in a game that was witnessed by *The Press* carriers, as part of their prize package. He was expected to do more of the same in San Diego in the Steelers' final regular season on Monday Night TV.

Bleier said his parents instilled the Puritan ethic of thriftiness and hard work in him at an early age. "Do your best in whatever you do," he said. "And don't be satisfied with this one success. The Steelers weren't satisfied to win the Super Bowl once, and we're not satisfied to have won it four times. So, we're still giving it our best."

He looked outside the window, and nodded toward Gateway Center. "This was a strange city to me when I first came here in 1968," he recalled. "I didn't know how long I'd be here. I've been lucky to have been with one team all this time, a championship team that could go down in history as maybe the greatest ever. And this has become a very special city for me since then. I've been fortunate to work and live here, and I hope to do the same for many more years."

One of the news-carriers, Shawn Hubbard, who plays for a midget football team in Wilkinsburg, was surprised by Bleier's size. He was listed at 5-11 on the roster, but admitted he was only 5-9½. "That makes him even more impressive to me," said Shawn. "I thought he'd be bigger."

After his heroics the previous Sunday, Bleier joked, "Young running backs have size, speed and ability, but age and cunning will beat youth and enthusiasm any time. Right?" For sure, Rocky has never been short on inspirational messages.

George Gojkovich

Joyous Steelers from left to right are Mike Webster (52), Moon Mullins (72). Rocky Bleier (20) and Franco Harris (32).

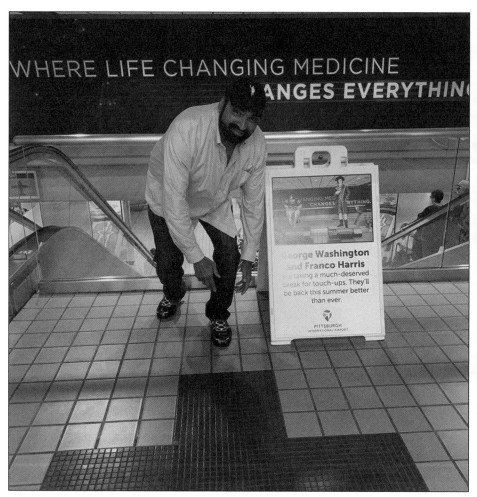

Franco Harris: "This is not what I had in mind when they offered me a 'position' at the Pittsburgh Airport."

GEORGE WASHINGTON
AND FRANCO HARRIS
ARE TAKING A MUCH-DESERVED
BREAK FOR TOUCH-UPS. THEY'LL
BE BACK THIS SUMMER BETTER
THAN EVER

Al Vento Sr.

He was a four-star general
in Franco's Italian Army

"He's a good man. I love that kid."

Al Vento said Franco Harris never forgot where he came from, and that Franco Harris has never forgotten old friends from his earliest days with the Steelers.

"He's a first-class individual," Vento said of Harris. "He never forgets me. He respects me. He was always good to me. If he's celebrating something—like the anniversary of his Immaculate Reception or some kind of Steelers' reunion—he invites me and my wife Rita and he always seats us with the best people. He always has time for us. He's a good man, so sincere. I love that kid."

Vento, who would turn 90 on July 26, 2018, owned and operated a pizzeria in East Liberty for 67 years. He and the late Tony Stagno, who owned a popular bakery on Auburn Street in the same neighborhood, founded Franco's Italian Army, a fan club like no other, to root for the rookie running back from Penn State during the 1972 season.

Vento grew up in that neighborhood. He and Rita rented a second-floor apartment there on St. Clair Street for $7 a week in the early years of their marriage. The building is still there and one of his workers lives there now. "It didn't have running water in the apartment when we were there," recalled Vento. "You had to go down the hall to a bathroom." They soon moved to a beautiful home in Whitehall, where they lived for 64 years.

Franco and Big Al Vento

Photos by Jim O'Brien

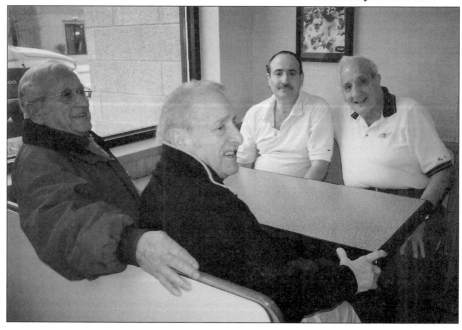

Vento's Pizza was meeting place for, left to right, Baldo Iorio, Bob Milie, former trainer with Steelers and Duquesne University, Al Vento Jr. and his father, Al Vento Sr.

Franco's Italian Army comes in for a mention on the first page of Dan Rooney's book, *My 75 Years With The Pittsburgh Steelers and the NFL,* and a full chapter in Myron Cope's memoir, *Double Yoi!* So, they are part of the Steelers' story, the team's history.

Franco's Italian Army came to the Steelers' games in full gear, wearing Army battle helmet liners, waving a full-size Italian flag, and bearing baskets of Italian cheeses and, buried beneath that, some homemade Italian wines. On one occasion at Three Rivers, they came onto the sidelines in Army tanks and jeeps they borrowed—hey, Vento had connections—from the Army Reserve unit at Hunt Armory in East Liberty.

When the Steelers spent a week in Palm Springs prior to a late-season contest with the San Diego Chargers in the 1972 season, Cope arranged for Frank Sinatra to come to a Steelers' practice. Ol' Blue Eyes was properly inducted into Franco's Italian Army by Vento and Stagno who flew there on a half-day's notice to conduct the ceremonies.

"Those years were the greatest time of my life," allows Vento. "I met a lot of nice people. It's something that will be in my memory bank forever. And I became a friend for life with Franco."

Vento was still waving an Italian flag for his friend Franco.

I visited Vento at his most recent restaurant location on 420 North Highland Avenue, his fifth location in that time span, back in 2008. City officials are always attempting to change the landscape in East Liberty and Vento's Pizza is one of the places that kept getting moved.

"It's 'For the Betterment of East Liberty' deal," he said with more than a hint of sarcasm in his voice, "and it just keeps getting worse. Right now, though, the neighborhood around our place never looked better."

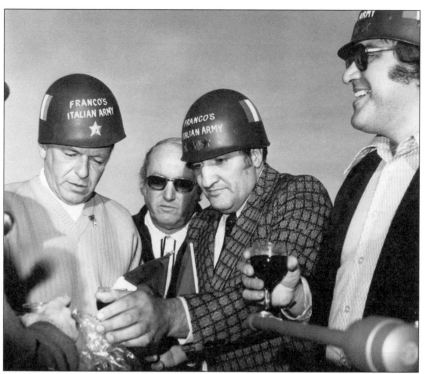

Frank Sinatra is inducted into Franco's Italian Army by Al Vento Sr. and Tony Stagno at Palm Springs meeting. Below, from left to right, Al Vento Jr., his dad, Tony Stagno, Armand Zottola and Dom Stagno at Franco's Italian Army banquet on December 4, 1972.

Vento voiced a lot of opinions about Pittsburgh. He loved to vent, so to speak. But he was fun to be with, and one could learn a lot about running a business successfully in the unforgiving streets of the inner-city, the Pittsburgh sports scene, the Pittsburgh political scene and the powers-that-be that call the shots. Vento and his pals were power brokers as well as hard-working citizens.

Vento had huge hands, working man's hands, and huge brown eyes. His hands and eyes were always moving to the beat of his stories, and he commanded and held one's attention. Anyone would have been comfortable in his company. He liked to say he was for real. He was a Pittsburgh guy, genuine to the core. He once was nearly 6-feet tall, but his shoulders were rounded now and he was a little stooped, probably from bending over to embrace his customers so often.

He once worked 18-hour days six and seven days a week. He had cut back to four-hour days. "I can't quit cold turkey," he told everyone. His son, Al Jr., 61, and his wife, Sherry, manage Vento's Pizza these days, but the old man remained the heart and soul of this East End institution. Al Jr. jives with the patrons non-stop at the front counter. He can speak Ease-sliberty with the best of them.

I love the sounds and smells of Vento's Pizza. Everybody's talking at once. The pots and pans are banging in the back of the kitchen. The aromas are wonderful, the red sauces, the hot sausages, the calzones, the garlic.

One of my favorite writers, Ernest Hemingway, told a friend in 1950, "If you are lucky enough to have lived in Paris as a young man, then wherever you go for the rest of your life, it stays with you, for Paris is a moveable feast."

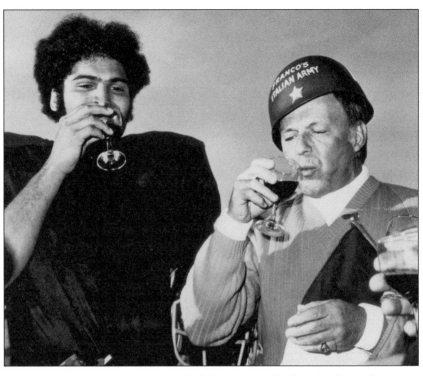

Franco Harris toasts Frank Sinatra at Palm Springs in 1972 when ol' Blue Eyes was inducted into Franco's Italian Army.

Franco Harris and Rocky Bleier exchange hugs with Terry Bradshaw at Steelers reunion at Heinz Field.

Vento's Pizza is like Paris, or maybe Rome, in that respect. The garlic goes with you, that much is certain. So does Al Vento's version of the world.

Al Sr. sold newspapers as a kid, and always hustled, doing whatever jobs he could find to make a few extra bucks. He saved some of it, and bought his own first car, a black 1950 Plymouth for $800. "I went to a Chrysler dealer on the North Side with Chippy DeStout, the old police chief," he recalled. "He knew the owner and he thought he could get me a good deal. I wanted a red car, but they couldn't get it for me. I went back with Chippy a couple of times, but no luck with getting a red one. So I took the black one. It was right there on the floor in front of me. Hey, when you're 16 years old your eyes light up at the sight of having your own car."

I visited Vento for the first time on Tuesday, January 29, 2008 to do an interview and returned a second time on Tuesday, March 18 to pick up some classic photos. We celebrated St. Patrick's Day one day late.

There are photos of Franco and Rocky Bleier and Terry Bradshaw on every wall at Vento's Pizza. There are even photos showing Vento as a teenager with some of the sandlot football teams he played for, such as Help of Christian, St. Peter and St. Paul, the Butler Cubs and Sto-Rox Cadets. He's one of the biggest fellows in most of the photos, the one with the dark-hooded eyes.

There are more framed photos in his back office, some showing him with the late Mayor Bob O'Connor, one of his favorites, and a photo with another late mayor, Richard Caliguiri. Vento can be viewed with other Pittsburgh dignitaries such as former County Executive Dan Onorato and sports celebrities such as Steelers' quarterback Ben Roethlisberger and former

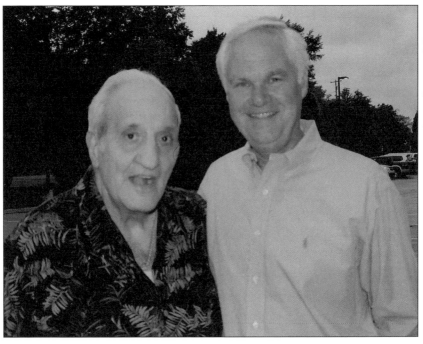

Al Vento at golf outing with Anthony Accamando

Al Vento Jr. with his dad at Vento's Pizza

Rams quarterback Marc Bulger, a local boy who followed in the Dan Marino tradition at Central Catholic High School.

Most of them have been to Vento's Pizza on more than one occasion. Vento and his friends have backed them all at one time or another.

I remember running into Al Vento in the fall of 2006 at Mayor O'Connor's funeral at Freyvogel's on Centre Avenue in Oakland, and he called out from the other side of the room, "You missed Myron Cope. He was just here. He doesn't look so good."

"He's the last of the Mohicans."

It was a pleasure to visit Vento's and to enjoy the pizza and hoagies and the owner's warm company. I brought along two good friends of Italian heritage that I thought would particularly enjoy him and his pizzeria. I told Al they were my bodyguards. Bob Milie, 81, was a part-time trainer with the Steelers when they won four Super Bowls in the '70s and a former trainer and sports information director at Duquesne University, and he had good stories to share with Al Vento. Baldo Iorio, 92, was the grandfather of my former son-in-law, Dr. Matthew Zirwas. Iorio was a car salesman in Bridgeville most of his working days and he could appreciate how Vento treated his loyal customers. Iorio and Vento spoke a little Italian to one another just because they could.

"He's the last of the Mohicans," said Iorio, after seeing Al Vento in action, shaking hands and patting customers on the back, and even reminding one of them that it was time to take his medicine. His place can seat about 50, counting the patio. On both of my visits, his customers looked about two-thirds African-American and one-third Caucasian. "Make that 60/40,"

173

advised Vento when I told him my observation. It was packed for lunch on both occasions.

He pressed the flesh with everyone, coming and going. "Thank you for coming," he'd say. "I appreciate you coming. Don't be a stranger."

His work ethic and the way he treated his customers—like family—is similar to that of Gus Kilaris, a proud Greek who operates an outdoor ice ball stand in West Park on the city's North Side and counted Dan Rooney and several Steelers, past and present, as customers and good friends.

"We're for real," said Vento. "I treat people the way I want to be treated. We treat everyone with love and respect. It's that simple and that demanding. The restaurant business is a tough business. You've got to be there all the time to make it work. And you've got to have good product. If your food isn't good the customers won't come back."

At my request, Vento inducted Milie and Iorio into Franco's Italian Army during our visit. They were both lieutenants. They, like Al Vento, have since passed and I miss them very much. Franco used to invite Bob and his wife Maureen to anniversary parties.

Al Vento brought out some glasses of homemade Italian red wine and calzones to mark the occasion. So it's official. He said, "Salud" as they sipped the dark red wine from plastic cups. "Good luck for a hundred years," he said. He repeated the toast in Italian. Iorio and Milie just smiled appreciatively.

They had some good stories of their own. Milie was telling us how Franco always wanted him, and him alone, to tape his ankles before a game. "He had the flattest feet I ever saw," said Milie. "I had to tape his arches up first, to give him a little boost."

Both Milie and Iorio served in the U.S. Army in World War II. Milie was in the Pacific Theatre along with two of his brothers, Jack and Louis, and Iorio was in Europe. (Al said his brother John served in the Pacific as well.) Milie was with the 24th Infantry Division that came into Southern Japan right after the peace treaty had been signed in 1946. He visited Hiroshima and Nagasaki, the cities that had been hit by the Atomic Bomb. "There were steel structures that melted to the ground, the heat was so intense from the blast," said Milie. "Everyone you saw in those two cities had some kind of bandage on them. It was unreal."

Iorio served in North Africa and Sicily. He had shown me photos from those days, and he was proud to have served his country. He was an NCO. He smiled and said he was also proud to be a lieutenant in Franco's Italian Army. "Now I'm an officer," he declared. "I'm moving up in the ranks."

Milie grew up in East Liberty and graduated from Peabody High School, a block away from Vento's Pizza. Milie was a good guide in that neighborhood, pointing out homes where Franco and Rocky Bleier once resided, where Sam Davis and Frenchy Fuqua once lived, as well as the boyhood homes of light-heavyweight boxing champion Billy Conn (Aurelia Street), singer-dancer Gene Kelly (Mellon Street) and singer Billy Eckstine (Bryant Street). We saw Motor Square Garden where Conn and Fritzie Zivic of Lawrenceville once fought.

There are a lot of stately, still-magnificent mansions lining Negley Avenue. "I'll bet Italian brick-layers built those homes," said Iorio.

We passed the corner of Penn and Negley where the Pennley Park Apartments once stood. They have given way to strips of townhouses in yet another renaissance in East Liberty. My wife Kathie and I lived at Pennley Park for a year-and-a-half when we first were married in 1967 and 1968. Our fellow tenants included Roberto

Clemente, Maury Wills, Juan Pizzaro and Alvin O'Neal McBean of the Pirates, and legendary basketball coach Moe Becker of Greensburg High School and Braddock High School. Those were great days, too.

I remember watching Sonny Liston train at a local gym there for a fight with Roger Rischer at the Civic Arena (November 12, 1968). He skipped rope to the sounds of "Night Train."

Rischer had declared before the fight that he was not afraid of Liston, despite his menacing reputation and baleful mask. "I fear no man who walks this earth," Rischer said in a pre-fight interview.

Liston KO'd Rischer in the third round with a lethal blow to the kidneys. I mentioned Rischer's remark to Liston after the fight, and Liston allowed, "Once he got up into that ring he wasn't on this earth no more." You don't forget lines like that.

That fight was for the benefit of Ben Anolik, a veteran fight promoter in Pittsburgh, who was one of the first heart transplant patients in America. Within two years, Liston, Rischer and Anolik all were dead.

We saw the East Liberty Presbyterian Church. It's still such a statuesque landmark. It was often referred to as "Mellon's fire escape" because it was built with Mellon money. Some thought it was built to keep the Mellons out of hell for their lending practices.

There's a lot of history in East Liberty. "There's no place quite like it," said Al Vento.

From an interview . . . Al Vento Sr.:

The Steelers went to Palm Springs, California late in the 1972 season for a big game with the San Diego Chargers. Chuck Noll wanted his team to get used to the warm weather in December, so they went there for a week to get ready.

My buddy Tony Stagno told Myron Cope that Frank Sinatra lived in Palm Springs. Stagno suggested that Cope use his connections to get hold of Sinatra, have him attend a practice, and induct him into Franco's Italian Army.

When the Steelers' party arrived in Palm Springs, Cope, quite by accident, spotted Sinatra at a dinner club. He wrote him a note explaining his mission. Sinatra came over to Cope's table and said he'd do it.

I remember Myron Cope calling me and telling me he had arranged for Frank Sinatra to come to a Steelers' practice in Palm Springs to meet Franco Harris. We jumped on a plane to get there. When we arrived, Sinatra hadn't shown up yet. Jim Boston, the business manager for the Steelers, made a flip remark

Art Rooney Sr. and Frank Sinatra check out Steelers' practice session in Palm Springs late in the 1972 season.

to Myron.

"Where's your Frankie-boy now?" said Boston, who could be counted on to say the wrong thing. "Sinatra's a no-show. Cope's a loser again."

No sooner had Boston berated Cope than Sinatra was there, tapping Boston on his shoulder. "When Sinatra says he'll show," said Sinatra, "he shows."

That was great and there were newspaper photographers there to capture the moment. That was one of the highlights for Franco's Italian Army. Here's how Al Vento Sr. told the story:

"It was a great day."

I had a special time this season, too. When Miami came here for a Monday night game (November 26, 2007), a lot of the former great Steelers were in town to mark the 75th anniversary season of the Steelers. They had a program that afternoon at the Heinz History Center to call attention to Dan Rooney's new book about his life with the Steelers during that time. He was born the same year (1933) the Steelers came into being.

My daughter, Mary Ann, bought a pair of tickets for my wife and I to go, and surprised us with this gift. She went with us. They have a display of all my stuff from Franco's Italian Army at the Sports Museum at the Heinz History Center. I gave them everything.

When we arrived just before the noon start, the Steeler Nation got there earlier and we had to sit in the back row of seats. We were split up, at first, but then someone moved so we could sit together.

Stan Savran interviewed Dan Rooney, and many of the Steeler greats were up there on the stage. Terry Bradshaw and Joe Greene were up there. When I saw Franco come out, I went up to say hello to him during a break in the program. I wanted to let him know I was

178

there. Franco was sitting on the end.

His wife Dana stops me and gives me a hug and a kiss. She tells me to get my wife and daughter and bring them down to the second row. There were more players sitting in the front row. Bradshaw told a good story about how he had once been asked to pose for a picture with someone and their baby in Ligonier. He said that 30 years later, he was in town and a guy came up to him, and said he had a picture to show him. The guy said, "I was the baby you were holding years ago." Bradshaw said stuff like that catches you up short. "That reminds me how long ago I was playing for the Steelers," Bradshaw said.

Then Dan Rooney said that Franco never should have been allowed to leave the Steelers to go to the Seattle Seahawks in his last season (1984) in the NFL. He said if he'd known what was going on he'd have paid Franco out of his own pocket to keep him here. What a bullshit story that was! I nearly fell out of my chair. Who was the owner of the Steelers then? Who was signing all the checks? That hit me the wrong way. Who'd he think he was talking to?

Franco shouldn't have been playing anywhere but Pittsburgh. He did so many good things for the Steelers and this community. The same is true now with Alan Faneca. These guys should be Steelers forever. Franco went to Seattle and they didn't want to block for a new guy. He'd taken the place of a teammate of theirs.

When Franco got up to speak at the History Center, he said, "We're fortunate today to have one of the generals of Franco's Italian Army with us." I stood up and the place went into an uproar. I hollered out, "Go, Steelers!" After the program was over, people asked me to sign Dan Rooney's book. They had me posing for pictures. My daughter had me posing and she was

179

taking pictures for them.

This one family was from Mexico and they asked, "Mr. Vento, will you take a picture with my family?" It made me feel pretty important. I shook hands with all the Steelers. It was a great day.

"They were so bad we rooted for the other team."

I remember when Franco had a one-room apartment near my pizza restaurant. It was a dingy-ass room, too. He liked my place and he was a regular. Sam Davis ate here all the time and I got to know him and his wife and kids. Her name was Gladys. It seemed like Sam was in here every day. They lived right behind that Home Depot building over there. That building wasn't there then. He was on Sheraden, I think. Rocky lived on Baum Boulevard, not far from here. Frenchy was on Negley. Willie Stargell and L.C. Greenwood came in a lot. I still see L.C. once in a while.

I asked Franco one day soon after I met him if he would mind if we would form an Italian Army to be his fan club, and he said it was okay with him. They already had fan clubs for Jack Ham and Roy Gerela. I'm not sure he knew what he was getting into. Our guys loved him. His mother was from Italy and his father was a black Army sergeant when he met her in Italy. When Franco had a big running day, we said he's all-Italian.

Tony Stagno and I started to go to Steelers' games in 1969 at Pitt Stadium. That was Chuck Noll's first season. They won their first game and lost the next 13. They were so bad we rooted for the other team so we'd be on the winning side.

Things got better when Franco came to town.

Franco had a one-room place on Stratford Avenue.

I would bring him two hoagies and a half-gallon bottle of Pepsi every other night. He went to the stadium by bus. He had no money. Dana was his girlfriend at Penn State and I got to meet her when she came to town.

"Joe got shafted real good."

One night I went with Joe Chiodo to a dinner for Bishop Wuerl at the Pittsburgh Hilton. We were sitting down front and all the Rooneys came by and they stopped at our table and they hugged and kissed Joe. You would have thought he was The Pope.

Some of the younger Rooneys were calling him "Uncle Joe" and stuff like that. I couldn't believe it. This is nice, I thought.

Joe Chiodo was one of their most loyal fans. He had season tickets—34, I think—when not too many people in Pittsburgh had season tickets. He sponsored bus trips to away games in Philadelphia, Cincinnati and Cleveland. He'd take two or three busloads of fans to those games.

Comes the seating for the new stadium (Heinz Field), he ends up with seats alongside the scoreboard, in the far corner. He couldn't get any of the Rooneys to change his seats. He called and no one called him back. He went to their offices on the South Side and no one would come out and see him. Joe got shafted real good. He was so upset about that. Finally, he gave up his seats. They put his picture on tickets for one of their games, but they didn't give him the time of day when he asked them to change his seats.

He was out in the sun and he wanted to be on the shady side of the stadium, and closer to the action. He deserved that much consideration. I told you about all the Rooneys hugging and kissing him, but where were they when he needed them? That wouldn't have happened, he said, if Mr. Rooney, the old man, had still been alive.

When Art was there Joe Chiodo could walk right into his office and talk to him about anything. Joe was proud of that.

Joe used to take me once in a while to the annual sports dinner at the Thompson Club in West Mifflin. There was nothing quite like it. Bob Prince and Pete Dimperio used to hold court there and they had everyone in stitches. Then Myron Cope and Bill Hillgrove became the big stars on the program. Lots of sports celebrities came to that dinner. I haven't been there since Joe died.

"I was making real money then."

Pizza goes back to 1937 or 1938. The first place around here I can remember where you could get pizza was at Delpizzo's Restaurant in East Liberty. That's the family that now owns Del's in Bloomfield. You could get a whole pie for a quarter. When I started in business in the '50s (1951), they were throwing surplus cheese in the ocean. They were giving every American family a five-pound block of American cheese. People would give it to me. I was selling it for 80 cents a pie, or 10 cents a slice. I was making real money then. Today, it's tough to make a buck. Everybody is greedy today. Everything costs so much. There's no way to make real money.

I got to meet a lot of good people. When I first met Bob O'Connor he was working for Lou Pappan. He had those Pappan's Retaurants and the Roy Rogers' Restaurants, and O'Connor oversaw their operations.

We have an Italian Club on Chislett Street in Morningside. My friend Joe Natoli lives on that same street. You can't belong to our club unless your family comes from Spingo, a town near Mt. Casino and Rome in Italy. We have about a hundred members and 47 of them are millionaires. There are some tremendous people that belong to the club.

Bob O'Connor came to me and said, "Do you know any people who can help me get on city council?"

My brother, John Vento, was the secretary-treasurer for the AFL-CIO union in Pittsburgh. We had a meeting among ourselves and Bob got the endorsement from the union. That helped. I got some of my friends to pool some money for his campaign. We liked Bob and what we liked best about him was that Bob's closet was clean.

He could have been the president of City Council right off the bat, but he'd given his word he wouldn't run for that office. His word was his bond. I told him he was foolish. This is politics, I told him. He might've been mayor one term earlier if he'd been the president of City Council right from the start.

Bob O'Connor used to come to our club when he was the mayor for special events. When he saw a photo of Mayor Caliguiri on the wall he asked if we'd put his picture up there, too. So we're going to do that this year. I've had Dan Onorato at our club, too. The drink tax didn't win him many friends, but he's a good man and he can go far in politics.

We liked Mayor Caliguiri. We went to him once to see if he could promote one of our guys, who had all the qualifications, for a higher position in the police department. He said he couldn't do it. When we asked him why, he said, "Because he's an Italian. Because I'm an Italian."

Most of the time—you can check it—the Irish have held the top political positions in Pittsburgh. Yeah, your guys. The Irish were calling the shots. Who had all the jobs?

When I was growing up, Italians had three options

in this town. You could be a numbers writer, you could be a pickup man, or you could join with the boys. Don't say "mob" because people don't like that connotation.

I have friends in high places; you never know. Some of my best friends have done me big favors, and I try to pay them back.

We had a friend named Col. John Danzilli. He went to school with me and graduated from Peabody High School. He was in charge of the Reserve Unit at Hunt Armory. That's how we managed to get those tanks and jeeps that we took to Three Rivers. We made him a Colonel in Franco's Italian Army. Maybe he was a general, I'm not sure.

Things are improving in this neighborhood. We have a lot of new stores that are thriving and drawing people from other places in Pittsburgh. They built some new homes nearby. I'm told a Target store is in the works. They're going to build a few hotels. There's money here now. It's headed in the right direction. It's coming back. I'm optimistic.

I always think the Steelers are going to win the Super Bowl.

Former Steelers running back Franco Harris and Jim Duratz, a cable TV executive from Meadville, met on an airplane traveling to Chicago where both were scheduled to attend the Italian-American Sports Hall of Fame Awards Dinner. Reflecting on "The Immaculate Reception," Franco offered:

"I played so much football in my life, and all I'm remembered for is a busted play. That doesn't seem right."

Randy Grossman

Randy was a reliable tight end
on those four Super Bowl winners

I knew Randy Grossman could give me some thoughtful insights into Franco Harris and Rocky Bleier, and he came through on that respect, but he offered so much more when we spoke over lunch at The Grant Bar & Lounge on Monday, January 4, 2019.

Grossman also shared stories and first-time insights into the likes of Jack Lambert, Dwight White and especially their coach, Chuck Noll, and Art Rooney Sr., the club owner. I had my "REPORTERS NOTEBOOK" from Office Depot at the ready and wrote notes while trying to manage an over-flowing club sandwich and onion rings.

I gave Grossman some newspaper clippings and photos of himself from my personal files, one showing him blocking for Franco, with Terry Bradshaw behind them. "You see that guy flying off to the side with a simple shoulder block by me?" he asked.

Grossman is great company. I hardly gave him the time of day when he was playing for the Steelers in the late '70s and early '80s. He was never a star and the Steelers had so many stars in those days. He shared the tight end position with Benny Cunningham, who died at age 63—same as my dad—on April 23, 2018. Cunningham was the first-round draft pick of the Steelers in 1976, coming from Clemson.

I missed something by not getting to know Grossman and Cunningham better in their playing days. I have gained a greater appreciation for Grossman after he retired as a player. I complimented him on his dry sense of humor. "I was always funny," he says now. "You just didn't know it then."

There were a lot of things we didn't know then that we both know now. Wisdom and perspective can only come with age. That's why Chuck Noll never liked to reminisce when he was still coaching. "There will be time enough to do that when we retire," he often said. Noll was 82 when he died in the summer of 2014 at his apartment in Sewickley. There wasn't time enough.

Randy Grossman was Noll's kind of player: dedicated, determined, intelligent and willing to sacrifice for the good of the team. Mike Tomlin needs to surround himself with players like that. To be models and leaders for the likes of Antonio Brown and LeVeon Bell. Joe Greene would have straightened out Brown and Bell long ago.

Randy Grossman is certainly one of the most intelligent players from that 70s era. Like his friend and former teammate, Mike Wagner, he thinks before he speaks and is careful in what stories he cares to share. Wagner has this to say about Grossman: "There were other guys like me who didn't look the part. You take someone like Randy Grossman. From Day One he was the longest shot for making it in the NFL. Yet he was a pivotal part of our offense. How's that happen? Randy just kept doing it."

Grossman protects the Steelers' legacy, as did Dwight White, L.C. Greenwood, Andy Russell, John Stallworth, Larry Brown, J.T. Thomas, Hines Ward, Jerome Bettis, Brett Keisel, Chris Hoke and some others. This is a skill lost on most of today's players who tweet and talk before they think.

"I don't know the Steelers of today," said Grossman. "They're not interested in hearing from me, or getting any advice, about football or how to handle their money and invest it prudently. That's the key word—prudently. When I was playing, would I have been interested in talking to someone who had played football for the Steelers in the '30s? I think not."

Grossman shared a story he thought showed how things have changed for players then and present. "Lynn Swann needed a bed for his apartment his rookie year and Franco told him he had an extra mattress he wasn't using," said Grossman.

"Lynn was our No. 1 draft choice and he was driving a used Chevy Camaro. I was driving a Ford pickup truck so Lynn asked me to go over to Franco's to help him get the mattress. Franco didn't even have a car. He took the bus. Well, we go over. In fact, it was just a mattress without box spring or frame. We picked it up and took it to Lynn's basically empty apartment. It was a case of previous No. 1 taking care of current No. 1. That's probably what Lynn slept on his rookie year, a mattress on the floor of a short-term rental. Most likely, a step down from what Lynn was used to at Southern Cal!"

*   *   *

As January gave way to February in 2019, Pittsburgh had experienced some of its coldest weather in all its winters. There was talk of a Polar Vortex, and a stretch of sub-zero days that closed schools and, worse yet, closed down bingos at church halls throughout Western Pennsylvania.

Grossman and I had to call off two other planned meetings because it made no sense to go out in the cold, and drive on ice-slicked roads. We're smarter and more cautious about that these days.

One day when it was particularly cold, I told Randy it was a good thing he didn't have to play football that day when the wind chill was minus 22 degrees. "I'd be glad to play today," he told me four days before Super

Bowl 53. "I'd be making more money this week than I made in eight seasons with the Steelers."

I knew that Grossman had signed as a free agent from Temple for $15,000 in 1974, the year the Steelers had what many consider to be the greatest draft in NFL history. He and Donnie Shell, from South Carolina State, both signed as free agents that year, and thanks to their skills and a player strike at the outset of the season, had a chance to make the team.

That 1974 class included Lynn Swann, Jack Lambert, John Stallworth and Mike Webster, all members now of the Pro Football Hall of Fame, and a seldom-mentioned but talented defensive back named Jimmy Allen from UCLA. Add Grossman and Shell to that lineup and you can appreciate how the Steelers won their first Super Bowl that year.

Rick Druschel, a guard from North Carolina State, was a sixth-round pick and played one season, including the Super Bowl IX victory over the Minnesota Vikings. He later became a coach and administrator at his alma mater, Hempfield Area High School. Jim Wolf, a defensive end from Prairie View A&M stuck with the Steelers for two seasons.

Randy later provided me with a breakdown of money that could be earned in the playoffs after the 2018 season: wildcard $28,000; division $28,000, conference $51,000, Super Bowl $112,000 for a total of $219,000, plus some individual bonuses. "Actually, I did make a little more than that in my eight seasons, but not by much," said Grossman.

* * *

It was warming up now. It was 52 degrees that day when I met Randy Grossman. He was still dressed for severe weather. He wore the kind of hat all men wore in the '50s, a woolen scarf, a dark woolen topcoat, and an ever-knowing smile, like the cat that killed the mouse. He had come from his nicely-decorated office at Wealth Management on Brilliant Avenue in Aspinwall. If it were Saturday morning, I might have thought by his appearance that Grossman was going to celebrate Shabbat at a local synagogue.

Grossman was born and grew up in Philadelphia, the son of a kosher butcher, raised in a Conservative Jewish home. When he was a youngster in school and he was asked what he wanted to be someday, he would always answer: "I want to be a professional football player."

There is still that little boy's twinkle in his dark eyes, and he likes to put you on your heels with some flippant observation. He often reminds me I am Irish, and when I told him a story about Franco crying in front of an audience of 800 Italians in Calgary, Canada, while sharing a story about visiting Italy with his mother, Grossman said, "Those Italian men and their mothers..." Randy pretended he was wiping away tears. He loves Franco for being so sentimental.

* * *

Grossman had been my featured guest at a Good Guys Luncheon on January 21, 2019. As I was walking through the parking lot alongside Atria's Restaurant & Tavern in McMurray, we spotted each other. I was carrying some boxes.

"Do you know one of the signs of guys getting old?" Randy asked me.

"We get gray hair," I responded. "We forget things."

"No, we forget to pull up our zipper," Randy said.

So, I did just that and kept walking. Randy is right, as usual. My wife often reminds me of that oversight.

Randy was a big hit with the good guys. "He must be good at what he does," observed Bill Flinn, whose son Jason is now running a well-established insurance business he built in Bethel Park. "Randy said he's been in the investment business for 30 years. He has to be good to still have customers." Flinn, and a few other of the Good Guys, offered other positive thoughts about Grossman, and many of his teammates they'd met at earlier luncheons, such as Franco Harris, Rocky Bleier, Edmund Nelson, J.T. Thomas, Robin Cole and Andy Russell, who had become a regular at these sessions.

"They're all coherent, up to date on what's going on in the world, and they are doing well in their business ventures. They are an impressive group." Grossman agrees with that assessment. Tom McGuire, another Good Guy, said, "I'd trust my money with Randy."

"Franco and Rocky are good guys; they are great guys," said Grossman, "and I feel the same way about many of my teammates. We were lucky to come along at the same time and the whole was greater than the sum of its parts, as Noll liked to say."

*　　*　　*

Millvale is one of those low-lying communities in Pittsburgh that always experiences floods when there is a lot of rain or in the aftermath of a snowstorm. So, the streets of Millvale were wet, with some puddles here and there, as I drove off a ramp from Route 28 and entered the community.

The Blarney Stone in neighboring Etna was once a popular dining and drinking spot, especially on St. Patrick's Day, but the owners gave up the ghost after it suffered great damage following the Ivan the Terrible Storm in 2004. Customers have helped clean up The Grant Street Bar and Lounge after it's been flooded.

I didn't know how long it would take me to get there, so I arrived a half hour earlier than our appointed 12:30 date. I like to give myself time for making a few U-turns these days because I don't like to be late.

I sat at the bar and checked out my surroundings. I saw a signed photo of Jim Sadowski, a former Pirates' pitcher from Lawrenceville, on the other side of the Allegheny River. I'd met and talked to him, as well as three relatives of his, the Sadowski Brothers, who left Lawrenceville for the major leagues long ago.

I was greeted by a waitress with a smile and a friendly manner and she handed me a menu. I learned from reading the cover of the menu that the restaurant at 114 Grant Avenue was "a Pittsburgh neighborhood gem, celebrating over 85 years of masterful preparation of simple foods at refreshingly reasonable prices. Everything is fresh and homemade. Genuine warmth and hospitality come from family pride and small town cordiality."

This is not a chain restaurant. It's for real, with a Pittsburgh accent. There are pennants from the Pirates, Steelers and Penguins on the walls, a plaque with Jerome Bettis' image on it, a Pittsburgh-ese dictionary of local words. It has a different, old-time feel about it. The wooden floors and walls look the inside hull of an old ship.

"Where else," wrote one critic I came across on the Internet, "can you get a breaded pork chop, liver and onions, homemade apple sauce or tapioca pudding?"

I went for "The Grant Bar Club," a triple decker combination of smoked turkey breast, crisp bacon, fried egg, lettuce, tomato and special dressing. It was the fried egg portion that sold me on this sandwich. I'd never had a fried egg on a turkey club sandwich. It came with onion rings. Randy had picked the right restaurant. There was great service with a smile. Our lunch came to about $22. Plus, a $6 tip.

A dear friend and patron of mine, Pat Santelli, a retired regional manager for Pfizer, recommended The Grant Street Bar and Lounge, where he has lunch on occasion with friends.

Two different people said hello as they passed, and Randy said he wasn't recognized there or most places in Pittsburgh. "Everyone knows Franco and Rocky, but I'm just an old Jewish guy in most places. There are advantages to being recognized, and there are disadvantages to being recognized."

I was sitting at the bar, the only one there, and certainly the only customer in the landmark joint enjoying an unsweetened iced tea with a slice of lemon.

There was a segment on the KDKA-TV noon news that Bob Friend, another esteemed Pirates pitcher of the past, had died at age 88. Highlights of his distinguished career were shown. Friend has been the Allegheny County Treasurer and a successful insurance agent for Babb, Inc., on the North Side. I had invited him and his wife Pat to accompany their son Bob and Hoddy Hanna of Hanna Real Estate Services, to be guests at my Good Guys Luncheon in the South Hills. Both mother and son were real estate sales reps at Howard Hanna. Pat had heart surgery the previous year. They couldn't come. Bob, the father, said he wasn't up to it.

Another friend and patron of mine, Armand Dellovade, who owned a sheet metal business that did international business out of Canonsburg, had also died over the weekend. Friend and Dellovade were good men in the community.

"When people you know start dying it gives you pause for thought," said Grossman. "It gives you something to think about. So many of my teammates on those great Steelers' teams have passed. It makes you think about your own mortality."

*   *   *

I told Grossman a story about Jack Lambert threating to kick my ass if I ever wrote another critical story about him, or brought up any scandalous tales. "You should have told him you had ten friends who'd kick his ass if he gave you any trouble," advised Grossman, ever the advisor. "He would have backed off. Jack didn't want to get into any fights; he just liked to annoy people."

When I told Randy that I had just read an article about how some financial advisors have to be therapists as well for their clients, he concurred.

I had heard that Dwight White and Jack Lambert didn't talk to each other for nearly ten years because of Lambert's attitude and behavior. He had a vanity license plate on his truck that read I DON'T BRAKE FOR LIBERALS, and he usually wore a policeman's ballcap and wrote some messages some would regard as racist remarks on the club blackboard. And there was that incident in the clubhouse at St. Vincent in their playing days.

Lambert was undressing and he tossed a soggy jock strap White's way. It struck White, who was then known as "Mad Dog," on his nose.

"Sorry, I'm not saying it's not true," related Randy, "but I have a hard time believing that story. Lambert liked to play the bad guy, but Dwight would've crushed him."

I recalled Grossman telling a story at a luncheon at a fire hall in Kennedy Township, near McKees Rocks, about how he threw up in Chuck Noll's lap while Noll was sleeping on a Steelers' chartered flight. When I asked him if that was true, he said "It's a good story."

When I later told Rocky Bleier about the story, he smiled and said, "It's a good story."

My boss at *The New York Post*, managing editor Paul Sann, used to say, "If you want it to be true, it probably isn't."

I've read that books of their personal experiences are written through a prism to shed light on their lives. They are suffused with nostalgia. The past is grafted into the present. They are a source of inspiration, about the struggle to be good, if not great, at something.

This is as true for Franco Harris and Rocky Bleier, as it is for Terry Bradshaw, Randy Grossman, John Banaszak, J. T. Thomas, and so many other Steelers.

Then Randy related a story about Lambert in the locker room at Three Rivers Stadium. "Saturday was always a light workout and we were permitted to bring our kids to practice that day," he said. "My Oliver is playing with a little toy truck on the rug in the locker room. He's about three or four years old, just a little guy. He pushes the toy truck and it goes across the room and stops at Lambert's feet. Lambert picks it up. I told Oliver to go get it. When he gets near Lambert, Lambert gives him his best Lambert glare. "That's my truck," Oliver says. To which Lambert says, 'Not anymore. Now it's mine.' Oliver starts to cry. I mean he was just a little kid. Lambert felt so bad about that; he didn't mean to make the kid cry. He was so apologetic."

Then I told Grossman about a Saturday morning when I brought my two daughters, Sarah, 7, and Rebecca, 3½, to the stadium. We were walking down a tunnelway to the field and L.C. Greenwood was hiding at the end of the tunnel. L.C. was 6-6½ and wore a black-tinted face mask, making him look like Darth Vader.

L.C. jumped out at us and went "Boo!!!"

My girls both folded into the back of my legs. L.C. then apologized for scaring them so much and became one of my girls' favorite Steelers, along with Joe Greene, Rocky Bleier and Lynn Swann.

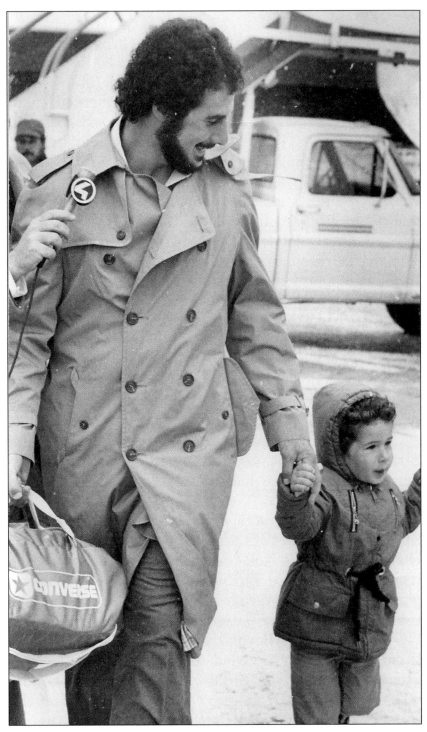

Randy Grossman holds hand of son Oliver upon return from Super Bowl victory in January 1979.

"He could see beyond the stars."

"I see where Gil Brandt got into the Football Hall of Fame this weekend, and it was well deserved," said Grossman. "But if Brandt belongs, then so does Bill Nunn Jr. and Art Rooney Jr. They had some of the best drafts ever in the NFL.

"Everybody was trying to get the best talent. There were so many variables to consider. The Cowboys were one of the first teams to come up with grading standards for prospects: size, weight, speed and such."

Then Grossman offered an insight into Noll that I had never heard before, not even from Joe Greene or Mike Wagner, or any sportswriters.

"Chuck Noll was different," said Grossman. "Maybe because he was an under-sized player himself, who played guard on offense and linebacker on defense, and brought in the plays (from Paul Brown), he knew that all things were not measurable. You had to have heart and some other intangibles.

"He was the opposite, say, of someone like Hank Stram, who had not played and had a different view of what he wanted in a football player. His way worked, too.

"But I could make Chuck Noll's team. Donnie Shell could make Noll's team. Mike Wagner and Rocky Bleier could make Noll's team. Noll saw in some guys who looked average, but were not really average—no one in the NFL is average or they wouldn't be there—that they could contribute.

"He could see beyond the stars. We had lots of them, too, and you needed to have the stars to be a great team. But Noll could classify guys beyond the stars. He wanted to see guys actually produce on the football field, not by how fast they could run the 40, or what their vertical jump is. Hank Stram loved specimens. So did (Tom) Landry in Dallas. Some of us Steelers might have been among the first cuts by the Cowboys who had a physical model in mind. We'd have been early scratches."

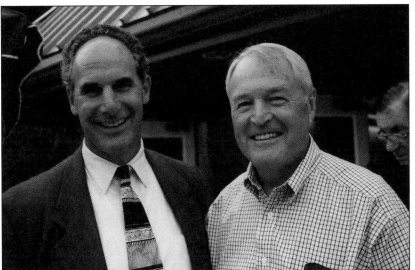

Jim O'Brien

Randy Grossman and Chuck Noll at fund-raising tennis tournament in Mt. Lebanon to benefit Guild for the Blind

Steelers Archives

Randy Grossman had a full head of hair and then some when he signed on with Steelers in 1974.

First Impressions

He wants everyone to like him

"I never learned to say no."

First impressions mean a lot, and Rocky Bleier is hell-bent on making a positive impression. He always had to be at his best, whether he was running with a football, blocking for Franco Harris and Terry Bradshaw, or providing a safety-valve pass outlet for the blond bomber from Louisiana. Rocky couldn't afford to slack off for a single play.

He had been reminded so often of his limitations that he knew where he stood. He was standing beside me one day, and I was standing as tall as I could, measuring myself next to him. I'm 5-8½ and I'm just a loose hair or so (of his) shorter.

"What's the deal, Rocky?" I said. "I'm damn near the same size as you and coaches always told me I was too small to play football."

"Your problem, O'Brien," Rocky replied, "is that you believed them."

He put a knuckle in my sternum as he made his point.

Always the motivational speaker.

Jim O'Brien

Rocky Bleier was a featured guest in 2018 at Good Guys Luncheon where he did a portion of "The Play."

"Every payday is a good payday," Rocky has often reminded me.

I went to the old Roosevelt Hotel near Gateway Center to interview Bleier for the first time back in July of 1979. The Pirates were on their way to winning the World Series, and the Steelers would soon open training camp to prepare for winning their fourth Super Bowl in six seasons.

My timing was always spot-on. I moved from Pittsburgh to Miami in 1969 in time to cover the Miami Dolphins in the final year of the American Football League and the second season of the American Basketball Association, and became the pro basketball columnist as a sideline for *The Sporting News*.

I moved from Miami to New York in 1970, arriving as the city was still basking in the "I guarantee it" Super Bowl victory of Broadway Joe Namath and the New York Jets over Johnny Unitas and Earl Morrall and the Baltimore Colts, and "The Miracle Mets" winning the World Series. I would be instantly assigned as the fourth member of a writing team to cover the New York Knicks in the NBA playoffs as they went on to win the team's first championship in club history.

I also covered the Nets of Rick Barry and then Julius Erving who would win two ABA titles, and later the New York Islanders who would build a team that, eventually, would win four consecutive (1980-83) Stanley Cup championships.

That team was assembled by general manager "Bow-tie" Bill Torrey, whom I had met when he worked for John Harris at the Civic Arena and managed the Pittsburgh Hornets and promoted the Harlem Globetrotters annual Christmas season visit to Pittsburgh. So, I had a great connection at the top to report on the Islanders, and sometimes the Rangers at Madison Square Garden in Manhattan. I could catch a train on the Long Island Railroad at a stop alongside our apartment building in East Rockaway, and arrive at Penn Station below the Garden in about an hour.

I bought a home on a cul-de-sac in Baldwin, just five miles from Hempstead (L.I.) Arena and Nassau Coliseum and even closer to Rockville Center. Those buildings framed the Hofstra University campus where Joe Namath and the Jets held practice.

Beaver Falls Joe wasn't a fan of Paul "Dr. Z" Zimmerman, who covered the Jets for *The New York Post*, and later was the pro football guru for *Sports Illustrated*. So, I was sent to the Jets' training camp each Tuesday to do a story on Joe Namath. It was a great beat.

Namath liked dealing with a sports writer from Western Pennsylvania. Namath knew some of the same nefarious characters from back home as I did, so we got along fine. And I did not have to write any critical stories about him. That was up to Dr. Z.

So, life was good, from Dr. J to Dr. Z.

I stayed one year in Miami and then nine years in New York before returning home to Pittsburgh to work for *The Pittsburgh Press*. I was not hired to cover the Steelers, but soon after I accepted the job and before I reported for duty, Glenn Sheeley, left *The Press* to join the *Atlanta-Journal Constitution*, one of America's more prominent and respected newspapers. Sheeley had been covering the Steelers.

I drew the prized assignment from editor John Troan and managing editor Leo Koeberlein to cover the Steelers.

That's how I met and got to report on the daily doings of Rocky Bleier and Franco Harris & Co. Robert Bleier was Rocky long before Sylvester Stallone came around.

My first interview with Rocky Bleier was interrupted by a phone call from his wife, Aleta, who was calling from their home in Fox Chapel. Aleta was the daughter of Dr. Giacobin, a highly-respected cardiologist at the former St. Francis Hospital in Lawrenceville. Children's Hospital of Pittsburgh now occupies that same campus.

Aleta was used to the good life and, as best I could judge, she was unhappy to hear she and Rocky were going to have to travel to a celebrity vacation getaway with regular airline tickets. The trip was free, but the seating arrangements were not to Aleta's liking. Judging by what Rocky was saying, he would call the sponsor and see about getting first-class tickets.

I could tell Rocky was backing down on one thing after another. It was fun to watch. Here's a guy named Rocky and he was a push-over, like me, when he was dealing with his wife.

I would later be introduced to Aleta by Rocky and she would say hello and goodbye in the same sentence. She dismissed me quicker than you can say Val Jansante.

I got back at Aleta about six months later. We were in attendance at a fund-raiser event at Christopher's Restaurant atop Mt. Washington. Christopher Passodellis, the restaurant owner, introduced us. "You know Aleta, I'm sure," he said.

"I'm sorry," I said to Aleta. "I didn't get your name…"

Aleta appeared annoyed, which was just the reaction I was seeking. Have you ever heard of Irish Alzheimer's Disease? If you are Irish, you forget everything but a grudge.

Rocky and Aleta would get divorced in 1996 after 20 years of marriage. She took him to the cleaners. She got married, for the third time, a month after she and

Rocky were divorced. Read that sentence a second time just to make sure you got it right the first time around. That had to hurt. She and Rocky had two children. She moved to San Diego.

I had no idea that day at The Roosevelt how interesting the story of Rocky Bleier was to become. When I first met his second wife, Janet, I told her I liked her better right away. Janet just smiled. She was from West Mifflin, not far from my hometown of Hazelwood and, like Rocky, she was so for real and instantly appealing. She appeared beautiful on the outside and inside. I know people familiar with her family and siblings and say nice things about them. She is easy to be around. Rocky deserved such a match. Our first meeting took place at a wine-tasting party at Station Square, also attended by Jack Ham, Bruce Van Dyke and Mel Blount, among other Steelers.

Rocky had just come away from his daily workout at Three Rivers Stadium when I visited him at his office at Roosevelt Arms. He limped as he moved toward the water cooler. He blamed it on bursitis in the knee.

In his book, *Fighting Back*, he revealed that he often limps when he's tired. This was a man, mind you, who was shot in the leg by hostile small arms fire in a rice paddy in Vietnam, and soon after had a hand grenade blow up near him, ripping part of his right foot away. Doctors didn't expect him to walk, let alone run. And they certainly didn't envision a return to the National Football League. But, then again, the doctors didn't know the real Rocky Bleier, either.

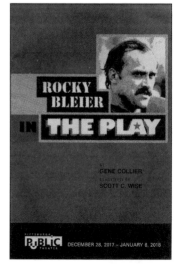

Andy Russell resists being referred to as a "veteran," saying the only danger he faced during a two-year stint in Germany in the mid-60s was driving a Porsche on the Autobahn. He says Rocky was a "real veteran."

Rocky wears a size 10½ left shoe and a size 10 right shoe. He also wears a Super Bowl ring on occasion, and has four such rings in his personal restored collection. He had to sell them to a friend for safekeeping when he ran into financial problems at the time of his divorce, but reclaimed them when he got his finances in order.

He was looking at a schedule that called for him to be in Mobile, Alabama, then Gainesville, Florida, back home to Appleton for a family gathering on a weekend, and another dinner in a town he couldn't recall at the moment. While in Appleton, he would present a scholarship named in his honor to the best young woman athlete at his old school. Are you out of breath? Not Rocky Bleier. "I look at speaking engagements as part of my off-season job. I've always had a story to tell, one I believe is inspirational to kids and reassuring to adults. We're all selling hope.

"After we won the Super Bowl the first time, and I played a part in it, I was just more in demand," Rocky continued. "My problem is I never learned to say no. I've always tried to get involved with the community. I think there's a responsibility for athletes to do that."

Steelers' publicist Joe Gordon got many requests for Rocky's presence at different events. "I have to believe his experience in Vietnam had a tremendous impact on him," said Gordon. "I also think he sincerely believes that athletes have a responsibility to give something back to the people. It sounds corny, but why else would he do it?

> *"Always do right. This will gratify some people and astonish the rest."*
> —Mark Twain

Randy Grossman

Reflecting on Fats Holmes

"Easy, Fats. Easy."

R andy Grossman was at another table at the luncheon. He was the first Steeler I spoke to when I showed up at the Best Western. We started sharing some stories about Ernie "Fats" Holmes, who had died a month earlier. I introduced someone to Grossman and told them he had a dry sense of humor that he discovered late in life.

At a Mel Blount celebrity roast, Grossman got on ESPN's Chris Berman and was surprised that Berman got hot over it.

I remembered a funny story Grossman had told me about getting together with Holmes at a team reunion a few years back. "I asked Ernie what he was up to," said Grossman, "and he told me he was studying to become a Baptist priest. I said to Ernie, 'You know, Ernie, I'm not of the faith, but I don't think Baptists have priests.'"

Grossman told me a new story. He said that he and Mike Wagner and Ernie had been honorary captains for a game dedicated to the Steelers of the '70s during the previous season in which the Steelers celebrated their 75th anniversary season.

You may remember how Holmes got into trouble with the law during his playing days by shooting at a police helicopter that was hovering overhead in Youngstown, near the Ohio Turnpike. Holmes ended up spending time at Western Psychiatric Institute in Oakland, where he was treated for a mental breakdown.

He once complained to teammate L.C. Greenwood, who was asked to visit him by owner Dan Rooney, "I got to get out of here. Everyone here's crazy."

Grossman told me this story:

"Before we went out onto the field, we're standing in a hallway, and Ernie is talking to me and Mike. He says, 'I'm really into hunting now. I've become a really good shot.' Mike and I just looked at each other and rolled our eyes.

"Later, we're standing out at midfield at Heinz Field," continued Grossman. "It's me and Mike and Ernie. Then three Army helicopters swooped in overhead during the playing of the National Anthem. Mike looked at Ernie and said, 'Easy, Fats. Easy. Don't get too excited.' Only guys who've played and lived together in a football setting can still have fun over a teammate having a nervous breakdown. It makes you wonder."

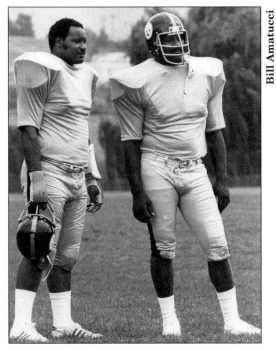

Bill Amatucci

Ernie Holmes and Joe Greene at St. Vincent practice field

ROCKY

"Every payday is a good payday."

Rocky Bleier from an interview:

Franco and I both lived in East Liberty in our early days with the Steelers. Franco didn't have a car for a time, and he used to take the bus to Three Rivers Stadium. Sometimes I'd drive over to his place and pick him up. I'm not sure, but I think he got his first car when he was named the NFL Rookie of the Year. Let's just say Franco was frugal in those first few years.

Andy Russell has always been my advisor. I was in business with him for awhile, as part of Russell, Rea, Zappalla & Bleier, a group that did bond issues out of the Roosevelt Hotel when you and I first met. Dwight White used to say he was smarter than the average bear, and Dwight has shown he was right about that. He's been a success in business. Well, the same is certainly true of Andy. He'd been around and he knew more than most about the real world. He helped a lot of us in that respect. We trusted what he was telling us.

I have benefited from playing with and, more importantly, becoming close to Andy and Franco.

I got so much value out of playing football, plus I got paid. I've always said that every payday is a good payday and that was certainly true of all my years with the Pittsburgh Steelers.

Once you pass 60 that makes you start to think about where you've been and what you've done. I am lucky to have a great wife in Jan (Gyurina), and we adopted two little girls that are going to make me keep plugging away. We have two great little girls who came from the Ukraine, Elly and Rosie and they're in college now. They'll keep me hustling. We needed a bigger home for them so we moved to another place near us in Mt. Lebanon.

You don't always realize the impression you leave or the impact of your actions. I just got an e-mail from a Notre Dame grad. He graduated in 1976. I was a senior class fellow when I was at Notre Dame and I came back to the campus to speak. This guy tells me he was there and that he remembers it to this day. He said he got my book, and he wanted to get it autographed. So, there's one person I made a positive impression with.

I wish I knew then what I know now and I would've given a better speech. It was so important to that fellow that he still remembered it.

You can't get all the details right about all the days in your life, but the football and the speaking are all part of my life. You think about that and what you've experienced.

Another guy e-mailed me and said his father played basketball with my father. He got hurt and he said my father loaned him the crutches I used when I came back from Vietnam. He wanted to know if I'd like to have those crutches now. He thought I could give them to some charity to auction off. I had no idea where those crutches were. I do know that my father never played basketball in his life. It must have been my uncle who did that. But those crutches were part of my life, too. Sometimes it's hard to separate fact from fiction with some of these stories.

We were all in our early 20s when we started with the Steelers. That's all you knew at that point in your life. In truth, you didn't know much. You were worried about yourself for the most part.

I've ended up making my living as a motivational speaker. Someone approached me and asked me if I thought I could get Franco to deliver a speech to his organization. They were willing to pay $15,000 for Franco to talk to them. He turned it down. He didn't want to do it. He said he wasn't confident about doing that sort of thing. I've heard him speak at several events and I thought he always handled himself well, just being Franco Harris, just being himself, and talking from the heart. That's all he has to do. But Franco has definite thoughts about what he will and won't do.

We used to refer to "Franco time." If he tells you he will be somewhere, he'll be there. But he'll show up on his time. He might delay you, but he won't disappoint you.

Franco is much more comfortable talking these days than he was when he was first with the Steelers. In the beginning, Franco didn't say anything. When I was a sportscaster at Channel 11, I tried to interview Franco a few times and it was never satisfactory. As a result, many in the media never talked to Franco.

Now he has questions. He wants to know, like we all do, what it was all about.

Going to a funeral for Myron Cope makes some of it come back to you. He was part of all of this. You went through a lot together. I always felt privileged and honored to hang around Myron. He was always connected to certain people and he'd been around a lot of interesting people and places. I liked to listen to Myron's stories. He was fun.

We all have stories about how we got to where we are today. The road was different for all of us, more difficult for some, but we all had our ups and downs. It wasn't a straight line.

We knew we couldn't always play football and we all dealt with the uncertainty differently. We didn't need Chuck Noll to needle us about preparing for our life's work. That would come soon enough and it was, or could be, frightening.

Football was part of the fabric of our lives. A game, a season, a career, a beginning, a middle and an end. When I am out talking to people, no matter what business they might be in, I tell them that we're all creating hope. I hope I can do this, I hope I can do that. No matter what you do, you are creating hope.

I had to have hope to come back after my Vietnam experience. I have never portrayed myself as a war hero; I wasn't. If my story has any meaning to anyone else it's how I worked so hard to get over the effects of the wounds I suffered on the battlefield in Vietnam.

I grew up in the backyard of the Green Bay Packers and the Lombardi years. My favorite pro football team was a championship team. I was the captain of a national championship team at Notre Dame. Not too many colleges can claim the history they have at Notre Dame. So I was well schooled in what it meant to be part of a championship program. I was lucky to get drafted by the Pittsburgh Steelers. They were patient with me and gave me a chance to get myself physically prepared to play again. Mr. Rooney was always in my corner. Chuck Noll might not have been sure about me, at first, but he certainly had my back during my stay with the Steelers.

At the funeral, I saw some of my teammates like Mel Blount and Lynn Swann, Mike Wagner, Randy Grossman, Tunch Ilkin and Craig Wolfley and, of course, Franco and Andy. They all serve as reminders of some of the best days in my life.

It also reminds you that too many of my teammates have died. You remember those funerals as well. Ray Mansfield was the first, at 56. He was the first one of our team to die. It kinda took your breath away.

We all face these things. But you didn't expect it to happen so soon. Then we lost Steve Furness. And Joe Gilliam. It hurt when you heard that Mike Webster died; he looked like he was getting his act together again. It was such a shame. He was working to get things back to where they were and he has a heart attack. Tyrone McGriff and Dan Turk were Steelers some people don't remember, but they're gone, too. We lost Theo Bell. We lost some of our coaches, Rollie Dotsch, and then Dennis Fitzgerald and Bud Carson. Then Steve Courson gets killed cutting down a tree. He tries to save his dog and the tree crushes him. Steve had worked so hard to stay alive after he had his heart problems. And now, just a month back, we lose Ernie Holmes. How could we ever forget him? Ernie had a good heart; he just had a hard time disciplining himself.

That's why I appreciate opportunities to get together with my teammates for reunions and dinners. It was nice to be invited to Myron's funeral—you had to be invited—and to see my teammates there.

Jack Lambert drew a lot of criticism for not coming to the 75th anniversary celebration. I keep in touch with Jack and I know what his issues are with the team. He makes his living doing signings and endorsements and he feels the team has not paid him properly for some of the throwback jerseys they sell, stuff like that. I understand where he's coming from and why he feels the way he does. I know Jack and he's a man of great principles.

The fans want Jack Lambert to be there. The fans want their world to be what it is. Should Jack have been there? Yes. I wish he'd have been there. He was such a big part of our success. Jack called me and he explained why he wasn't coming. He wanted me to understand his spin on the situation. He just wanted to let me know why. I know he told Dan Rooney why he wasn't coming. I think Dan tried to square things with Jack.

The image he has with the fans is not the real Jack Lambert. Jack is a very disciplined guy in his beliefs. To him, everything is black and white, and he doesn't yield on too many things. He has his own ideas of right and wrong and he doesn't waiver. I believe he has the right to make money and to be paid for his appearances and for his jersey and things like that.

Jack was my roommate. We've been through a lot together. Jack is my friend. I'm proud to say that. We're different in our approach. But I would never attempt to tell Jack what he ought to do. Hell, I'd be afraid to. You think I want him to get mad at me?

Jack wasn't very pleased when you wrote that book about him. You know how he is about such things. He'll never tell you this, but deep down I think he liked most of what you wrote. Personally, I thought it was a nice tribute to him. But I wouldn't tell that to Jack. He believes that No. 58 belongs to him.

There are only two numbers—70 and 75—that are officially retired by the Steelers. The number 70 was worn by Ernie Stautner and Number 75 was worn by Joe Greene. But there are jerseys that are not given out to players anymore. Tony Parisi, the equipment man, and now Rodgers Freyvogel, don't give out Bradshaw's No. 12, Lambert's No. 58, Ham's No. 59, Franco's 32. They may hold back Jerome Bettis' 33 now.

Sometimes they need to use those numbers during training camp because they have so many players then. I found out they gave them to guys they didn't think had a prayer of making the team.

The next guy to wear No. 20 after me was Dwight Stone (1987-1994). I was told they didn't think he'd make the team.

I had three different numbers during my days with the Steelers. I had No. 24 when I first went to training camp. Then I got 26 before the season (1968) started. When Preston Pearson was traded by the Colts to the Steelers in 1970 he got No. 26. When I came back from Vietnam and rejoined the team in 1971 I was given No. 20. No one had worn No. 20 the year before. Paul Martha had worn it for six years (1964-1969).

It took awhile, but I finally realized that I was given No. 20 because they didn't think I'd make the team the second time around.

Harry Homa/Pittsburgh Steelers

Franco, Terry and Rocky formed quite the backfield.

Moon Mullins

Moon Mullins was among the many former Steelers who showed up to support the Mel Blount Youth Home at a dinner on Friday, April 5, 2019 at Heinz Field.

It was a celebrity roast for Casey Hampton, the All-Pro nose tackle on the generation of Steelers that followed Moon's team of the '70s. Hampton wore No. 98 of the Steelers for 12 seasons, from 2001 to 2012. He weighed 325 pounds or so before breakfast and his nickname was "Big Snack," so there were lots of "fat-guy" jokes and anecdotes about his insatiable appetite and how he'd pilfer other players' snacks during breaks in team meetings. "It was the best dinner yet," said Randy Grossman.

Brett Keisel, who can be quite funny, said "Casey had muscles on the sides of his head from exercising his jaw so much."

Former defensive line coach John Mitchell said Hampton was always sitting next to his back-up, Chris Hoke, because Hoke was smart and knew the playbook well, and the answer to most questions. "Once, when I picked up the written tests, there were two for Chris Hoke. Turns out that Casey copied everything including Hoke's signature."

"He's still a big man, but I was surprised to see how much weight some of the guys have shed, especially Aaron Smith," said Mullins a few days after the dinner. "He's a different looking man. I come because I want to see our guys. The program gets a bit redundant, but Joanie and I had a good time. We like to see Mike Wagner and his wife, Becky. She and Joanie have hit it off."

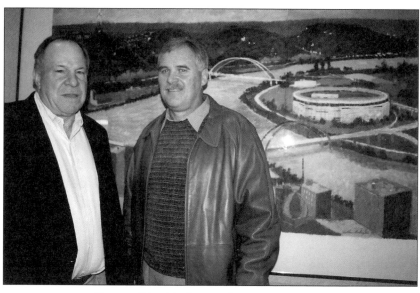

Bruce Van Dyke and Moon Mullins

Moon and Joanie Mullins at Heinz Field dinner.

Mullins told me that he and Mike Wagner shared a two-bedroom apartment in their rookie season (1971) in the neighborhood of the west side of the Squirrel Hill Tunnels. Terry Bradshaw was with them for awhile but Terry had a St. Bernard dog.

Terry had to stay late after practice for strategy sessions so he wasn't in the apartment that much. So, the dog left a mess that Terry neglected to clean up on occasion. Terry and the St. Bernard had to go. "Terry just didn't give a shit," said Mullins. But apparently the St. Bernard did, all too frequently.

Moon said he and Joanie had been to too many funerals, just since I had seen them a week earlier, one for a friend and one for an aunt, his mother's sister.

Art Rooney Sr., the founder of the Steelers, may have attended more funerals than anyone in Pittsburgh, and urged others to do the same. "You have to show up," he'd say. Moon mentioned that he had attended a funeral service in March for Lynn Hoak, the wife of 54 years to retired backfield coach Dick Hoak. She had died on March 9, at age 75, and the funeral service was on March 13. "Franco was there," said Mullins, "and some other guys from our team. Mike Wagner was there. Rocky Bleier was there.

"Dick is a great guy. I remember driving with him once for nearly three hours each way, and we talked more than we ever had before, and he's just easy company. He always seemed like the quiet type at the Steelers' facility, but he opened up to me and told me some great stories about when he played for the Steelers, and what the guys were like in those days. They sounded like a free-wheeling bunch of characters. They went out regularly for hamburgers and beers. No one needed drugs to get high in those days.

"We had some characters of our own on our team," added Mullins. "If we had cell phones and all these communication devices like they have today we might all have been in jail. A few people at the dinner told me the guys on the team don't spend much time with their teammates away from the field. They're into themselves."

Lynn Hoak was familiar with the Steelers of at least three generations. She was a cheerleader in high school and grew to love football. She grew up in Greensburg and met Dick at a cafe there. Dick was the star quarterback of the high school team in neighboring Jeannette.

He went off to Penn State. He coached a high school team in Wheeling for one year after his Steelers' playing days (11 years) and he returned to the Steelers and never left them or Greensburg. Lynn was in the stands for nearly all of the Steelers' home games at several different venues in Pittsburgh.

Hoak went back to the Steelers of Pitt Stadium and Forbes Field, as well as Three Rivers Stadium and Heinz Field.

"There was a lunch after the service at DeNunzio's Restaurant in Jeannette, and Dick pointed to a spot on a hill nearby where he grew up. I'm glad we were there."

Hoak could go home and spend time with his wife and family when the Steelers spent their summers at St. Vincent College in Latrobe.

He was a favorite of Art Rooney. "I heard that Art Rooney told him he'd always have a job with the Steelers. Hoak was the only coach to remain on staff when Bill Cowher gave way to Mike Tomlin," said Mullins.

Actually, John Mitchell, one of the unlikely stars of the Hampton Roast, also stayed on the staff when Tomlin took over for Cowher, and stayed 25 seasons to be second only to Hoak in staying on the coaching staff that long.

* * *

Mullins and Sam Davis were the guards on the Chuck Noll-coached team that won four Super Bowls in six years. I think about Davis often. I visited him in a rehab facility in Oakdale after he was found badly beaten and bruised at the bottom of the steps in his home. I remember there was a timeline of important events in his life as a border around the room's ceiling. Just to jog his memory. I visited and talked to him at a personal care home in McKeesport, in my wife's hometown of White Oak.

The Sam Davis I knew from his Steelers' days was long gone. He told me he was going to play on Sunday, and how much he liked playing for Chuck Noll. When he said that, he had not played for several years. His teeth had gone bad from too much sugar—too much Mountain Dew—and neglect. He often took a walk down the street to a store where he purchased candy bars and stopped to talk to the female crossing guard.

Mullins and Mel Blount and John Banaszak visited him as well and they all believe Davis was beaten by mob guys after he failed to pay a debt. "He was black and blue from head to toe," Mel remembered. "You don't get like that falling down steps."

Sam's wife, Tamara Davis, who remained faithfully loyal to her husband after he suffered brain damage, has told me repeatedly that Sam suffered his injuries in a fall down the steps of their home in Gibsonia. She insists her story is true. I've met their two daughters and both are most attractive young women.

For some unexplained reason, when the Steelers announced an all-time Steelers' team in 2014, the offensive guards were Alan Faneca and John Nisby. Sam Davis deserved to be on that team, if not Mullins. It was as if the Steelers didn't want to put a spotlight on Davis.

"I have not visited him," admitted Mullins. "I did see him at some function a few years ago. He looked bright-eyed and was all smiles when he approached me. I thought maybe the old Sam was back, but the man looking after him was shaking his head, standing behind Sam, indicating that Sam was not himself. Then his eyes just drifted off and he wasn't there. This was a different Sam. He was so smart and so sharp when he was with us, and what happened to him is a damn shame. I was told he was wrapped in chains and dragged across a stony driveway, and got all torn up. These were nasty guys. He borrowed money from the wrong guys.

"Some of our guys, like Stallworth, have gone on to real success in their business careers. Some didn't fare too well. It was a tragedy what happened to Mike Webster, living out of a car, and stuff like that. It all turned out bad for him. We all had to get jobs. We weren't on scholarship forever."

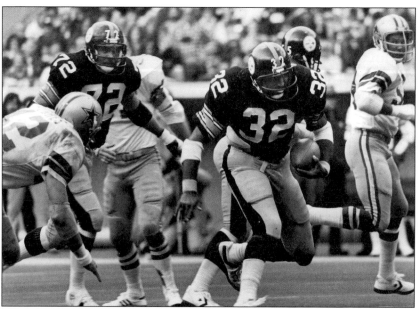

Moon opens hole for Franco

ANDY

*"I seldom ran the play the way
it was drawn up."*
—Franco Harris

A ndy Russell was now 66. Rocky Bleier was a week away from his 62nd birthday. Both were grandfathers. Franco Harris would have his 58th birthday two days later. I was 65. I was a senior at Pitt when Andy Russell was a rookie with the Steelers and they were playing their home games at Forbes Field. They would move to Pitt Stadium a year later.

Russell was working in high finance, a managing director at Laurel Mountain Partners, L.L.C., merchant bankers with offices at 625 Liberty Avenue, formerly the Dominion Tower. Bleier was still traveling the country commanding nice fees as a motivational speaker. His story of a comeback from wounds suffered in combat in Vietnam to make and then star for the Steelers still played well with corporate types who were looking for something to spark their enthusiasm and work ethic. Russell and Bleier both got started on their business careers while they were playing for the Steelers. Andy gave up football when he was making more money on the side than he was with the Steelers. Franco was the president of Super Bakery, which produced special high nutrition donuts for school children's government-sponsored breakfast programs and had an office in the North Hills.

Russell, who did a two-year stint as an officer in the U.S. Army, is credited with 14 years in the NFL. Bleier is credited with 13 years and Franco, who finished up with a half-season in Seattle, is also credited with 13 years.

Russell was living in a beautiful home alongside the 18th hole at The Club at Nevillewood. Bleier had just moved from one home to a larger home in Mt. Lebanon's Virginia Manor neighborhood. He needed a bigger home since he and Jan adopted two little girls from the Ukraine a few years earlier and needed more room. Franco had a home in Sewickley, not far from the homes of his teammates Lynn Swann and Jack Ham.

So, needless to say, they were all doing well.

Franco was talking the most. Franco and Rocky later told me that Franco was more confident these days, more likely to start a conversation. He had come over to where I was standing in the room getting a can of Diet Coke and he had initiated a conversation. That led to me joining him at that table.

Franco offered insights into his running style. "I was 6-3 and I thought that gave me an advantage in seeing the opposing side," he said. For the record, he was always listed as 6-2 in the press guide and game program, which seems right.

"I don't think I was the size they were looking for, at first," he continued. "I heard Noll wanted someone else, someone stockier like the big running backs of that era."

Chuck Noll favored Robert Newhouse, who became a fine back for the Dallas Cowboys, but not the Hall of Fame back that Harris turned out to be. "I started picking up my reads before I even got the ball," said Harris, initiating a lengthy reflection on his running style. It was fascinating football insiders' stuff.

"I seldom ran the play the same way it was drawn up. If plays went the way they were drawn up every play would go for a touchdown. The defenses foul things up. They move around and they disrupt everything. I wanted to see where they were, not where they were supposed to be."

He smiled at Andy and explained. "I don't think I ever ran the 19-straight play the way I was supposed to. I looked for openings. And when I found one I'd go that way. If I ran it ten times I might run ten different ways"

Steelers' offensive linemen of that era told me that they had to block differently for Franco than they did for Rocky. "When Rocky got the ball and he was supposed to come behind you that meant he'd be on your ass in a second or two, and you better plow straight ahead. Rocky would be where he was supposed to be. With Franco, even if he wasn't supposed to run the ball behind you it was a good idea to try and hold your block a little longer. Any second, he might be coming back your way. It worked for both of them."

There were games when they both rushed for more than 100 yards and at least one season when they both rushed for more than 1,000 yards. They were quite the backfield tandem.

Steelers' fans have fond memories of the two-back offense when Franco was paired with Rocky. Franco had been effective with Preston Pearson as well, but Pearson wanted to be the featured back and that caused some difficulty with the coaches.

Dick Hoak, who was the backfield coach at the time, said they noticed that Franco was more productive when he had Rocky in there because Rocky was a better blocker, and more willing to accept that supporting role. I talked to Hoak, who had retired the year before, at DeNunzio's Restaurant in Jeannette before going to see Terrelle Pryor play for the Jeannette basketball team in a PIAA playoff game with Kane at Hempfield High in February of 2008.

"I was fortunate to become the backfield coach with the Steelers the same year (1972) that Franco came to the team," said Hoak. "He didn't impress people right away because Franco didn't look good when guys were going at half-speed like they did on the practice field. He was at his best when everybody was going full-speed.

"Franco had a unique running style. He was quick. He'd find an opening and he could accelerate fast and get through it. He did it his way and his way worked. It was a privilege to coach him."

When Franco and Dana were departing the banquet room later that day, members of the kitchen staff intercepted them and asked if he would pose for a picture with them. Franco obliged and put his arms over the shoulders of two of them. Dana did the picture taking. They couldn't have been nicer to Franco's fans.

Dana and Franco Harris

Robert Pavuchak/The Pittsburgh Press

Dick Hoak

Bleier or Thornton with Franco for Super Bowl XIV in Pasadena

W e were in the Los Angeles area, and the Steelers were practicing at Newport Beach and getting ready to play the Los Angeles Rams in Pasadena at the iconic Rose Bowl. Only this was Super Bowl XIV—No. 14, and No. 4 for the Pittsburgh Steelers.

It was Friday, January 18, 1980, two days before the big game.

Chuck Noll and Dick Hoak had a big decision to make, and they were keeping it to themselves. Hoak, the Steelers' offensive backfield coach, had to choose between Rocky Bleier and Sidney Thornton to start alongside Franco Harris.

This is from a bygone era, so you understand, when football coaches believed you could win games with two backs behind the quarterback.

This was a prestigious assignment and Noll would go along with however Hoak thought it would give the Steelers the best chance of winning their fourth Super Bowl in as many outings, something no other NFL team had ever done. He trusted Hoak's judgment.

There would be more than 100,000 in attendance and there would be more than 100 million viewers watching it on television, or what figured to be the largest audience ever to watch a sporting event.

Pittsburghers and Steelers' fans could be seen everywhere in the LA region. The wives of the players and coaches had arrived by a charter jet that Friday, and my wife Kathie was among them, courtesy of the

223

Rookie backfield coach Dick Hoak has two prize players to work with in 1972 season in Rocky Bleier and Franco Harris.

John Henry Johnson and Bobby Layne were teammates of Dick Hoak in 1962.

Steelers. This would be her first and last Super Bowl, so it was special, right up there with being in the 34th row for "The Fight of the Century" between Muhammad Ali and Joe Frazier at Madison Square Garden in New York back on March 8, 1971.

This was a big decision for Dick Hoak. It was not like trying to decide whether to have bacon or sausage with your eggs at breakfast at Eat'n Park.

Both Bleier and Thornton were healthy. That was not the case in the AFC championship game with the Oakland Raiders in 1976—the year that Art Rooney Sr. believed the Steelers had their best ballclub.

Franco Harris was hurt. So was Rocky Bleier. The Steelers had to go with Reggie Harrison and they lost 24-7. This time around they were missing two of their most valuable defensive players, linebacker Jack Ham and safety Mike Wagner, but the Steelers were deep at their positions and managed to overcome their absence.

"What makes it even more difficult," Hoak said of the decision as to start Bleier or Thornton, "is that they are both such great team players."

I thought the Steelers would go with Bleier. "We'll have to wait and see," said Hoak, not hearing or caring about my choice. "If anybody gets nicked up, they'll both play."

Bleier believed he would start. "That's my gut feeling," he said. "Of course, I felt that way before the first playoff game with the Miami Dolphins, and I didn't start. But I have a stronger gut feeling this time."

Thornton started against the Dolphins and did well, but reinjured a sprained ankle which had caused him to miss five games late in the season. Bleier started against the Houston Oilers and was one of the heroes as the Steelers won the American Football Conference championship.

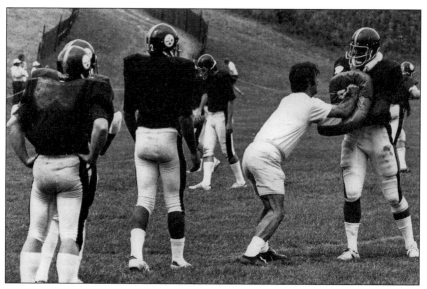

Dick Hoak demonstrates proper blocking technique to Franco Harris (32 on back of his helmet).

Dick Hoak is flanked by two great head football coaches, Joe Paterno of Penn State, and Chuck Noll at Steelers' summer training camp at St. Vincent.

A personal note here: I was one of several sportswriters who covered the Steelers who were standing at the back of the end zone in the closing minutes of the game and had an up-close view of Bleier running behind Ted Petersen to score the final and clinching touchdown.

My eyes must have been misty. Joe Gordon, the team publicist, turned and saw me. "Are you okay?" he said.

In honesty, I was overcome with the thought that I had returned to Pittsburgh that summer after ten years away, a year in Miami followed by nine years in New York, and now I would be going to the Super Bowl with the Steelers. How's that for timing?

Hoak is still talking about whether they would start Bleier or Thornton at Newport Beach. "Having both of them, we've gotten an awful lot out of that half-back spot," said Hoak.

He had been a halfback for the Steelers when people called them halfbacks, and when there were true fullbacks and even ends.

"The two guys combined for over 1,000 yards rushing and caught 50 passes. They averaged close to five yards a carry. You can't do much better than that."

Here are the actual numbers: Thornton was second to Harris in rushing, gaining 585 yards on 118 carries for a 5-yards-per-carry clip and scored six touchdowns on the ground. Bleier rushed for 434 yards on 92 carries, or 4.7 a crack, and had four touchdowns. So, they totaled 1,019 yards or 4.9 a try, and ten touchdowns. That compared favorably with Franco Harris' 1,186 yards on 267 carries for a 4.4 average and 11 touchdowns.

All of them broke off big TD runs during the season, Thornton going 75 yards, Harris 71 and Bleier 70.

Harris caught a career-high 36 passes for 291 yards and a touchdown, while Bleier had his best season with 31 catches for 277 yards, and Thornton improved on his pass-catching ability tremendously, snagging 16 for 231 yards and four touchdowns.

"Both would like to start," said Hoak. "But it's not a problem because both accept whatever we decide. It's a team thing. Sidney gives you some things Rocky doesn't, but that works both ways."

Bleier would be 34 in March of 1980, and this was his 11th season, while Thornton was 25 and in his third year. Bleier was 5-10, 210 and Thornton was 5-10, 230.

"Rocky doesn't make mistakes," said Hoak. "And I've seen him come through so many times. On Sunday after Sunday. He's always prepared and he'll make the big play. He's not the greatest practice player, but he's a winner."

And, right there, without meaning to tip his hand, Hoak gave the best reason for starting Bleier on Sunday. Sidney would have his day, or so it was thought, in some other Super Bowl.

"I just wish Rocky would quit talking about retiring," volunteered Hoak, who put in ten years as a halfback for the Steelers before calling it quits. "If he keeps talking about retiring, Chuck will tell him to quit. I wish he'd keep quiet about that. He hasn't talked to me, and he hasn't talked to Chuck about it.

"Even if he didn't start for us next season, he could be so valuable. Him not having to play all the time has helped him this year. There were times before when he was hurt, and he had to play because we had no one else to turn to.

"Even banged up, Rocky was better than anybody else we had. We're fortunate now to have Sidney. And if Greg Hawthorne's healthy and with Anthony Anderson around, we're deeper that we've been in the

Dick Hoak, backfield coach of Pittsburgh Steelers

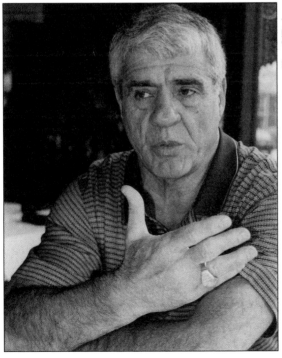

Dick Hoak during interview with author at DeNunzio's Restaurant in Hoak's hometown of Jeannette.

backfield. If I told Rocky he had to play fullback, he could do that, too."

There were some who believed Bleier was too involved in outside business interests. He was trying to peddle some bonds and investments to businessmen in Houston when the Steelers were there for a big late-season game. But Bleier didn't miss a beat when he switched from his business suit to a Steelers' uniform.

"Rocky studies the game," said Hoak, "and he forgets all those outside interests. This is still his main interest. He's had a great year, all things considered, and I don't know why he's even talking about retiring."

Then Hoak turned his attention to Harris, his prize stallion, and one of the greatest big-game players in NFL history. There was concern about Franco early in the season, and Hoak had to admit he was looking for Franco to have a return to form, to see Franco find the holes and 15-yard gains, instead of going from sideline to sideline.

"Everybody was making such a big deal about it," said Hoak, "and I was a little concerned, yeah, you had to be. But he's gone through that every year. He'll have three or four bad games. It just stood out so much because it was the beginning of the season."

Years later, I would visit with Hoak in his hometown of Jeannette where he had been a high school star before going off to Penn State. We sat at a table and talked over lunch at DeNunzio's Restaurant, with his good friend Tony DeNunzio nearby. Other than that, our conversation at Newport Beach had to be a record for Hoak talking to a sportswriter.

> *"When you are retired you wake up in the morning with nothing to do, and when you go to bed at night you have half of it done."*
> **—Steelers' coach Chuck Noll**

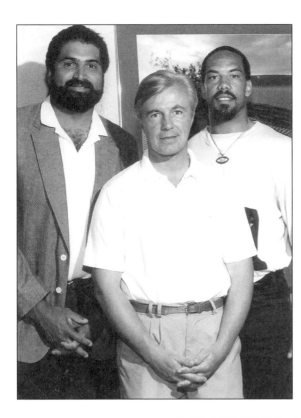

Pittsburgh Mayor Bob O'Connor is flanked by Franco Harris and Louis Lipps.

Photos by Bill Kovach

Former Pittsburgh Mayor Bob O'Connor with Roy Rogers and Jim O'Brien in pressbox at Pitt Stadium. O'Connor was a regional manager for Roy Rogers Restaurants and Lou Pappan's Restaurants.

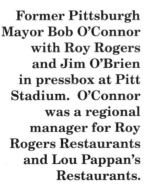

Jack Lambert

Bleier believed Lambert would be key to Super Bowl XIV in Pasadena

The Steelers were in Newport Beach, California, along the Pacific Coast shoreline, staying at a hotel there and practicing a bit and posing for pictures on a football field at a local school. It's an hour's drive north to Pasadena, where the Steelers were scheduled to play the Los Angeles Rams in Super Bowl XIV that weekend.

They would travel past Long Beach and Irvine and Los Angeles to get there. The game was on everybody's mind.

Rocky Bleier comes upon his buddy, Jack Lambert. They had been roommates on the road for years. Talk about "The Odd Couple." They were nothing alike except for the passion they shared for playing football and wanting to win.

Lambert had just been named the season's out-standing defensive player in the American Football Conference by the UPI. United Press International was a major media source along with the Associated Press back then, but has been out of business now for some time.

"What do you think of the Rams?" Rocky asked Jack.

Lambert shrugged his broad-beamed shoulders and said, "We're ready! We'll do our job. You guys have to do yours!"

Lambert's bullish posture was a good sign for the Steelers, as Rocky read the picture. Lambert was one of the big keys, one of the Steelers Bleier believed the most when he made a confident observation about an upcoming game.

The Steelers were favored by 12 points over the Rams. The Steelers were even more confident of their chances and Bleier pointed to Lambert, Joe Greene, Franco Harris and Terry Bradshaw as the best indicators of the club's confidence that it would win its fourth championship in as many tries.

There were other tip-offs or things to look for, which Bleier offered exclusively to *The Pittsburgh Press* as the kick-off neared for the final and biggest pro football game of the season on January 20, 1980.

If Jon Kolb gets sick to his stomach before the game, that would be a good sign, according to Bleier. Kolb had missed the previous three games with an injury but was slotted to start at left offensive tackle against the Rams.

George Gojkovich

Jon Kolb

Other good signs would be Franco Harris pacing the clubhouse at the Rose Bowl in Pasadena, Mel Blount boasting about how he'd be shutting down Preston Dennard and Billy Waddy, the Rams' young receivers, and that Lynn Swann hadn't gotten sunburned from being under the harsh lights of TV interviews back home, where he once starred at Southern Cal.

Bleier was encouraged because L.C. Greenwood and Dwight White were so loose a few days earlier when the annual team picture was taken. The Steelers were supposed to be the best-organized franchise in pro football back then, but one would never know it to see how difficult it was for them to line up properly and smile at the same time for team photographer Harry Homa. White wanted to know how they could take a team picture without Jack Hart, the field manager who quit the club in a huff halfway through the season and was told by Dan Rooney he was done.

Bleier brought along a professional-looking movie camera. He had been kidded about that. Some insisted that he was filming "The Rocky Bleier Story" for TV on his own. But Bleier did have an ability to bring the Steelers' scene into sharp focus. This was his 11th season with the Steelers, his fourth Super Bowl, and he knew the team as well as anyone.

Lambert mystified most people by his behavior, but he was a hero to Bleier, a neighbor in Fox Chapel. Lambert was one of the most visible of the Steelers during this span, disco-ing the night away. The legendary Steelers' quarterback Bobby Layne never spent more time at a bar, but Bobby wasn't usually as well-behaved as Lambert had been at the team's hotel. He was just always in sight, if one spent enough time in the cocktail lounge.

The hotel lounge was supposed to be off-limits to the players wherever the Steelers were staying on the road, but Lambert

Bobby Layne

ignored that rule, and Chuck Noll ignored the fact that Lambert was lawless. Noll was careful to choose his battles wisely, not willing to make a stink over something that wouldn't matter in the end. He knew when Lambert stayed out late at training camp, but chose to look the other way. Lambert was best left alone.

"Maybe he's a throw-back," said Bleier of Lambert. "He's a player first. Nothing will affect his play when he's on the football field. Whether he had a bad night the night before, or a bad week. You know he'll be there. He's so consistent. So, people don't care what he does off the field.

"Jack has a unique make-up and relationship with some of our players. He'll call people anything that comes to mind, and some of it sounds rough, even racist, and he says stuff to the black ballplayers that nobody else could get away with, but he does. He pulls no punches with anybody."

Lambert liked to wear a police ballcap and had a bumper sticker that read: I DON'T BRAKE FOR LIBERALS. Teammate Jack Ham once wrote an invitation to a team party at his house in Green Tree on a blackboard in the clubhouse, and Lambert added a line in chalk, "Blacks not included."

"I know where the hell he's coming from," White once told me, "and I don't care for his shit. He doesn't fool me."

That sort of thing went on, unpublicized, behind the Steel Curtain.

Lynn Swann and John Stallworth had a fierce rivalry and Stallworth felt Noll and Bradshaw favored Swann, but that never escaped the clubhouse. It's not that way these days.

> **"Everyone wants a joyful life."**
> **—Dalai Lama, 2019**

Bradshaw dressed near Bleier in the clubhouse and Rocky regarded him as the single most important player on the Pittsburgh team. "If he's going good, we're in great shape," said Bleier. "If he's not, we're in trouble.

"When Terry's nervous before a game, and has some difficulty sleeping the night before, and he worries, well, those are good signs. On the day of the game, if he's confident and loose it bodes well for us. I think Terry does such a great job of handling his whole situation. I wish you could have seen him earlier in his career, and could see the transformation that has taken place. He's come a long way in great fashion."

I didn't know it at the time, but several members of the team's support staff stayed up with Terry the night before the Super Bowl to calm him and help him get some needed rest. Lou Riecke, the team's strength and conditioning coach, even hypnotized Terry a few times on the eve of big games.

Bleier expected he would be in the starting lineup, even though Noll and Dick Hoak, the team's offensive backfield coach, had not offered any hints as to whether Bleier or Sidney Thornton would get the nod.

"This is my turf, so to speak," observed Bleier. "Sidney will be playing long after I'm gone from the game. I can call upon past experiences in the Super Bowl, and I think that's important. I've always played well in big games."

If Bleier was in the starting lineup – and he was – he would find it reassuring to see Kolb in the huddle. He had been there before as well. "It's just a confidence factor," said Bleier. "Not to take anything away from Ted Petersen, Jon's just been there before. Jon hates to be taken out of a game. Jon cannot stand still, and he wants so badly to play.

"He's a habitual vomiter, before big games like this. You can hear his stomach turning. He's just a nervous kind of guy."

For a long time, I didn't think Kolb cared for me, but Sam Davis, the wise old man on the offensive line who roomed with Kolb, told me not to take it personally. "Jon just gets into a tunnel of his own in the week leading up the game," said Davis. "He's so focused; he hardly talks to any of us."

Players have their own rooms these days.

Others were nervous but demonstrated it in a different way. Dwight White was a good example of that. "He gets into a preacher-type role," related Rocky. "He gets vociferous, and he'll be talking about how Jack Youngblood of the Rams has been playing on a broken leg, but how he hadn't played yet against the likes of Larry "Bubba" Brown. He really gets after Larry. Larry is the quietest guy on the team. J.T. Thomas tells some great stories about Larry. How he goes to bed at 9 o'clock and never gets out and how it's tough for J.T. to sleep because Bubba is already snoring when J.T. first lays his head on his pillow."

Then Bleier talked about Joe Greene. "Joe has a very positive attitude about this game," he said. "He's the leader of the front four, and they are going to be putting some kind of pressure on Vince Ferragamo, the Rams' quarterback.

"I think Bud Carson, the Rams' defensive coach who used to be with us, made a big mistake when he said the Rams had a better front four than the Steelers, and that their linebackers were about even. That sort of thing has a tendency to get our defense psyched up."

He mentioned that George Perles and Woody Widenhofer were really hot about Carson's comments, and also resented the attention before afforded the former Steelers' assistants who were now on the Rams' staff, Dan Radakovich and Lionel Taylor, in addition to Carson.

Bleier also spoke about Steve Courson, who had come a long way during the season and was thought ready to start at right guard. Courson was an ardent weight-lifter and he missed, while on this trip, working out in the weight room at Three Rivers Stadium, or the weight room in the basement of Curinga's Restaurant out in Washington, Pennsylvania.

Courson stayed in shape lifting young women off their feet and into the rafters at the hotel lounge, getting a laugh from Lambert. Courson looked as strong as ever.

Wide receivers Lynn Swann and John Stallworth, and tight ends Randy Grossman and Bennie Cunningham, could be counted upon to score a touchdown or two, and they were pushing each other to greatness.

All in all, Bleier believed that he and the Steelers were super ready for Super Bowl XIV.

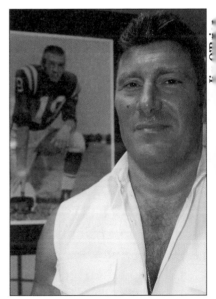

George Gojkovich

Two faces of guard Steve Courson.

238

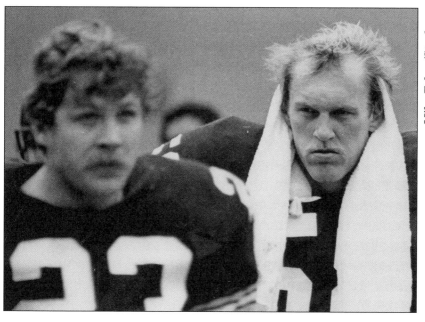

Mike Wagner says Jack Lambert was one of the smartest of the Steelers.

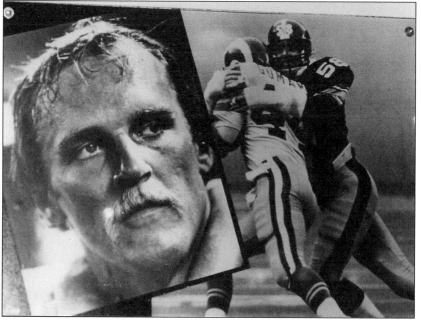

Mike Wagner

He says the Steelers of his day remain a close bunch

Mike Wagner wants to improve his golf game—make his swing higher and more consistent—learn how to read music to play the piano, do bicycling in a safer manner, and read books about all the U.S. Presidents.

"I'm a big believer in setting goals," he said while eating a plate of spaghetti bolognese bravo at Bravo on Rt. 19 in Cranberry Township, not that far from his home in Mars, Pennsylvania. I had a personal favorite, eggplant parmigiana with a chopped salad and it was sensational.

I met Mike at 1 p.m. and we both pulled into our parking spots at 12:58. There was one car between our vehicles. Talk about good timing. I reminded him that we had once met at Bravo in North Fayette. I looked it up in my book *Steelers Forever,* and the date was Wednesday, April 10, 2002. Mike had suggested 1 p.m. that time, too. And that seemed like only yesterday. Now we were meeting on Wednesday, January 6, 2019.

So Wednesdays were good for meeting Mike Wagner. Remember the movie *Any Wednesday*? It starred Jason Robards as a well-to-do Manhattan businessman who had a mistress (Jane Fonda) in a New York hotel. I told Wagner that I once attempted to interview Kordell Stewart in the Steelers' locker room and he snubbed me. "Don't you know the rules," Stewart scolded me, "I only do interviews on Wednesday."

* * *

That previous visit with Wagner was on a bright, sunny day. This was on a day when it never stopped raining. Never. Pittsburgh had experienced record rainfall in 2018 and it looked like it was already on its way to setting a new record. The parking lots along the rivers were shut down. They were flooded.

As Wagner walked toward me in the parking lot, he looked much like the fellow I had talked to in 2002, still walking ramrod straight, still taut, looking like he could chase down, say, Antonio Brown on the Steelers' practice fields on the city's South Side.

Wagner weighed 170 pounds this Wednesday. "Every decade I make a conscious effort to drop ten pounds," he said. "I bicycle 20 miles each day and, yes, I've fallen off my bike more than a few times. Bicycle people will tell you that's par for the course. Uneven roads, pot holes, cars suddenly moving in on you, lots of obstacles."

His hair—including his eyebrows and mustache—may have a little more curl to them and there's some gray on the sides of his handsome head—but he looked terrific, as always. Mike has been most accommodating, while careful in what he says, still recalling how Chuck Noll told the players to be careful in speaking to sportswriters. I tell Mike he still looks like he just walked out of a window at Brooks Brothers. Even when he's wearing a dark blue jersey.

I noticed that he slid the chair to his left away from the table so he could extend his left leg. "It was rubbing against my knee," he said. He still has some wounds and soreness from his playing days with the Steelers. He's had his share of surgeries and repairs and rehabilitation.

He had asked the hostess to seat us in a corner where we could talk better, without anyone eavesdropping on us.

Mike still smiles at some of my questions, as Noll often did during press conferences, but he tells good stories. Sometimes the smiles are smug smiles. "You still want me to tell you about something relating to me not playing in Super Bowl XIV," he said for openers once we were seated in Bravos. Mike still hasn't told me that story. I just know that he and Jack Ham did not play in that Super Bowl and, worse yet, they were not in the team photo for that season.

Injured players and players on the reserve squad were never on the sidelines when Chuck Noll was the coach. Today, mostly in hoodies and sweat-suits, those players appear to be directly behind Mike Tomlin. Why? Noll had those guys sit in the last row of the press box at home games.

Wagner was eager to tell me about Franco Harris and Rocky Bleier, two of his favorite Steelers this side of his former roommate, Jack Ham. He smiled when I told him I had spoken to Randy Grossman on the phone earlier that morning and that Randy had requested I be sure to give Mike his regards. Randy is also one of Mike's favorites.

"He's a smart man," said Wagner. "And he makes funny observations. That's Randy.

"They are all good guys," added Wagner. "We had a lot of good guys on our teams back then.

"One of the things that says a lot about the Steelers of my day," said Wagner, "is that we genuinely care about one another. I just went to a funeral for Ron Johnson in Detroit, and many of the guys were there. I didn't call anyone to go out with me; I just felt I had to be there. When we see each other, it's not just a hi or hello. We hug one another, and we mean it."

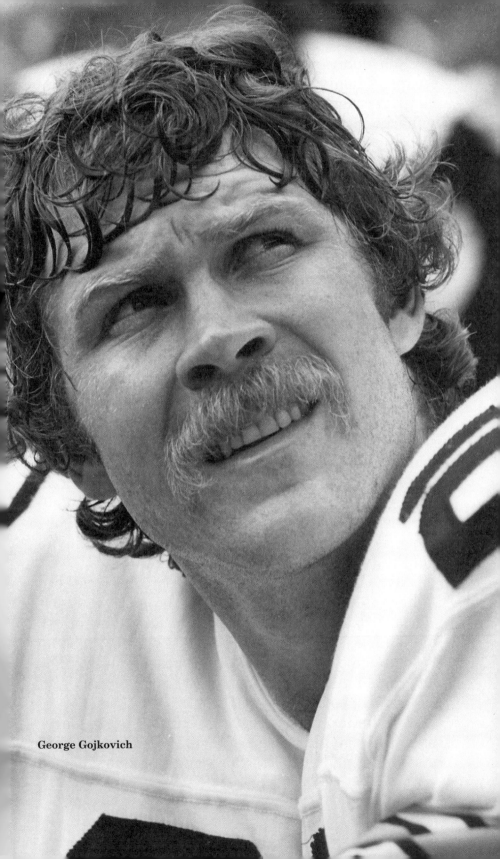

George Gojkovich

Ron Johnson was the No. 1 draft choice out of Eastern Michigan in 1978, the year before I came to camp to cover the Steelers. He had a mean look and he backed it up. He played seven seasons (until 1984) with the Steelers, mostly as a cornerback but some at free safety. Wagner was a free safety with those same teams. Johnson had played with two Super Bowl winners—XII and XIV. I know, from talking to them, that J.T. Thomas and Mel Blount both attended the funeral service for Johnson.

I thought Johnson was from Michigan, but that was Ron Johnson of the New York Giants, whom I had interviewed in my New York days. Wagner said it was Eastern Michigan and checked his Smartphone to certify it. Wagner was right.

Wagner is a smart guy. He graduated from Western Illinois and he has an MBA from Pitt. He had recently retired after nearly 40 years in the financial services field with several Pittsburgh banks and corporate entities. He and Andy Russell were good friends and called on one another about business.

"It was hard when we lost Dwight White and Ernie Holmes in such a short period of time (in early 2008) and then (in 2013) we lost L.C.," said Wagner. "I got to know those guys more after we retired from playing, and they were special in their own ways.

"Jack Lambert tells me that every time I call him, he hesitates to pick up the phone because he figures someone has died. I'm 60 now and Ron Johnson was just 53. It's scary. All those guys had gifts. J.T. Thomas was a much under-valued cornerback—he was solid—and you should hear him play the piano or an organ. He's really good.

"We had so many great players, and great players make average players great. One year, Glen Edwards and I both made the Pro Bowl and the following year

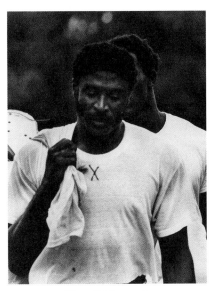

Glen Edwards

Glen gave way to Donnie Shell as a starter at strong safety. I was wondering how that happened. But Shell is now under consideration for the Hall of Fame."

Edwards was in the Pro Bowl in both 1974 and 1975 and surrendered his position to Shell the following season. Shell started for the Steelers for 11 seasons and was a five-time Pro Bowl participant.

"I often wondered how or why coaches made decisions about who played or where they played," added Wagner. "We had four to five weeks of training camp then and you could test and sort out the players better than you can now. We had full contact practices; we had the Oklahoma Drill—one-on-one helmet-first collisions—and now everyone is more safety-conscious and avoid what is deemed unnecessary contact. I saw a play in the (2019) Super Bowl where a defensive back hit a receiver one second after he caught the ball, and there was a penalty for hitting a defenseless player. How do you know when you can tackle a player now? It's ridiculous."

Wagner has always been proud of being a Pittsburgh Steeler. He likes to talk about those days and his teammates, but he is always careful to protect the franchise, and the legacy of his teammates, the Rooneys and Chuck Noll.

"It's different today," he said. "Yes, it bothers me when I hear about some of the things that go on today.

The players are so into themselves. I'm a big believer in team, and good sportsmanship.

"There's so much money in the game today, and with free agency the players have a lot more to say about where they are going to play. They have more power. Most pro athletes have come from poor or humble circumstances, and they have little knowledge about handling money. They are not mature. We weren't so mature at their age, either. I did some stupid things in my life I wish I could change. That's what you do when you're young. We thought we had a lot of money.

"The Steelers are a great franchise. They are pretty good in the entertainment business. And they put a pretty capable product on the field. The Rooneys are no longer in control of the club like they were for most of the team's existence. There are more stakeholders. That's what happens with a lot of pro teams. They have to spread the wealth. The Rooneys had no way of knowing how big this thing would get, how much the franchise would be worth."

Then, from somewhere out of the blue or his marinara sauce, he asked, "Who's Antonio Brown's friend on the Steelers?"

I told him I didn't know, but that it was a good question.

I e-mailed that question to Ed Bouchette of the *Post-Gazette*, a long-time observer of the Steelers' scene, indeed a member of the writers' wing of the Pro Football Hall of Fame, and he answered: "I don't know. Maybe Ely Rodgers."

When I told Wagner, I thought Brown was the best catch-and-run receiver in Steelers' history, I thought I had kicked Mike in the leg under the table.

"Antonio Brown is one of the best receivers in the game today," said Wagner, "but in no way can he

Mike Wagner joins his good friend Rocky Bleier at Andy Russell's Celebrity Golf Outing at The Club at Nevillewood. Russell and his wife Cindy reside at villa by 18th hole.

George Gojkovich

Wagner gets to run with football.

compare with Lynn Swann and John Stallworth. The rules are different today. You can't hit anybody. The receivers are all in a 'defenseless' position. You can't hit them too hard.

"Swann and Stallworth would have so many more catches to their credit if they had played with today's rules. The NFL is in the entertainment business and they favor offense over defense these days. People thought the Super Bowl (53) was boring because it was all defense. I didn't see it that way.

"Terry Bradshaw would be smoking 'em with these rules. He would've been throwing 50 passes a game. Don't get me started on that. I would have had more interceptions, too, because they're throwing the ball more these days."

* * *

When Wagner and I were talking about some of the defensive backs—such as Donnie Shell, J.T. Thomas, Jimmy Allen and John Rowser—he said he had seen Rowser at Johnson's funeral but wasn't sure Rowser remembered him.

Wagner was an eye witness at the camp cafeteria the day Jimmy Allen slammed his dish into Joe Greene's head. "We had shrimp that day and Joe took a piece of shrimp off Jimmy's plate because he was displeased that Jimmy didn't show up at a party Joe was hosting the night before. We couldn't believe how Jimmy reacted to Joe's taking his shrimp. Joe grabbed Jimmy in a chokehold and pushed him to the floor with Jimmy's neck in his grasp. The guys all jumped in and pulled them apart."

I mentioned to Wagner that Allen told me he had spaghetti on his plate. Wagner wags his head. "How could Joe have grabbed spaghetti in his hand?"

Wagner had heard Jimmy was a homeless person somewhere in LA. I told Wagner I found Allen when I was visiting my daughter Rebecca in LA, and that we have kept in touch. I visited Allen in Victorville a few years earlier, and was able to tell Mike that Jimmy had a nice home, and had been estranged from his late wife. He was in good spirits and wearing his Steelers' jersey (No. 45) when I saw him.

A researcher named John Bennett from Vermont had sent me some information about Allen that enabled me to connect with Cora Allen, Jimmy's wife, and she led me to Jimmy. "He can always come back here," she told me. "He will always be welcome." Cora has since died.

Allen has called me a few times, once on Christmas day, and he always is delightful. He played behind Mel Blount and thought he deserved to start. "You were playing behind the wrong guy," I advised him.

My wife Kathie could overhear some of the conversation as she stood in the hallway just off my office. "Who'd he play behind?" asked Kathie. "Mel Blount," I said. "He was playing behind the wrong guy," Kathie came back.

Jimmy was an outstanding swimmer but lost out to Mark Spitz for a spot on our 1972 Olympic team. Spitz set a record by winning seven gold medals in the Munich Games. "Once again, Jimmy, you were behind the wrong guy," I kidded him.

Jimmy still had his Steelers' jersey. I showed Mike a black and white photo of a dozen Steelers standing on the sideline in rain gear, and Mike confessed that he still had his heavy rain cloak from his playing days. "That's one thing I took with me," he said.

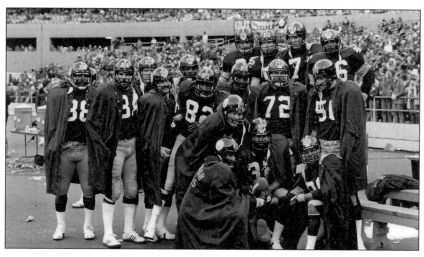

You won't find Waldo in here, but see if you can find Franco and Rocky, and maybe Lynn Swann in this sideline shot by photographer on a bitter cold day at Three Rivers Stadium.

*   *   *

I showed Mike some other photos I was giving to him as a keepsake, one showing him holding a football tightly as he returned an interception, one showing him picking up a fumble, one showing him sitting next to a grim Jack Lambert on the bench.

Mike thanked me for giving him the photos. Lunch was also my treat, but then I was so embarrassed to discover I didn't have my wallet. I'm thinking Mike is thinking "that's a sportswriter for you," but he didn't say anything. He offered to pick up lunch, but I assured Denice, our waitress, that I would call in my credit card number when I got home. They knew Mike as a frequent customer, so they were understanding and confident they would get paid.

My wallet was in my nightstand by my bed and I don't ever remember storing it there before. That's why I forgot it. That, plus my memory is fading on today's events, even though I can remember Steelers' stories from the past in great detail.

I'm not perfect in that respect. I thought Ron Johnson had played his college ball at Michigan, but Mike thought it was Eastern Michigan—"same as John Banaszak"—and Mike was right. He checked it on his Smartphone just to be sure.

Mike Wagner comes from Waukegan, Illinois and went to Western Illinois and was an 11th round draft choice of the Steelers in 1972.

When I asked him of his first impressions of Rocky Bleier and Franco Harris, and how they looked at training camp, he said, "I wasn't worried about how they were performing. That was Chuck Noll's concern. When you're an 11th round draft pick, you worry about yourself. I wanted to make sure I made the team. Every year."

* * *

We left Bravo at 3:30 p.m. We had talked for two and a half hours. That morning, after I told Randy Grossman that both Dave Parker of the Pirates and Jerome Bettis of the Steelers had given me a four-hour interview. "You give too much credit to yourself on that account," said the always forthright Grossman. "They probably got to talk maybe a half hour."

Grossman was right on the mark. I like tell stories to set the proper tone and rhythm. My story makes them think of a similar story, or offers cues to what comes next from their memory and mouth. It works well for me. But I do talk too much; I know that. I can't help myself. I blame it on being Irish.

* * *

I told Mike a story about why I transferred from Central Catholic High School to Taylor Allderdice High School midway through my sophomore year (1958). "I was on the student newspaper staff at Central. It was called *The Viking*. I wrote a fairly lengthy story on cross-country and my byline was not above the story. I asked Brother Francis Emery why my byline was missing. His response to my query was to slap me hard across my cheek. I walked away from him and went to a telephone on the wall and called my mother and told her what had happened.

"I was not out of line, and I didn't raise my voice or swear," I said. "Dad doesn't hit me and I'm not going to stay here. I'm going to Allderdice, where I wanted to go in the first place." Two days later, I was at Allderdice.

I was a better student, an honor roll student, at Central because there was more discipline there. I was freer to explore the city at Allderdice. Looking back, I enjoyed the best of two worlds in my high school days.

"If I had come home," said Wagner, "and told my dad that a brother had slapped me, he would have slapped me himself, and he'd have called the school and told them to slap me again when I showed up the next day. My dad didn't fool around when it came to disciplining me. He hit me hard and often.

"When I would recall those days to him later on, and why I thought he was too tough on me, he'd say, 'You turned out all right, didn't you?'"

Wagner's story about his father punishing him caught me by surprise. His story was similar to that of so many of the Steelers I talked to for this book. Does getting your ass whipped as a kid contribute to you becoming fit for the violent game of football? It's worthy of a research paper.

> **"I am sure my tutor kept a whip to threaten me. If the whip worked... holy pain!"**
> **—Dalai Lama, 2019**

*   *   *

That's also why it took awhile before I got Wagner to tell me about his feelings about Franco and Rocky. Bleier had been in bad shape when he returned from Vietnam in 1970 and he was put on injured reserve for the entire season.

"When Rocky returned to the team in 1971, he had bulked up considerably. He obviously worked out so hard that year because he knew it would be hard for him to make the team.

"He was broad across the chest and he could lift weights with the best of them. He looked more like a fullback than a running back and, of course, Franco ran more like a halfback than a fullback. But they ran well together. Franco still hasn't made his first block—I still get after him about that—but Rocky often blocked for Franco and helped open holes for him. Rocky ran behind the offensive line; Franco often ended up running behind Rocky. Franco was feinting this way and that way, looking for an opening.

"We weren't allowed to touch Franco in our drills. I call that 'the Lynn Swann rule.' They didn't want anyone hitting them. You could grab them or touch them, but that was it. That was fine with me. Who wants to hit those guys, especially Franco?

"Noll had us playing a type of offense and defense that was different from most teams. Everyone in the stands knew we were going to run a trap play in certain situations and we still ran it. Noll liked undersized linemen who were quick and had good feet, and were effective at running traps or running on sweeps. It all came together at the end of the day.

"It took a while, but Franco and Rocky became quite the running tandem. They complemented one another."

Marianne Noll with Mike and Becky Wagner.

*   *   *

Mike and his wife Becky have been married for 15 years, Mike thought aloud, but they have been together more like 25 years. She offers pilates classes in their home and wishes Mike would spend less time at home, so he's not in the way, or a distraction, when women come there for a workout session.

I advised him to spend time at the local library, where he can get those books about the U.S. Presidents and read—at no cost—*The New York Times, The Wall Street Journal, Barron's, Money* and *Fortune* magazines, and other publications that would be of interest.

Recommended Reading

Anyone interested in reading about U.S. Presidents should check out this list that I provided to Mike Wagner:

Grant, about Ulysses S. Grant by Ron Chernow

The Accidental President, about Harry S. Truman, by A.J. Baime

The American Lion, about Andrew Jackson by Jon Meacham

American Sphinx, about Thomas Jefferson by John J. Ellis

His Excellency, about George Washington, by John J. Ellis

Truman, about President Truman, by David McCullough

John Adams, by David McCullough

Jim O'Brien

Mike Wagner at the Clark Bar on North Side under ink sketch of Pirates' Hall of Famer Willie Stargell.

FRANCO

Q. AND A.

This is a reprint of an Inside Interview by Jim O'Brien for the August 1984 issue of Inside Sports:

A little old brown automobile that would not turn a head on its own came to a stop at the curb, and from it emerged the unmistakable figure of Franco Harris, a sure-fire Hall of Fame fullback who had starred for 12 seasons with the Pittsburgh Steelers.

There was no hint at this time that Franco would finish his career with a half-season with the Seattle Seahawks after a salary squabble with the Steelers sent him packing.

Harris was headed this sunny afternoon for the Trees Hall gymnasium on the upper campus of the University of Pittsburgh to play in a pickup basketball game, part of his off-season conditioning and get-away-from-football-and-have-some-fun routine.

A middle-aged woman smiled in recognition as Harris passed by. He smiled his warm smile, said something softly in greeting, and then smiled again when he heard the spirited hoots and hollers from five or six young men in ragtag basketball attire who were headed for the same door.

"I'm sorry, I'm a little late," he said to me.

Harris stopped to speak to some students he had come to know from his frequent visits. Harris had time for everybody. Time seemed to be on his side.

Besides playing basketball, Harris also skipped rope, ran around the oval track at Pitt Stadium and in the Pitt Field House, and lifted weights when he was at Pitt. He said the facilities were better than what the Steelers had at Three Rivers Stadium. *That is no longer the case since the Steelers moved their training complex to the South Side which they share with Pitt.*

"He works out hard when he's here," said a student, "but he looks like a guy who doesn't have a care or concern in the world. He looks like he's doing exactly what he wants to be doing."

Harris sat down in the front row of some bleacher seats in the gym, noted the activity around one of the hoops, and hollered out, "I'm going to sit this one out. But I've got the winners for the next game."

Q. You have always been reluctant to discuss personal records, yet you definitely have set your sights on surpassing Jim Brown's record, haven't you?

A. I'm not one to worry about records. They take care of themselves. But this one would be something very special.

Q. Has Jim Brown been a special sports figure in your life?

A. In high school, I wore No. 32 because of Jim Brown.

Q. Have you ever watched him in action on film?

A. Very little.

Q. Did it mean much to you to meet him in person?

A. Not much. He was a great athlete, and a great runner. But it didn't mean much to me.

Q. Do you think Jim Brown is serious about making a comeback in order to keep you from breaking his record?

A. Not really.

Q. Do you think Jim Brown can make good his boast that he can still beat you in a 40-yard dash?

A. What do you think?

Q. I'd bet on you. But I'm asking the questions. Could he beat you?

A. Never.

Q. Don't you think, because you will have played four more seasons than Brown, and played in more games, and carried the ball more often, that you will run into the same sort of harsh criticism encountered by Henry Aaron when he beat Babe Ruth's home run record?

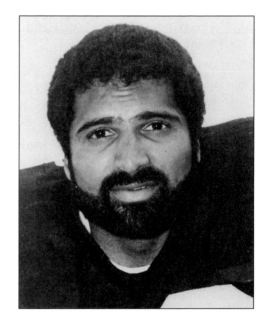

A. Of course, but I still want it. The thing that would feel good would be that I'd be the first one to break Jim Brown's record. I'm certain someone else will break mine if I get it.

Q. Already, some critics are saying you can't compare yourself to Jim Brown. Do you anticipate that kind of negative response?

A. I'll know it was done. If it took a longer time, it makes me think I had to endure more. I had to work harder. It makes me feel better. It's not something that came easy.

Q. What's your reaction when they say the NFL was a much tougher league when Jim Brown was playing?

A. During the '70s, we had some tough defenses, and some tough football. It makes it something to be cherished.

Q. Do you think you've lost a step?

A. What's a step? Even if I'm not slower, they'll say I am. I can probably run a 40 better now than I did my first year with the Steelers.

Q. Do you think athletes should retire at the peak of their game? Why do the media and the fans seem to demand that?

A. Why? That's a question I ask all the time. Why? If I get to be No. 1, that's just another achievement. It doesn't mean it's the end.

Q. I can assure you that sportswriters don't feel compelled to quit at the peak of their game. So why do you think there's a persistent pleading for athletes to retire when they're on top?

A. Sometimes it just makes for a story. They want a happy ending. Like once you've accomplished something great, you shouldn't want any more. You should be satisfied. People want to remember you at your best But life's not like that. You have your ups and downs.

Q. Does that kind of thinking bother you?

A. If the only thing you thought about was how people think, then you should end it. If you're not afraid of what people think, you do what you think is right and best for you.

Q. Do you anticipate all this coming down on you this season?

A. We all go through that. I know how hard I work. No matter what, they won't be able to take that away from me. They can write things. But I know—and that's a great feeling.

Q. None of this should be new to you. You've been criticized right along for your running style, going down at times without an apparent struggle, or stepping out of bounds to avoid a hit...

A. Those people just don't understand the game, or our offense. We don't have many plays where you're supposed to just run straight ahead. A lot of our plays call for us to "read" the defense—see what they're doing—before we make our moves. If you put blinders on, you just can't "read." But I don't have time to worry about that stuff.

Q. Doesn't that second-guessing get old?

A. People really not close to it say I've lost a step and stuff like that. I just don't pay any attention to it. I know what I have to do, what has to be done to get ready for each season. Right now, I feel good. I don't go around thinking about it. I don't have the same concerns as some other people. If you ever think too much, that's when you have problems.

Q. You've always been reluctant to reflect on records in the past. Why is that?

A. If records can't be part of the winning formula, they're not that important. I definitely want people to look back and say, "Hey, he was part of the Pittsburgh Steelers team that was probably one of the greatest ever assembled."

Q. How would you reflect on your career?

A. I just keep passing certain milestones. As long as I can keep playing, there is no finish line. I'm just never done. When I leave, I'd like to be known as being on one of the best teams ever. More than anything else. I'll still feel like our team was the best when it's over, and I feel very proud to be a part of it.

Q. What will determine when you do decide to retire?

A. I'll look at it each year, and I'll continue to play if I feel like it. God willing. If I can still jump out of bed in the morning, I'll still want to play for the Steelers.

Q. Does that mean you don't have any retirement plans?

A. I've always heard that if you take care of little things day to day the bigger things will fall into place. A lot has been accomplished. Wherever I am rated when I hang 'em up, nothing's going to take away the job, or everything we accomplished.

Q. What about the sniping at your running style?

A. I never listen. Anybody wants to run with the football, they're welcome to it. Some people complain just to complain. Maybe something else is bothering them. Your teammates, and maybe a few people close to you, realize what it all means.

Q. Is your shake-and-bake style something you developed intentionally, or did you feel it best suited you?

A. It's kind of hard to think about how you're going to run when you're running. It has to be instinctive. You can't plot how you're going to run, or practice it. It's just the way I play football.

Q. At practice, though, you always run the ball an extra 40 or so yards when you run through a play. What's that all about?

A. That's just part of the training. You know you have to be in extra good shape. It's a tough position, the way I see it. You have to be ready with all that's required of a running back.

Q. Was Jim Brown the best running back?

A. I still consider O.J. Simpson *the* running back. I'd like to look at myself in the same light. He, to me, had so much natural ability. I know there's no way I can touch him.

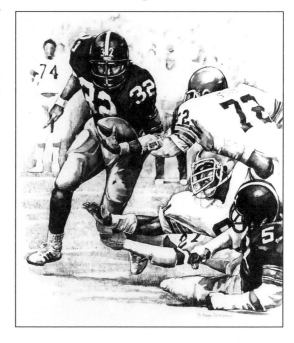

Jack Ham

Ham and Harris put on
their happy faces

The temperature in Pittsburgh had been zero overnight, but it spiked sharply to get up to 30 degrees by game time. Jack Ham and Franco Harris were warmed by a 24-0 victory at Three Rivers Stadium over the Los Angeles Rams in a rematch of Super Bowl XIV, and a stunning 48-14 victory by Penn State, their alma mater, over Pitt the previous day at Pitt Stadium.

That was when we had a Three Rivers Stadium —what a great name we took for granted—and a Pitt Stadium, when it was on the campus where it belongs. This was in late November of 1981.

The two former Penn State stars were normally two of the most reluctant talkers on the team, but they were positively gloating and it wasn't any wonder.

They were especially jacked up because they knew I was a Pitt grad. So, they were bright-eyed and smiling from start to finish in our post-game interviews in the Steelers' locker room.

On Saturday, their favorite college football team came to town and knocked Pitt off its No. 1 ranking in the nation. I was at that game, sitting in the stands with my wife Kathie because I was not covering the game for *The Pittsburgh Press*. I was just a fan. Pitt was 10-0 and on a 17-game winning streak. The Panthers were a touchdown favorite over the Nittany Lions, 8-2 record. They thought they could win another national championship.

I never saw such a turnaround in a game in my life. Danny Marino, the prize Pitt quarterback, began the game by throwing two touchdown passes that looked like something out of Star Wars. He threw what should have been a third TD pass into the end zone, but it bounced off the chest of Julius Dawkins, one of the team's best receivers, and into the hands of a Penn State player for an interception.

It was all Penn State the rest of the way, with Todd Blackledge outdueling Marino. Even though Pitt lost, I can't understand how or why any Steelers' scouts in the press box could have passed on Marino in the draft of 1983. Blackledge was one of five quarterbacks chosen ahead of Marino.

The others were John Elway, Jim Kelly—both in the Football Hall of Fame—and Tony Eason and Ken O'Brien. I think Marino was fortunate to go to Miami where he had a great coach in Don Shula, great receivers, few stellar running backs and great weather.

* * *

I can still see that locker room at Three Rivers Stadium, and make up a seating chart as to where each of the Steelers was sitting on a stool at game's end, and I can picture Pitt Stadium on a cold winter's day when there was some snow in the air.

"It was a great day, a great weekend," said Harris. "There's no doubt that Penn State's win really got me fired up. I knew there'd be a lot of Penn Staters here today, and I wanted them to see I haven't slowed up too much." Harris showed everyone he could still hoof it pretty good. After ten years with the Steelers, he still had something left in him.

About 5½ minutes into the game, he went off left guard for three yards to pass O.J. Simpson as the running back who carried the ball more than any other in

National Football League history. "I find that hard to believe," said Harris.

Simpson, who had retired two years earlier, had carried the ball 2,806 times in regular season games. Franco finished his career with 2,949 carries, which ranked 15th all-time going into the 2019 season. Emmitt Smith of the Dallas Cowboys was the all-time leader with 4,409, followed by Walter Payton (3,838), Curtis Martin (3,518) and Jerome Bettis (3,479).

Martin grew up in my hometown of Hazelwood and went to Taylor Allderdice High School and Pitt, same as I did. I saw him run for 251 yards against Texas on Dorsett Day at Pitt Stadium in early September of 1994. No one on an opposing team ever ran for more yardage in 101 years of Texas football. Martin sprained an ankle and played in only two games his senior season. He could have taken a red-shirt and returned but he chose to enter the 1995 draft. Bettis was a favorite of mine during his long stay with the Steelers.

*   *   *

Jerome Bettis

Harris also scored the first touchdown in the victory over the Rams, from one yard out midway through the first quarter, his 84th TD by rushing in his All-Pro career, moving him into second place on the all-time list behind Jim Brown. Brown had 106 in nine seasons.

Later, in the same period, Harris broke off a 50-yard run, his longest of the season to that point. He also caught a 26-yard pass from Terry Bradshaw on a big-play day. Harris carried the ball 18 times for 114 yards—his 39th 100-yard game.

"I'm awed by the public address announcements

Jack Ham had his own fan club.

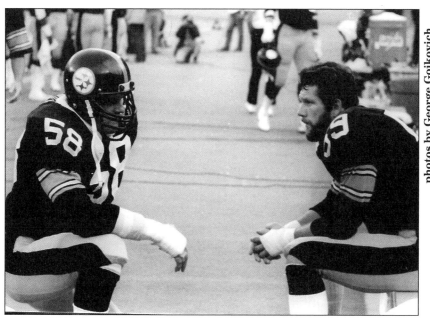

photos by George Gojkovich

Jack Lambert and Jack Ham discuss defensive strategy.

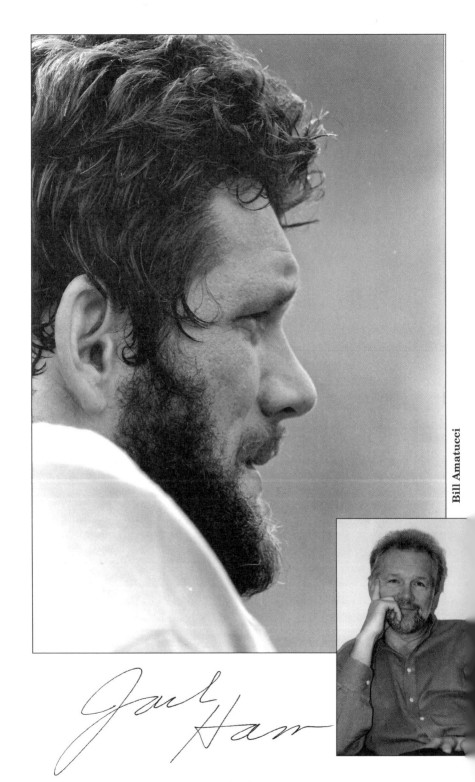

266

about him, just one record after another every time he touches the ball," said Ham. "It's been ten years now, and he's going down in history.

"Yet he hasn't changed from his freshman year in college, except he's gained miles of yardage for the Steelers."

(Ham's comment got me thinking. Franco totaled 12,120 yards in his career which comes out to 36,360 feet. There are 5,280 feet in a mile. So, Franco rushed for 6.8 miles in regular season games.)

"He's still a low-key guy," continued Ham, an All-Pro without peer at outside linebacker. The Steelers had quite the linebacking threesome early on when they had Andy Russell, Jack Lambert and Ham. Russell still insists that Ham was the best of the bunch.

Ham had his first interception of the season against the Rams and became the active linebacker with the most career interceptions (31). That was also flashed on the scoreboard.

"I'm just glad we got points out of it," said Ham, who hauled in a pass from Pat Haden that was intended for Wendell Tyler, and returned it 23 yards to the LA two-yard line, setting up the Steelers' third touchdown and their second in less than two minutes at the outset of the second quarter. "That's all I care about," said Ham.

There were more achievements cited on the message board and by the stadium announcer when Mel Blount intercepted two passes, the 50th and 51st of his career, which put him one behind Jack Butler, the team's all-time record-holder.

"Mel's only regret," said Ham," is that he didn't go to Penn State."

Ham and Harris both made the point that Pitt is their second-favorite college football team, and that they are close to several of the players. They rooted for Pitt except when Pitt was playing Penn State. Fair enough.

"They're taking me to glory."

Continuing on an important theme, Ham said, "We've all been around here long enough, and we've been to so many Super Bowls, that we know what we want to accomplish here. You can ask Mel or Franco or anybody. The individual records are secondary to the success of the team."

Harris had the same mindset, for sure. He said he believed he had more desire than ever to win the Super Bowl again. The Steelers weren't in a good position to accomplish that goal. They lost two of their final three games and ended up with a 9-7 record and missed the playoffs for the second year in a row and only the second time since 1971.

"You have to feel something will happen," Harris said at the time, but it didn't happen.

Asked how he felt about all the records he was establishing, Harris smiled and said, "No doubt, I'm proud of them. But they'll be broken someday. I'm enjoying it now because it came with a win.

"I thank God I haven't had any serious injuries. But I'm also giving credit to our team, to our defense for getting the ball, and to the offensive line for what they've done for me. I'm just following them, and they're taking me to glory."

As for the individual records, Harris said, "You can't put it ahead of other things, like playing for a championship team. Right now, we're as good as our old team. If we didn't have a championship here, and we didn't have a great line, these ten years wouldn't have been as much fun."

Ham and Harris got used to winning at Penn State, and they wouldn't settle for anything less with the

Steelers. Ham came to Pittsburgh in 1971 and Franco the following year.

"In my sophomore and junior seasons at Penn State," recalled Ham, "we went undefeated both years, and finished No. 2 in the country both times. We weren't national champions, but we were satisfied, and Franco and I got a lot of publicity when we were there. But we knew back then that team accomplishments mattered the most."

Harris and Ham were also two of Chuck Noll's favorite players. He would have loved to have more of them.

"They both have talent and they're both quiet guys," said Noll. "Their actions speak louder than words. A lot of people like to talk a lot, but they don't get it done. They are doers."

Mike Fabus/Pittsburgh Steelers

1988 HALL OF FAME CLASS—All four inductees had local roots with, left to right, Fred Biletnikoff of Erie, Mike Ditka of Aliquippa, Jack Ham of Johnstown and Alan Page of Canton, Ohio. "Biletnikoff didn't look like much," said Steelers' defensive back J.T. Thomas, "but he was so hard to keep up with."

Art Rooney Jr.

"Franco and Rocky were like my dad"

It was Thursday, March 28, 2019. The phone rang and it was Art Rooney Jr., calling me from his condominium apartment in Palm Beach, Florida, a nice address.

Better than his boyhood home, even though it was one of the better homes on that stretch of the North Side, just up the hill from Heinz Field. It is on North Lincoln Avenue in what is known as Allegheny West, near the Thaw Mansion. His dad used to refer to it as the First Ward. Dan and Pat Rooney resided there in more recent years. They moved there from Virginia Manor in Mt. Lebanon, a high end community.

"I used to ask my dad why we had to live in a ghetto when he had lots of money," I recall Art Jr. telling me over lunch one day at the St. Clair Country Club, where he and his wife Kathleen are frequent diners.

"He never wanted us to show any signs of wealth" said Art Jr. "We were not allowed to buy Cadillacs. So, we all drove 'loaded' Buicks we bought from a relative of my mother. His name was McNulty and he had a Buick dealership on the North Side."

The Rooneys never realized they were millionaires, and that helped them fit well with the team's blue-collar fans. Dick Schaap, the outstanding sports author and commentator, once told me in Tampa at the site of Super Bowl 35 that "Art Rooney looks like Pittsburgh." So does Art Jr., more so than any of the Rooney Boys.

Kay Rooney convinced her husband that they should rent a limo to ride to the unveiling of the statue of Art Rooney Sr. in 1990 with some out-of-town visitors.

The Chief checks out Steelers' locker room at Three Rivers Stadium in the '70s.

The Rooneys

Dan Rooney

Art Rooney II

As they neared the spot where the statue would stand, Art Jr. asked the driver to stop, and he jumped out of the car and walked the rest of the way. "I didn't want my father to see me in a limousine," he told me. You can't make up this stuff.

* * *

I remember a lot of things Art Jr. has told me—some of them are real gems—and he has good anecdotes to share, though he always calls them "antidotes." I knew I was in for a fun session and he didn't disappoint me in any manner.

"I just got in," he said. "I was looking at the view of the beach. It's pretty nice down here."

The Rooneys would remain there another month. They might make a short trip now and then to visit the Palm Beach Kennel Club, overseen and operated by his twin brothers, Pat and John. It's a well-established greyhound racing track with dining and a view of the track, simulcast gambling of racing everywhere and a poker room. His other brother, Tim Rooney, runs Yonkers Race Track & Casino in New York. When gambling rules were relaxed in 2004, it opened up a whole new source of revenue to the Rooneys. The race tracks transitioned into casinos and, then in 2018, sports betting could be done on every level at such venues. Once again, more money.

John Rooney is married to Sandy Sully, whose sister Suzanne Sully, was a classmate of mine for eight years at St. Stephen's Grade School in Hazelwood in the inner-city of Pittsburgh. Their father, a sturdily-built man with a Roman Centurion's profile, was a security guard at Western Penitentiary in Woods Run on the city's North Side. He looked the part.

Pat Rooney, the widow of Dan Rooney, and her sister-in-law Kathleen, are always dressed for a ball, but their husbands always dressed in the manner of retired priests, baggy ill-fitting slacks and casual shirts, seldom coordinated. They weren't dressed for job interviews.

Art Rooney Jr. is just as relaxed and casual in conversation. Some times he says the same things he told you the last time, but I am doing that more often myself. He uses a cane to get around these days, but he does get around.

* * *

"Every day, I think about my dad," he said from Florida. "Even now, talking to you, I wonder what The Chief would say, how he'd handle that last question. Every decision I make, I think about my dad."

I was already aware of this. As a young man, he majored in theatrical arts at St. Vincent College in Latrobe. He took a brief attempt at acting in New York, but he didn't get many stage calls. He was a 90-day wonder in the U. S. Marines and was later in the Marine Reserves, like the Pirates' Roberto Clemente.

He still thinks of himself as an actor, a Marine, a tough guy. That's the North Side in him even though he lives in a grand Tudor home near Mt. Lebanon High School in the South Hills of Pittsburgh.

He remembers his dad scolding him for getting into a fight, more of a wrestling match, with field manager Jackie Hart. He tried to drown Hart in a large vat filled with water, ice cubes and soft drinks in the Steelers' clubhouse at Three Rivers Stadium. It was one of those red Coca-Cola coolers; get the picture?

Hart had insulted Rooney in front of his good friend, Mort Schattiner of *Sports Illustrated*, whom he had brought with him to the Steelers' clubhouse. "Hart told me Noll didn't want anyone in the locker room," related Rooney. "I'm one of the owners! I was embarrassed the way Hart had talked to me in front of a writer."

His Dad had been a boxer of some notoriety and skill, and had been known to slug it out on a train (in 1934) with Head Coach Luby DeMeleo, but he thought it wasn't a good idea for his son to be feuding with the help.

"My dad told us to be nice to people, but never to allow anyone to mistake kindness for a weakness."

Art Rooney has found his acting role. He plays the part of his dad every day. He goes to Mass almost as much as his dad. He doesn't attend as many funerals —no one ever did—but he does his best, even when he doesn't move as well as he once did. He is well into what Chuck Noll would call "his life's work."

He went to see *The Chief*—the one-man show starring Pittsburgh actor Tom Atkins as his dad—and he saw it several times at the O'Reilly Theatre. "It was like going to town to have dinner with my Dad," he told me.

* * *

We talked about Roy McHugh, who had helped him write and edit a book about the Rooney Clan called *Ruanaidh,* which is Gaelic for Rooney. McHugh had died at age 103 on February 25 of 2019 at Marion Manor in Green Tree.

"You captured him well," said Rooney in reference to an article I had written about McHugh, someone who

Roy McHugh

had helped me with my own writing. "He loved my Kathleen. He was great to work with, though he was often critical of my writing ability."

In truth, they were a great team. Art Jr. remembered the stories well and McHugh had the talent and patience to put the words in their proper order. It's worth reading. So is Dan Rooney's book, *My 75 Years in the NFL*. So is Rocky Bleier's book, *Fighting Back*.

McHugh told Art Jr. it was not necessary to have swear words sprinkled throughout their book. "You have good stories and you don't need to have bad language in there spoiling it," said McHugh.

"I told him," added Art Jr. that my favorite Irish writer was James Joyce, and that I liked his style. To which, Roy said, "There's a big difference in that regard. He was a genius and you're not."

"We were an odd couple, for sure," said Art Jr.

*   *   *

He sends postcards to all his friends, and they are many, sometimes as often as once a week to his favorites. His secretary, Dee Harrod, told me that Mr. Rooney handwrites and mails out about 60 postcards a week.

She has been his secretary for 22½ years, as of April, 2019 and she lives in a home with her husband Wayne, a real sports enthusiast as a writer and photographer, a tenth of a mile from the office. She drives to work, but because she is surrounded by steep streets, "I'm in trouble when it snows."

Maureen Maier, the office bookkeeper, occupies a neighboring office on the third floor of a building on the border shared by Upper St. Clair and Mt. Lebanon. She is a daughter of Football Hall of Famer Jack Butler, who played end and defensive back for the Steelers in the '50s, and was a frequent companion of Art Jr. on the scouting trails.

"My parents had a gift that everyone they knew thought they were their favorite," said Art Jr. "I had four brothers and they all thought they were the favorite of our parents. I didn't worry about that. I knew I was my mother's favorite."

That brought to mind one of his favorite stories about his mother, Kathleen McNulty Rooney. "She was special," recalled Rooney. "She was a saint in so many ways, though I'm not sure that saints swear like an old sailor. I never heard her use the f-word, but she used a few that began with the letter b.

"One time I picked her up at the airport in Pittsburgh when she was returning from a trip to Ireland. She was complaining about my brother Tim, even though he had paid for her trip."

His mother said to Art Jr.: "Your brother and his wife fly first class all over the world. But me, he sends by steerage, the same way my parents got from Ireland to America in the first place."

That's vintage Kathleen Rooney and vintage Art Jr.

"My one regret," continued Art Jr., "is that I didn't go up to the house more often and have lunch with my mother. I had a standing invitation. But I didn't want to be looked upon as someone who was a momma's boy, or leaned on their mother too much as an adult. I didn't want to be seen that way. I very seldom did it.

"My wife Kathleen is like my mom. Not a hair out of place. Always dressed just right.

"Franco Harris and Rocky Bleier are both like my parents," he said, focusing on the story theme I wanted to talk about in the first place. "Rocky embraces people.

"They genuinely like people. They care about people. They talk to everybody, from A to Z. They want to know how you're doing. It's a gift. It's not easy to do. Franco has that type of thing. He likes you without being a phony about it. Rocky was always like that."

Art Rooney Jr. at book signing at Heinz History Center.

Art Rooney Jr. pictured with dad in Art's office in Upper St. Clair.

Art Rooney Jr. with Bill Nunn Jr.

Art Jr. does his best to emulate his old man, but he's not in the spotlight. He does not attract the kind of local and national attention his dad did during the glory days of the Steelers in the '70s. In that sense, Art Jr. is like an underground railroad. Under the radar, he has been nominated for the Pro Football Hall of Fame, and he and Bill Nunn Jr. might come up again for consideration now that Gil Brandt, the super scout of the Dallas Cowboys, has been so honored.

When I told Art Jr. that Andy Russell, Randy Grossman, Mike Wagner, Franco Harris and Rocky Bleier all thought he and Nunn should be in the Hall of Fame, he said, "That's really nice of them to say so."

Then a thought entered his mind. "You know Rocky worked for me one year in our scouting department," said Art Jr. "He had just come back from getting wounded in Vietnam, and needed crutches and then a cane to get around.

"My dad wanted to keep him around. He wanted to give him time to recover so he could play for us again. He wasn't in Chuck Noll's plans, but he went along with what my dad wanted to do. Rocky was good at scouting. He wrote thorough well-written reports. I told him he could be a general manager someday. I wanted him to stay with me. 'Stick with me and you'll be a general manager,' I told him more than once. When he was taken off the physically-unable-to-perform list, I told him not to do it. I didn't think he could ever play again.

"Rocky was upset and he said, 'I don't want to be a scout! I don't want to be a general manager! I want to play in the NFL!' And he ran down the hall, hollering at me like that. I guess I was wrong."

He was as wrong as the doctors who told Rocky he'd be lucky enough to walk again let alone play football. Rocky didn't do much running with the football in his first five years. He was a demon, a leader, a captain on special teams. He liked to take out blocking wedges on kick returns.

"Franco is like that. He is a team player all the way. I wanted him in the 1972 draft. Noll favored Robert Newhouse, who had a solid career with the Cowboys. But he was no Franco. I didn't want to get on the wrong side of Noll, but this was a pick I was confident about. When Franco got off to a slow start with us, I kept a safe distance from Noll until Franco finally came around and showed his true self.

"Franco is a first-class act. He was great with his teammates and he's been great with the fans. He has time for everybody. He and Rocky were two of my dad's favorites, but my dad favored everyone."

When the Steelers selected Franco on the first round of the 1972 draft, the 13th pick overall, Noll spoke briefly to Franco on the phone. When Noll got off the phone, he said to no one in particular, "He sounds like a dud to me."

Art Jr. related a story that Rocky Bleier had told him when they were having breakfast at Sea Island, Georgia. Bleier said he was trying to get some extra money from his first Steelers' contract with our business manager Fran Fogarty.

"Fogarty was a great guy who pretty much ran all of dad's day-to-day business," said Art Jr. "He knew the value of a buck and, in particular, where every dollar and cent in the organization was going. We didn't have the kind of dollars in those days like we do now.

"To an outsider, Fran could seem outspoken and cynical, and rough around the edges. In fact, he was, indeed, a tough ex-hockey player and a combat veteran of World War II. Fogarty was captured by the Germans, escaped from a moving railroad train and spent time with the French underground before making his way back to the American lines.

"This was before Rocky became a war hero in his own right. He was just a kid from Wisconsin and Notre Dame trying out for the Steelers. In those days, the Steelers' offices were in the Roosevelt Hotel. I saw you there from time to time, so I know you know the layout."

I do, indeed, they had two huge desks up against each other that filled the room. The ticket office was next door. The lobby of the hotel could be entered by a door in their office. I was there one day, when an old guy came through the door, pulling his zipper down, and Art Rooney, without missing a beat, said, "Next door!"

Art Rooney Jr. is relating his story: "Rocky Bleier said dad had been out of the office while he was talking to Mr. Fogarty. Rocky was trying to get a $1500 bonus he hadn't technically earned his rookie year. He

Art Rooney Jr. at St. Clair Country Club and, below, with Tom Atkins who was "the Chief" in one-man play, when they appeared at book-signing at Atria's Restaurant in Mt. Lebanon.

wanted Fogarty to take some other things into consideration. ("Hey, I needed the money," said Rocky.) The meeting was going nowhere. Neither Rocky nor Fran would budge an inch. Rocky had been a late draft pick so Fran was not going to be too excited about re-signing the kid even if he had been the captain of the Notre Dame team. Rocky said that all of a sudden, he heard a low, but forceful voice from another office call out, 'Who is that?'

"Bleier cringed because he recognized the voice belonging to The Chief.

"It's Rocky," replied Fogarty. "Give him what he wants," Rooney hollered. "OK," said Fogarty.

Rocky was drafted into the U.S. Army in December of 1968 during the Vietnam War. The rest is history.

Jim O'Brien

Art Rooney Jr. on the sidewalk outside his office on Highland Road in Upper St. Clair.

Rogel, Motley & John Henry

The Steelers had some great fullbacks before Franco

Before there was Franco Harris, the Steelers had some hard-running, hard blocking fullbacks by the names Fran Rogel, John Henry Johnson and Marion Motley.

Two of them, Johnson and Motley, are enshrined in the Pro Football Hall of Fame in Canton, Ohio. Motley is one of three men in the Hall who grew up in Canton. Alan Page and Dan Dierdorf are the others who call Canton their hometown.

I met Rogel and Johnson and I know as a kid I had Motley's bubble gum card, but in a Browns' uniform.

I found a newspaper clipping from the early '80s in which Pat Livingston, the sports editor of *The Pittsburgh Press* and a long-time observer of the National Football League, introduced me to Paul Brown, who founded and coached the Browns, but was now the owner and president of the Cincinnati Bengals.

Livingston was talking to Brown about one of his original stars with the Browns, Marion Motley, and Jimmy Brown. I was sitting next to them, eavesdropping on their conversation. Livingston is in the writers' wing of the Pro Football Hall of Fame.

Just then Franco Harris took a handoff from Terry Bradshaw "as he had done so many times in the last nine years," Livingston later wrote in his column about the game.

Harris "swung acutely to his left, cut back to daylight, and rambled awesomely downfield 34 yards to the Cincinnati Bengals' five-yard line," continued Livingston in his column.

That run prompted Livingston to ask Paul Brown how Franco compared to Jim Brown and Marion Motley, two of his greatest running backs from his days with the Cleveland Browns, who were named for him.

"There's a jiggle in him," Brown said of Harris. "He's not like Jimmy Brown at all. He doesn't have Brown's power or straight-ahead speed. Brown would take the ball and go. Franco's different. He gets to the same place, but he does it a different way.

"They're hard to compare," concluded Brown. "Franco's a great back, though, and he's been one for a long time. He's one of those unusual runners who doesn't come along every day."

Then Livingston asked about Marion Motley. "They're different ball players," said Brown. "Motley could do it all—run the ball, block—Marion was as good a blocker as ever played the game—and he played linebacker. He was a great defensive player, as well as a great offensive player."

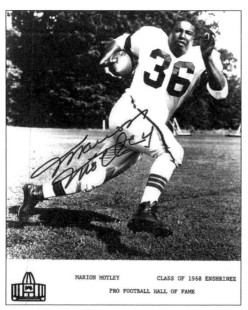

MARION MOTLEY   CLASS OF 1968 ENSHRINEE
PRO FOOTBALL HALL OF FAME

I recall that Brown had a defensive end named Horace Gillom who was a great punter and a two-way reserve end, and a Pro Bowl tackle named Lou Groza who was also a great place-kicker. That's why Noll hated specialists such as long-snappers. Noll hated to have to give up a roster spot for a specialist.

Jim O'Brien

John Henry and Tony D at Pro Football Hall of Fame.

*   *   *

Fran Rogel, in fact, who came out of North Braddock to star at California University of Pennsylvania and then Penn State, was the first Steelers' player I ever met. This happened at Frankie Gustine's bar and restaurant in Oakland, not far from Forbes Field. My father, Dan O'Brien, had to hoist me to stand on a burgundy-colored bar stool seat so I could look Rogel in the eyes.

He was listed at 5-11, 210 in the Steelers' press guide, but I doubt he was ever more than 5-9, maybe 5-9½. He was short and compact, heavily-muscled. Bobby Layne, the Hall of Fame quarterback for the Detroit Lions and Steelers, said Rogel was the toughest football player he ever saw.

John Henry Johnson played with Layne in Detroit and in Pittsburgh, and, I think, was even tougher than Rogel because he was bigger, at 6-2, 210. John Henry used to block oncoming rushers by lifting his locked fists up hard under their chins. There was another occasion when a raging-mad opponent chased John Henry to the sidelines and the Steelers' fullback grabbed the ten-yard marker and pointed the spear-end at his pursuer.

Layne called John Henry "my body-guard."

Before he played for the Lions, Johnson was a member of the San Francisco 49ers' so-called "Million Dollar Backfield" with Y.A. Tittle, Joe Perry and Hugh McElhenny, who didn't make a million dollars as a group for their careers. They are all in the Pro Football Hall of Fame.

Johnson had two 1,000-yard rushing seasons for the Steelers, the oldest ever to do that and to have a 200-yard rushing game at the age of 34.

* * *

Marion Motley was 6-1, 240 pounds and played fullback and linebacker for the Cleveland Browns when it was not uncommon for a player to go both ways. He was a teammate of Chuck Noll, who played guard and linebacker and was a "messenger guard," bringing in plays from Coach Paul Brown on the sideline.

Motley made a comeback after a year in retirement to play for the Steelers in 1955. He averaged 5.7 yards a carry in his career, still the best mark for a fullback.

From all I have known, I think it's fair to say that Rogel, Johnson and Motley were all better blockers than Franco Harris. Franco avoided

Browns Archives

Coach Paul Brown and Marion Motley.

286

contact which explains why he was such a great and smart runner. Rocky Bleier was a better blocker, but he had to be to keep his job.

Franco recalls that Preston Pearson, who preceded Bleier as the running back for the Steelers, made a half-hearted effort to block for Terry Bradshaw and allowed a pass-rusher to hit and hurt Bradshaw. Pearson was dispatched soon after to the Dallas Cowboys, and that created an opening for Bleier in the starting backfield. That's what Harris heard, anyhow. He didn't know if it was true.

Merril Hoge was once called out by Coach Chuck Noll at the Steelers' training camp for not looking to block somebody. Hoge was lined up at the left side of the backfield, and he was to block a linebacker expected to rush from that side but the linebacker never came. Hoge just stood there.

"What were you doing on that play?" asked Noll.

"I just stood my ground," answered Hoge. "I had nothing to do."

"Next time," Noll said, "find something to do."

It was finding something to do, of course, that led Franco to finding a football floating his way and turned it into what became famously known as "The Immaculate Reception."

"Joe Paterno told us to follow the ball," offers Franco, when explaining the busted play these days.

*　*　*

I was just 21 and finally of legal age to go into a bar for a drink when I accompanied John Henry Johnson to a black after-hours club in the Hill District. John Henry had taken teammates such as Layne and Tom "The Bomb" Tracy with him to the Aurora Club, but I was the only white man in the room this particular night. I am there again as I write this sentence. And definitely the youngest. Years later, I joined John Henry at the bar one night at Froggy's near Market Square, and we reminisced about that night at the Aurora Club.

We sat at a table together and had a few drinks. I wish I could remember John Henry's drink choice, but I can't. After a while, a brash waitress approached our table and shouted in John Henry's face.

"John Henry, when the hell are you going to pay your bill? You're always running out of here without paying, and you never leave a tip."

John Henry and I backed out of the room like Butch Cassidy and the Sundance Kid.

And you thought that was something that started with Ben Roethlisberger. Layne, by the way, went to his wallet a lot and was known as a big tipper. Bob Drum, a sportswriter for *The Pittsburgh Press*, observed once that if Bobby Layne and Arnold Palmer both broke their shoelaces that Palmer would tie them back together and Layne would buy a new pair of shoes.

Most players didn't wear face masks in those days and if a pass-rusher hit Layne or was coming close to hitting him, Layne would fire the football directly into his face. That had to sting.

When Layne went out drinking, he was usually accompanied by Ernie Stautner, a hard-hitting Bavarian linebacker and several other Steelers such as Lou Cordileone, Tom Tracy, Gary Ballman and Myron Pottios.

Myron Cope once asked Layne how he could stay out late on a Saturday night and still play so well on Sunday. "I sleep fast," allowed Layne.

Layne once drove his car into a trolley and told the police the trolley had swerved into his path, not an easy feat for a trolley on tracks.

Another time four Steelers were squeezed into the backseat of a driverless car when the cops came calling at the window. Then there was the night Myron Cope was called before a district magistrate after he had driven his car into a telephone pole on the way home from Dante's. Cope could be feisty and he reportedly spit in the magistrate's face and still escaped cell time. There was another night when Cope was upset with Layne and challenged him to a fight. Myron Pottios picked up Cope and carried him out to the sidewalk on Brownsville Road and deposited him at the curb.

When I was 18 and 19 and 20, I used to go to Dante's, a popular bar on the Brentwood-Whitehall border, that was frequented on a nightly basis by those Steelers, as well as sportswriters and sports broadcasters, such as Pat Livingston, Tom Bender, Ed Conway, Bob Drum, Doc Giffin and Myron Cope.

I went there because I wanted to keep company with the sports media, not because the Steelers were there. But I did sit in on a few sessions of a game called "buzz," in which drinking shots was involved. It was more fun than Monopoly, but you were in danger if you took too long to say the right number because Layne had little patience. You weren't allowed to say seven or multiples of seven. You sat in a circle. So, someone started with one, the person next to him said two, and when it came time for seven you would say buzz. Then it reversed until it was time to say 14. Get it? And Stautner was sitting next to him for body-guard purposes. If you screwed up, you had to drink a glass of whiskey. The more you drank the more you screwed up.

I always thought Rogel was a big beer drinker—he had a beer belly—but I later learned he did not drink alcoholic beverages. I also thought he was a life-long bachelor but I learned from one of his edgy brothers that he was married for two weeks, and then decided he didn't want to be married and just walked away and abandoned his bride.

I learned about that at the viewing for Fran Rogel at a funeral home in North Braddock. My pal Bill Priatko was present at the viewing. He idolized Fran Rogel.

He remembered Rogel in his heyday and when he coached high school football teams in the area while living on a farm near Bakerstown.

Rogel's body was dark and shrunken and laying deep in the casket when I saw him. I made up my mind that day that I did not want to be viewed. A display of my grade school and high school photos would have to suffice to satisfy anyone's curiosity.

Art Rooney Sr. liked to say "no one looks good in the box." Rooney loved Fran Rogel. He even named one of his race horses "Our Man Rogel," and said, "I hope he has as big a heart as our man Rogel."

When Rogel died, Priatko was called upon by Ed Bouchette of the *Pittsburgh Post-Gazette* to eulogize Rogel, a task Priatko performed at the church service.

"The saying at Penn State was that he never heard the whistle," said Priatko, "that he never believed he was down. He was one of the toughest guys, mentally, I've ever known in my life. He didn't know how to quit. He had so much heart and desire."

* * *

Jerry Nuzum was another tough halfback and fullback for the Steelers from 1948 to 1951. Nuzum rented a room in an apartment in my hometown of Hazelwood during his stay. Year later, when he owned a Chevrolet dealership in Wilkinsburg and was a frequent visitor to Art Rooney's office, he took a liking to me.

On one occasion, Nuzum invited my wife Kathie and I to join him and some of his former Steelers teammates at the Pittsburgh Athletic Association (PAA) in Oakland. We sat at a table with Rogel, Lynn Chandnois and his wife, "Bullet Bill" Dudley and his wife Libba, and Joe Gasparella. I recall that Vee Toner, a vocal Pitt booster and AAU official was there that night, wearing a bright red Chinese gown with gold threading. It went well with her shoe-polish black hair. I think she dyed it.

Nuzum and Chandnois would later trade the wives who were with them that night. Nuzum later gave me a provocative photo of his wife for my amusement, I suppose. She had on a low-cut top that revealed an ample bosom. It's nowhere to be found in my current photo files. One of my proofreaders has urged me to find it.

When he was playing for the Steelers, Nuzum was a "person of interest" in the murder of an 18-year-old waitress and notorious barfly known as "Cricket" back home in Las Cruces, New Mexico where Nuzum had played his college ball and where he resided in the off-season. Nuzum was the first NFL player ever to go on trial for murder—and he went on trial twice for the charge. It's a case that was never solved seventy years later. The Rooneys got him out of that mess, but his wife often wondered about that story. The second wife, that is.

"Well you know," she once told me, "everyone thought he killed that girl back home. I didn't know what to expect."

When I was covering the New York Yankees back in the early '80s, two of their pitchers, Mike Kekich and Fritz Peterson, swapped wives. When I brought that up one night after a game in Milwaukee, Yankees' manager Ralph Houk hollered at me in front of the entire team, and then apologized to me the next day one-on-one in his office.

I asked him to apologize to me in front of the team, but the tough soldier didn't oblige me.

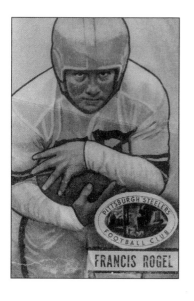

"Fran Rogel—or Rogie Bear as I called him—was my boyhood hero and remained my friend for life."
—Former Steeler Bill Priatko

Jim O'Brien

Tony Ferraro and Don DeBlasio talk to Merril Hoge at Atria's Restaurant & Tavern in Wexford, now known as Ditka's.

292

Antonio Brown

AB won't be happy in Oakland; wait till Raiders move to Las Vegas

G ertrude Stein once said of Oakland, California, "There is no there *there*." I doubt that Antonio Brown is familiar with Gertrude Stein, but surely he has heard of John Banaszak, who played on three Super Bowl title teams with the Steelers and is proud to be a Marine forever, and has an American flag flying high over his new home in Peters Township, about 20 miles south of Pittsburgh.

"Antonio Brown is a spoiled brat!" observed Banaszak at a luncheon I hosted in February, 2019 at Atria's Restaurant & Tavern, on Washington Road, just two miles from Banaszak's home.

Banaszak is one of several Steelers' alumni I have interviewed for this book. To a man, they were critical of Brown's behavior, and that of Le'Veon Bell as well.

"We're trying to get more African-American coaches and administrators in the NFL ranks," said J.T. Thomas, "and they've put Mike Tomlin in a bad spot, and may have jeopardized his job as coach of the Steelers. People are saying he can't control his own people, whatever that means."

* * *

Even a former Pirates' star chimed in on this issue when I spoke to Al Oliver, whom I met at a baseball clinic in Greentree a few months earllier.

"When I played for the Pirates," said Oliver, who lives in his hometown of Portsmouth, Ohio, also the hometown of Chuck Noll's wife, Marianne, "Mr. Rooney —The Chief—used to come out on the field at Three Rivers Stadium when we held practice and talk to me and Willie Stargell. And other guys.

"He was a grand old man, and he knew his baseball. You had to like him. I heard he was one of the best owners in sports. I hate to see the Rooneys and Pittsburgh get pulled through the mud and look bad on a national scope. These guys aren't respecting the Rooneys or the Steelers. It's a shame."

Al Oliver

Brown and Bell had both worn out their welcome in the Steelers' locker room.

I would place a bet in Las Vegas that Antonio Brown won't be happy in Oakland, or a year later—2020—when the Raiders relocate to Las Vegas. Brown will be a danger to himself in Las Vegas.

It'll be a great place for him to blow the big money he's getting from the Raiders on a three-year deal worth between $50 million and $54 million, with incentives, in exchange for three draft picks. Some local writers are calling the deal a "disaster for the Steelers," but I think they ought to be able to draft some useful players with those picks.

* * *

There's also the thought that there is addition by subtraction. Brown had become a bad seed in the Steelers' clubhouse. He abandoned them before the final game of the 2018 season.

Ben Roethlisberger has to be relieved. He must feel like he's had a painful, throbbing toothache removed from his mouth. He did everything he could to calm Brown down, and deliver passes his way, but Brown had an insatiable appetite to be the star of stars with the Steelers.

Antonio Brown will miss Big Ben and he will miss Mike Tomlin, too. I don't care for Jon Gruden's in-your-face with his reddened, heated mask abrasive style. Gruden thinks he invented football, the way the worst coaches do. Anyone who ever watched his TV series where he rated quarterbacks in one-on-one sessions should know what I am talking about.

Trust me on this, Brown won't like Gruden. They will be in each other's face before too long.

Gruden will want Brown to get his act together before the Raiders leave Oakland and a great fan base much like the Steelers' to start all over in Sin City. If you want to get a preview of what's going to happen to Brown in the self-destruction game go see the movie "Bohemian Rhapsody" before it's gone. Brown is Freddy Mercury of the music group "Queen."

The Raiders are set to move to Las Vegas and play in a palatial $1.9 billion 65,000-seat domed stadium with natural grass and a see-through roof with a view of The Strip for the 2020 season. The Raiders don't have a lease at this moment to play anywhere in 2019.

I believe Brown would have been better off in Buffalo, where he might have stayed home more and stayed out of trouble. But he wanted no part of Buffalo, which is more like Pittsburgh than Oakland or Las Vegas.

It's a shame. I met Brown soon after he reported to Pittsburgh and he was a bright-eyed, ever-smiling, charming and handsome young man. He lit up every room he walked into and, of course, that changed him.

Someone asked me whether AB had suffered a concussion and that this might have contributed to the change in his personality. I don't know.

I have attended seminars that shed some serious light on the subject. David Eagleman, the presenter of "The Brain," an Emmy-nominated TV series, was the final speaker in the Town Hall South series at Upper St. Clair High School. At Pitt a few days later, I heard author Jean Marie Laskas talk about her book "Concussion," which is the story of the Steelers' Mike Webster and Dr. Bennet Omalu, who examined his brain during an autopsy.

The brain is a busy place with trillions of connections and wires and such, and Brown's brain has to be more complex than most.

My wife Kathie and I were shopping one day and we were walking through the aisles at a Target store in Washington County. I came upon a display of Steelers' jerseys for children.

Le'Veon Bell

296

There were three different jerseys: those of BROWN 84, BELL 26 and CONNER 30. Most of the jerseys belonged to Brown. What's going to happen to those jerseys?

You can still find the jerseys of Lamar Woodley and Santonio Holmes at sporting goods stores and department stores around here. They are on sale at a deep discount.

I think Brown's jersey had become the most popular jersey in Pittsburgh, right up there with ROETHLISBERGER 7 jerseys. Now JU SMITH-SCHUSTER 19 will be one of the hottest sellers.

Brown will never be as big anywhere as he had been in Pittsburgh. The Steelers should still have a contending team this coming season, and Mike Tomlin must gain control of his team, or like Antonio Brown, he will be gone.

It's a shame the way this story of Antonio Brown and Le'Veon Bell has ended in Pittsburgh. They will both discover that the grass is not always greener on the other side, and that money won't buy them happiness or contentment.

Rocky returns to Vietnam

Through the years, I have often come across my friend Anthony Accamando in the company of former Steelers Rocky Bleier and Andy Russell. They shared a bond; they all served in the U.S. Army during the Vietnam Era.

Russell is reluctant to call himself a veteran because he served in Germany, far from the danger of battlefields, while Accamando and Bleier both saw combat in Vietnam, and Bleier was wounded in action.

Accamando lives on the same street as I do these days, on Hunt Club Drive in Waterdam Farms, Washington County, 20 miles south of Pittsburgh. When we were both living in Upper St. Clair, Accamando asked me on several occasions if I would like to accompany him on a trip to Vietnam to help build schools there. I had no interest whatsoever in going to Vietnam. He asked Rocky if he wanted to return to Vietnam with him, and he declined the offer as well.

Anthony Accamando

"The last place I want to go to is Vietnam," Bleier told me at the time. "The last time I was there I got my legs and ass shot up. Why would I want to go back?"

I told Accamando I felt fortunate that I didn't get assigned to military action in Vietnam in the mid-60s, after I had graduated from the University of Pittsburgh and was drafted into the U.S. Army. I spent ten weeks at Fort Knox, Kentucky for basic training, ten months as an editor at the U.S. Army Home Town News Center in Kansas City, Missouri and ten months at Fort Greely, Alaska, site of the U.S. Army's Arctic Weather Testing Center.

I was lucky and I knew it. A soldier shot and killed himself in the barracks on the eve of my arrival at Fort Greely. The Army could be a dangerous place, no matter where you served. You could easily get frostbite if you were out in the Artic weather too long. You could get court martialed if you were caught running on the post because that increased the wind chill factor.

In any case, I was willing to support Tony Accamando's efforts to assist veterans on a financial level. I have attended his annual Veterans Day Breakfast at his alma mater, Duquesne University, thought to be the biggest event of its kind in the state of Pennsylvania.

At his breakfast, now coordinated by his younger brother, Don Accamando, they ask people who served in different eras to stand and be recognized. I asked him to create a new category "Vietnam Era" because I didn't feel right when called to stand as "Vietnam." I have too much respect for people who actually served in Vietnam to have anyone think that I did.

Russell feels the same way. Russell and Bleier both show up for the Veterans Day Breakfast at Duquesne University and are big hits with the crowd. Some of the veterans share their stories, some are harrowing, and it makes you realize again how lucky you were.

I donated to Friends of DaNang, which he and another Vietnam veteran, George D'Angelo, helped found, which helped kids in Vietnam. D'Angelo was a fighter pilot in Vietnam. Tony is tall and George is a little guy, but both have the hearts of lions.

Both do whatever they can to support veterans. Accamando, who is retired after spending most of his adult life as an executive of Adelphia Cable Services, co-founded Veterans Cable Services over 30 year ago, and more recently he co-founded a Western Pennsylvania Support Group for Guardian Angel Medical Service Dogs that are given to veterans who suffer from post-traumatic stress syndrome and other disabling causes. The dogs have a calming effect on these veterans and help them in other ways, life-saving ways.

I founded a Good Guys Luncheon Group in 2015, at the urging of Accamando and Pat Santelli, and we send a monthly check for $125 to $175 to Williston, Florida in support of the program. This has convinced the folks in Florida who train these dogs—at a whopping cost of $22,000 per dog—to establish another training center in Washington County.

This will mean more service dogs for veterans in Western Pennsylvania. Rocky Bleier appeared at one of our luncheons, as did Franco Harris and many of their teammates, and they like a program that helps veterans.

Bleier updated his book *Fighting Back*, co-authored with another Notre Dame grad, Terry O'Neill, and the proceeds are going to support veterans' assistance programs. Bleier has become one of the National Football League's poster boys for military-related programs.

In September of 2018, Bleier went back to Vietnam for a different reason. He was invited by ESPN to go there and do a documentary about what happened to him there, and Bleier felt he could be more effective in his support of veterans' issues if such a story was aired on network television.

At a press conference on September 4, 2018 at the Heinz History Center, Bleier spoke about his second go-round of the southeast Asia area.

"We were able to go where we got hit and where we had met the enemy and where I got wounded," Bleier told KDKA-TV reporter Jon Delano.

"It was helpful in realizing the post-traumatic stress disorder that affects so many veterans of war.

"For the first time, probably, I understood what post-traumatic stress is all about, and how it can come back later on and grab you," said Bleier.

There are a quarter-million veterans in Western Pennsylvania, and one of the most standout figures of that group is Alejandro Villanueva, a 6-8 offensive tackle for the Steelers.

Villanueva was a tight end for the U.S. Military Academy football team, and a veteran of three military tours of Afghanistan. He was the one who proudly stood outside the hallway when the National Anthem was being played prior to Steelers' football game. "I had to be there," he said.

Villanueva said that when he first reported to the Steelers, Rocky Bleier stopped by to see him and introduce himself to the latest veteran on the Steelers' roster. "Sometimes I have to go back and look at a photo of Rocky in uniform and find a picture of myself in uniform to see that I am very fortunate and lucky to be an American, to live in this country, and have all the freedoms that I have," said Villanueva.

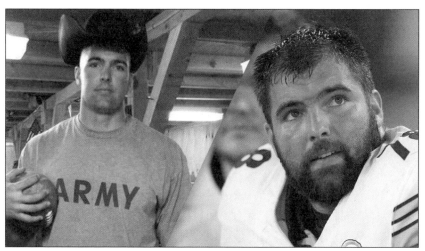

Alejandro Villanueva

Babe Parilli

Babe Parilli sent in play that became "The Immaculate Reception"

Vito "Babe" Parilli, the pride of Rochester, Pennsylvania, was one of the most prolific passers in college and pro football history, along with Johnny Lujack of Connellsville, Arnold Galiffa of Donora and George Blanda of Youngwood, one of the first quarterbacks from Western Pennsylvania to distinguish himself on a national level.

He died in Parker, Colorado, a suburb of Denver at age 87 on July 15, 2017, and it got me thinking about the personal history I had with this man who was inducted into the College Football Hall of Fame in 1982 and might merit inclusion in the Pro Football Hall of Fame as well. He was a great story-teller.

- I saw him play in 1965 for the Boston Patriots against the Kansas City Chiefs at Municipal Stadium when I was serving as an editor at the U. S. Army Hometown News Center, 601 Hardesty Avenue, Kansas City, Missouri.
- I was at the press conference in New York in August of 1970 when he announced his retirement at age 40 after 18 years in professional football. He had been the backup to Joe Namath of Beaver Falls in the stunning upset of the Baltimore Colts in Super Bowl III in his last season.
- I covered the New York Stars in 1974 for *The New York Post* when Parilli was the head coach of the World Football League team. The Stars wore black and gold uniforms. Tom Moore, later a backfield coach with the Steelers, was on the staff.

- In 2014, when he was nearing his 85th birthday, he revealed to me in a telephone interview how he called the play as the quarterback coach of the Steelers that turned into "The Immaculate Reception," voted the No. 1 play in pro football history, and how the play went awry even before anyone else saw it go awry.

I was working on a book called "Golden Arms —Six Hall of Fame Quarterbacks from Western Pennsylvania," and Parilli might have provided the best chapter in the book. He was so honest, so revealing, good humored, good hearted, humble.

* * *

He would turn 85 on May 7, 2015, was still playing a pretty good game of golf, and his voice was strong and cheerful as he spoke over the telephone from his home in suburban Denver on February 16, 2015.

Jim O'Brien

He was generous with his time and his tales; he's a Hall of Famer as a story-teller. Parilli proved a great source in reflecting on the quarterbacks he has known well, from Blanda to Joe Namath, to Terry Bradshaw, Joe Gilliam and Terry Hanratty,

Vito "Babe" Parilli

with rave reviews on the passing abilities of Johnny Unitas, Danny Marino, Joe Montana and Jim Kelly. He's known most of them up close and personal.

I got more than I bargained for when I spoke with Babe Parilli.

Parilli followed Blanda as the quarterback for legendary coach Paul "Bear" Bryant at the University of Kentucky, and was inducted into the Kentucky Sports Hall of Fame along with Unitas, who played his college ball at the University of Louisville. Parilli has been inducted into the University of Kentucky Hall of Fame, the College Football Hall of Fame, the Italian-American Sports Hall of Fame, and the Western Chapter of the Pennsylvania Sports Hall of Fame.

He is not, however, in the Pro Football Hall of Fame but he has the numbers and achievements that might merit such an honor. Yes, he was that good. But every NFL town can claim a player or two whom the local fans feel has been overlooked by the Hall of Fame.

Parilli was a consensus All-America at Kentucky in 1950 and 1951 when Vic Janowicz of Ohio State and Dick Kazmaier of Princeton were the Heisman Trophy winners in those respective years. Parilli finished in the top four in the balloting both years. At Kentucky, Parilli led the Wildcats to a victory over No. 1 ranked Oklahoma in the Sugar Bowl. He was one of those quarterbacks pictured throwing a jump pass in publicity photos that were popular in that era.

In talking to Parilli, I learned several things I did not previously know, and that's exactly what I aim to offer in my books.

For instance, Parilli, as the quarterback coach on Chuck Noll's staff in 1972, called the play that resulted in "The Immaculate Reception." It didn't work the way Parilli wanted it to work, but it has been called the greatest play in NFL history.

Parilli told me how he was a party to having Bradshaw hypnotized on the eve of three games to settle his pre-game jitters. I was aware that some of the Steelers' insiders used to stay up late, and literally hold Bradshaw's hand to calm him on the eve of some

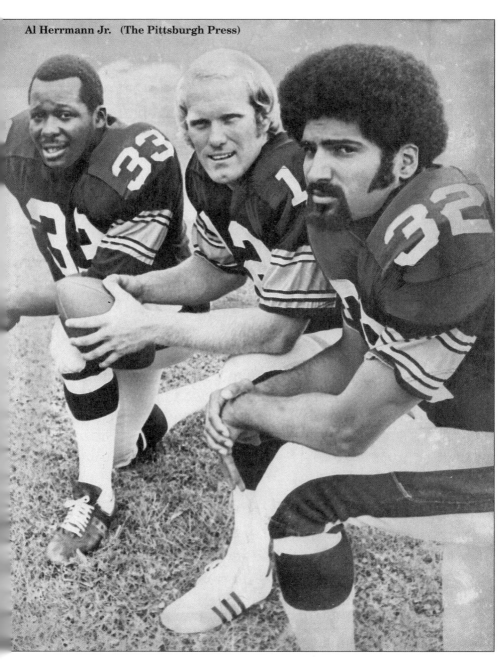

HOLY TRINITY—The threesome that figured in "The Immaculate Reception" in 1972 reunites at St. Vincent training camp in 1973, left to right, John "Frenchy" Fuqua, Terry Bradshaw and Franco Harris.

big games, including his fourth Super Bowl triumph in 1980 against the LA Rams at the Rose Bowl in Pasadena, California when I was covering the Steelers for *The Pittsburgh Press*.

Here's how Parilli remembers "The Immaculate Reception":

"I called the play from up in the press box. I noticed Willie Brown of the Raiders was playing off Frank Lewis, who was our fastest receiver. I wanted us to throw to Frank Lewis and have him step out of bounds to save some time. I didn't communicate that to Chuck Noll, though. I just called the play. I didn't mention Lewis. It was a fourth-and-ten situation with enough time for about two more plays.

"Noll sent in Barry Pearson, who had not caught a single pass that season, in place of Lewis. When I saw that, I took my headset off and slammed it down on the table in front of me. Pearson wasn't open so Bradshaw found Frenchy Fuqua downfield and threw the ball to him. Jack Tatum was closing on him, and Franco had the great instincts to run downfield to see if he could do something. He didn't quit on the play. The rest is history. Maybe that's why Noll is in the Hall of Fame and I'm not."

The play Parilli called – mind you – was half right, split opposite, 66 out end in, or 66 option circle. It was designed to be a 12-yard pass to get a first down and keep the last-minute drive alive. Fuqua was running a curl, Al Young 18 yards and out, and John McMakin was running a short route, and Franco was flaring off in the backfield. "They were blitzing Bradshaw like all hell," recalled Parilli, "and he got flushed out of the pocket. I don't know how he spotted Fuqua."

If Barry Pearson had caught a pass in that situation maybe he would be among the better known players in Steelers' history instead of a mere footnote. I wish I could ask Chuck Noll why he put Pearson in the game for Lewis at that critical point.

Parilli did not have an answer for that question.

He died after a long bout with multiple myeloma.

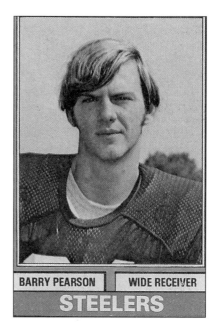

Franco and the unknown soldier's story

The late Frank Haller, a friend of mine, used to forward stories, jokes and you name it to his pals on his e-mail hit list. Here's a keeper that he sent me regarding Franco Harris and a soldier. I made efforts to find out who wrote the following message—the soldier's aunt—and the name of the soldier, but was unable to get that. So this is a story about Franco and an unknown soldier. There was a photo attached, but without identification.

It's a feel-good story about someone in sports who has never thumped his chest, but went about his work with a quiet dignity. "It ain't charity if you talk about it," Art Rooney Sr. used to say.

This is the text of the woman's letter:
Let me tell you about one soldier's return flight to Iraq. He saw a man who went into the bathroom at the Pittsburgh Airport and thought he recognized him. When the man came out he went over to him and said, "Excuse me, sir, but are you Franco Harris?"

The man replied, "Yes, I am," and then, being such a big Steelers' fan, the soldier asked him if he could have a pic of him. Franco was agreeable to this. After taking the pic, they talked for a few minutes and (the soldier) told him he was on his way back to Iraq. Franco acknowledged his sadness and gave him encouragement and wishes for a safe return.

Then they shook hands and parted on their ways. The end of the story you would think, but not so...

You see, after a while the soldier's name was announced over the loud speaker to come to the desk...which he did...Once there the lady behind the counter informed him that there was an empty seat in first class and she was going to bump him up to that seat if it was OK with him. He said he didn't care where he sat in the plane, as long as he made it to Atlanta to catch the Army plane. So she informed him that he was now going first-class to Atlanta.

He thanked her and went back to tell everyone (in his family) as he waited to board the plane. Once he was seated on the plane, he was waving out the window to his Dad and Pap. He felt a hand on his left leg. He turned to his side and there was Franco sitting in the seat next to him!!!

Needless to say, they talked all the way to Atlanta about the Steelers and then parted with Franco taking his address and giving his signed ticket stub to the soldier as validation of their trip together. This was a trip not of sadness and loneliness, but one this soldier will never forget and will talk about forever thanks to Franco Harris.

This act of kindness and generosity from this man is one that words cannot express. In my opinion, Franco Harris is 'the man of all men.' I wish I could thank him for making a soldier's lonely flight back to war one of his ultimate lifetime experiences that he will talk about forever.

Thank you, Mr. Franco Harris.

I'm happy to have real pen pals on the opposite side of the wall

Rocky Bleier has never been behind bars, but he did turn up in conversations at a prison where a friend of mine was doing time. This requires an explanation.

I have had six "pen pals" over a period of 16 years. These are friends or acquaintances, even a relative, who have done time in prisons and I have written them monthly letters. Writing is easy for me, so it's my way of helping some people through difficult times.

These are not real bad guys, just misguided guys, at least in my mind. People you knew when you were young are never as bad as some others see them.

When I was in eighth grade at St. Stephen's Grade School in the Hazelwood section of Pittsburgh, my teacher, Sister Mary Leo, told my mother "Someday your son is going to end up in Sing Sing."

My mother, Mary O'Brien, sent a formal invitation to my graduation ceremony at the University of Pittsburgh and wrote this note: "See, Sister, he didn't end up in Sing Sing after all."

My friend Myron Cope cautioned my mother's enthusiasm, saying I still had a shot at it. So I guess I am grateful to still be on the outside and not behind bars. Sing Sing, by the way is the name for a prison in upstate New York, Ossining, New York that is.

When I was working on a recent book, and going through files for newspaper and magazine clippings and photographs, I stumbled across a letter that was hand-written on yellow legal paper from a friend named Joe, who was doing six months in Moundsville, West Virginia Penitentiary for income tax evasion.

This letter was dated July 7, 2005.

Dear Jim, I'm very sorry I haven't written to you in a while. I think about you often. Thanks again for your help and support and concern. I really appreciate it.

I can't believe I have less than one month to go. Time has gone fast. I have adjusted well and met some really good guys. July 29th is now my release date. My weight is down to 215 lbs. now from 255 lbs. when I came in on March 2nd. I feel good.

My good Irish buddy, Jim Connor, 60 years old, from Uniontown let me look through a book called *Pittsburgh Sports—Stories from the Steel City,* edited by Randy Roberts (University of Pittsburgh Press). Your name and quotes are in the book. I also read a book called *1960—The Last Pure Season (Baseball).*

In prison language, when you get close to leaving, everyone asks you, "How long?" In prison jargon, one always says, for example, "24 and a wake-up." My buddy Jim asked me the other day (July 4th), and I told him, "24 and a wake-up." He then said, "Willie Mays and a wake- up." Everyone thought that was unique. So we did our own prison jargon to count down the days till I leave. The players' jersey numbers are the key to it:

24 Willie Mays and a wake-up......................July 4
23 Michael Jordan and a wake-up................July 5
22 Doug Flutie and a wake-up..................... July 6
21 Roberto Clemente and a wake-up ....July 7
20 Rocky Bleier and a wake-up ....July 8
19 Johnny Unitas and a wake-up................ July 9
18 Roman Gabriel ánd a wake-up .... July 10
17 John Havlicek and a wake-up................ July 11
16 Joe Montana and a wake-up .... July 12
15 Bart Starr and a wake-up .... July 13
14 Pete Rose and a wake-up .... July 14
13 Dan Marino and a wake-up .... July 15

And on July 29th when I wake up, it's Roberto Duran—"No mas! No mas!"

See you soon, Joe

Jim O'Brien

Myron Cope

Cope claims Immaculate Reception was a legal sequence

Maybe government officials should have had Myron Cope check out the Zapruder film to determine exactly what happened in Dallas the day President Kennedy was assassinated.

Cope and Cyril Wecht, the once-and-forever coroner of Pittsburgh and a respected forensic scientist, could have teamed up to find out if there was just one shooter in a book warehouse above that grassy knoll in downtown Dallas on November 22, 1963. If you are old enough, what were you doing that day when you heard the shocking news?

Cope claimed he had positive proof that "The Immaculate Reception" of Franco Harris was within the then-rules of the National Football League. Back then, during the playoffs of the 1972 season, the rules said that a football could not touch two players on the same team. In short, in this case, the ball could not have bounced off Frenchy Fuqua into the hands of Franco Harris. It had to touch Tatum to be legal. That rule has since been changed. It would not be a controversial call today.

Cope got hold of game film taken by one of the WTAE cinematographers and went over it slowly, one frame at a time. Cope said with conviction that the ball struck the shoulder pad of Jack "The Assassin" Tatum, a defensive safety for the Raiders, and bounced back in the direction of Franco Harris, who was following the play, thinking he might be able to throw a block for Frenchy Fuqua.

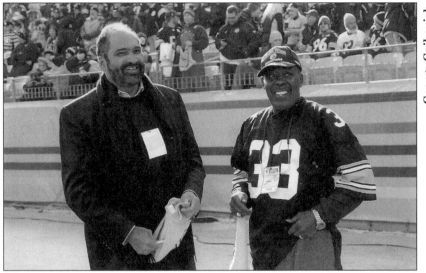

Franco Harris catches up with Frenchy Fuqua at 2012 reunion at Heinz Field.

I've seen the film sequence many times and I have never been able to determine with conviction what actually occurred. Frenchy Fuqua has said many times he is going to carry the secret with him to his grave. Then Frenchy gets a few drinks and he gives his version of the sequence of events.

I don't think Frenchy knew what happened that play that is now regarded as "the greatest play in NFL history," though I maintain it wasn't a play. It wasn't the play that was called in the huddle. It was a broken play.

In fact, Babe Parilli, a great quarterback from Rochester, Pennsylvania, told me something I had not previously heard when I was working on the book *Golden Arms*, about the six Hall of Fame quarterbacks from Western Pennsylvania.

Parilli called the play from the press box and he had Terry Bradshaw throwing a down-and-out pass to Frank Lewis, the team's top receiver. He thought there'd be time to call another play after that one, to get closer for a field goal.

Then, to his disbelief, Parilli sees Lewis running off the field in favor of Barry Pearson, who had been on the reserve squad most of the season and had no receptions to his credit for the season, come on the field. Parilli said he threw his headset onto the shelf in front of him in anger.

What was Noll doing? Now Noll is gone, so I can't ask him. Parilli, who might have been the best interview in my book, has died as well.

*   *   *

Myron Cope didn't come up with the name "Immaculate Reception" but he was the first to say it on the air and he definitely was most responsible for popularizing the name. The Terrible Towel wasn't completely his idea either—station management at WTAE pressed Cope to come up with a gimmick to link the station with the Steelers—but he made it stick with his relentless promotion of the towel.

Being a Jew, Cope was nervous about possibly offending Christians by calling it "The Immaculate Reception," a play on the Immaculate Conception, the virgin birth of Jesus by Mary.

He checked with a few Catholic friends and they gave him the green light. Cope did not check with the bishop.

Cope and Franco became forever linked, the way Howard Cosell and Muhammad Ali were allied in the public consciousness.

Cope created lifetime logos with his "Immaculate Reception" and "Terrible Towel" proclamations. He gave legs to the logos.

Jim O'Brien and Myron Cope at Pitt's pre-season training camp at Allegheny College in Meadville, Pa. in summer of 1962.

Today, I think of Cope every time I see fans waving towels or flags or pom poms in ballparks across America. Even though that practice goes back to Shakespeare's stage productions. It was thought to be "a sacred cloth," and Cope came to regard his Terrible Towel in much the same manner or spiritual light.

Bill Hillgrove gives Cope credit for "inventing" the Terrible Towel. "The difference between our towel and

Bill Hillgrove and Dick Groat at Champion Lakes Golf Club in Bolivar, Pa.

those at other venues," says Hillgrove, "is that Steelers' fans pay $10 or $12 for those towels, whereas they are given to fans in other cities as part of promotions."

Cope was in the WTAE studio after the playoff win over the Oakland Raiders. A fan named Sharon Levosky called the newsroom and asked for Cope. She told him her friend Michael Ord, a young man in his late 20s, had made a proclamation at a Downtown bar, "This day," announced Ord, climbing upon a bar stool and tapping a glass to get attention, "will forever be known as the Feast of the Immaculate Reception!"

Cope loved it, as only Cope could do.

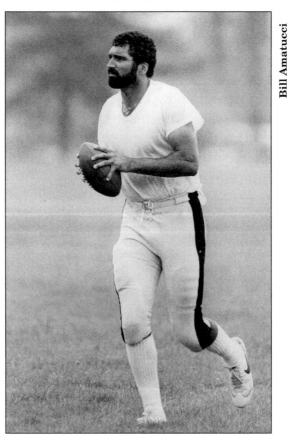

Bill Amatucci

Franco on St. Vincent field.

Cleveland Browns

Browns always brought out
Franco's finest performances

D ick Hoak was telling the other Steelers' assistant coaches about a National Football League film he had seen the night before on cable TV about great running backs.

This was during a lunch break at Three Rivers Stadium as the Steelers prepared for a game in Cleveland with the arch-rival Browns of the Art Modell era. The game would be played on Sunday, December 19, 1982, the week before Christmas.

Hoak talked about Jim Brown, who used to work for the Browns. Some folks thought the team was named after Jim Brown and not the team's owner, Paul Brown.

"He was the best I ever saw," said Hoak, the Steelers' offensive backfield coach. "What I didn't realize until I watched the film, though, was that he never missed a game in nine seasons.

"He never even laid on the field once with an injury. He always got up slowly, but he always got up."

Hoak mentioned the highlights he saw of Gale Sayers, O.J. Simpson and Earl Campbell.

Asked if Franco Harris had been in the film, Hoak flinched. He cocked his head the way a jeweler does when he's about to inspect a diamond. Or maybe when a jeweler finds a flaw in a diamond.

"Doing what? Catching a pass?" asked Hoak, showing a side of himself even darker than the ever-present stubble on his chin. "Throwing a block?"

It's important to know that Hoak was not being critical of Franco, his favorite running back, along with Rocky Bleier. This was not a "Franco who?" flippant remark by head coach Chuck Noll, not recognizing that he was not a comedian.

This was a rare outburst by Hoak, who was not happy with the way Franco Harris was being utilized or not being utilized during the first half of the 1982 season. No one knew at the time that this would be Franco's final season with the Steelers.

Hoak came out of Jeannette to play at Penn State and was the Steelers' seventh round draft pick in 1961. He played for the Steelers from 1961 to 1970. He was more like Rocky Bleier than Franco Harris, but he was one of the most respected players on the team. Bobby Layne was the quarterback of the Steelers when Hoak joined the team and there was a strong mutual respect. Hoak wore the same stoic face to work when he was a player—I go back to the days when they played at Pitt Stadium and Forbes Field—and often appeared zombie-like in his coaching days. But he was a man's man and the players had great respect for him.

Hoak stuck with the Steelers for ten seasons as a player, and 35 years as a coach. He managed to make the Steelers his *life's work* because he did his job to the best of his ability and he kept most of his opinions to himself. Hoak was as wary of the writers as Harris, running to daylight when he saw members of the media approaching him for a comment. Franco picked up on that and could be just as shy or reserved about speaking to the media.

That's why this show of emotion and unhappiness with the way things were going was so unusual, and stays with me.

Chuck Noll would often warn his coaches and players to watch what they said to the sportswriters. Noll

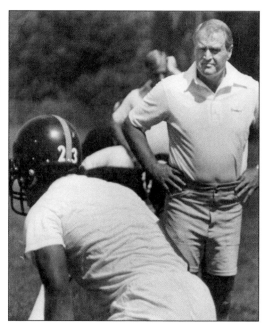

Chuck Noll at St. Vincent's training camp in Latrobe, Pa.

was not a fan of the media, but he was always available, sometimes at the urging of publicist Joe Gordon, and was cooperative.

If you wanted someone who actually enjoyed talking to the media you could visit with Art Rooney, the owner, who enjoyed talking to anybody. The Chief had often said that if he wasn't a team owner, he would have liked to have been a sportswriter.

"And I'd go to the losing locker room first after a game, added Rooney, showing just how sharp he was, "because that's where the action is."

Hoak had been critical, in his own non-confrontational and non-controversial way, about Harris not getting to carry the ball more in the Steelers' new-fangled offense, and this was merely Hoak's way of blowing off some steam. No one, not even our President, was tweeting their thoughts in those days.

* * *

A 57-day strike in the NFL reduced the 1982 season from 16 games to nine games. In six games, Harris had carried the ball 80 times for 318 yards, a 4-yard a carry average. That was just over 13 carries a game. He led the Steelers in receiving with 23 receptions for 168 yards.

Art Rooney with Franco

It was as a willing pass-catcher that Harris had an edge, say over Tony Dorsett of Pitt and the Dallas Cowboys, because Dorsett didn't want to catch passes over the middle where receivers were most vulnerable to smashing tackles in their back side.

Unlike Earl Campbell of the Houston Oilers, Franco felt there was no sense in taking on tacklers all the time, and would simply step out of bounds when he thought it prudent to do so.

That's why Franco can walk freely today, with some discomfort, while Campbell requires a walker to get around, with much discomfort.

*   *   *

Harris had always been Hoak's man. Hoak was hired by Chuck Noll to join his staff in 1972, the same season Harris came to Pittsburgh from Penn State, so there was strong mutual support.

"Harris has to carry the ball 20 times to be effective," said Hoak. "He has to get a feel for the game."

"Even when he was younger, he might not get more than three yards on 15 carries, then he'd break one for 10, 15 yards, and then maybe all the way. That's the way he's always been."

Hoak was now sitting in the dimly-lit screening room, moments before his charges were to come back from lunch and study film of the Browns' defense against the San Diego Chargers.

What offensive backs could learn from watching the pass-happy Chargers' offense was beyond my grasp.

Writing about Hoak having time to talk to me in a screening room reminds me of why the Steelers' beat was such a gift to sportswriters who truly worked at their job.

Thanks to Art Rooney and Joe Gordon, the Steelers had doors-always-open policy, and we enjoyed freedom to roam that was rare for our contemporaries in other NFL cities. One writer, John Clayton, who worked the Steelers beat with me at *The Pittsburgh Press*, ruined that situation by going where we weren't allowed to go.

Clayton reported on the Steelers wearing pads when they were not permitted to do so, and that cost the club a draft choice as a penalty from the league office. Clayton also got caught sneaking in to Bill Nunn's office to check the waiver wire on a cutdown date.

To his credit, Clayton was one of the hardest-working reporters, and was always on the telephone with someone seeking information. It led to a great career as an analyst and insider for ESPN, both the cable TV sports station and its national magazine. Like draft guru Mel Kiper, Clayton created a niche for himself. He left his mark with the Steelers, that's for sure.

Today, the media are housed in a different dorm than the players during training camp at St. Vincent, are restricted as to where they can stand to watch practice, aren't allowed to ask questions of coaches or scouts on the sideline, and do not travel with the team on airplanes or buses. They have to make requests to interview players at camp, and can't visit them in their dorm rooms as we often did.

They stand on the sidewalk outside the cafeteria and catch players as they pass by, getting little more than soundbites. I found a way to get around that, without breaking any rules, simply by appealing to the players that I needed more personal time to write the best possible story. So, we sat in grottos, behind high hedges, all by ourselves, and simply talked. On a Catholic college campus, those hideaways were like confession boxes. You can't write books with soundbites.

In short, sportswriters don't have the access they enjoyed when I was covering the club from 1979 to 1984. Then again, I used to hear stories from older writers about how we missed out on traveling on a train with the players back in the early years. "It was better in the old days;" that's a quote that will be heard in decades to come.

Then again, those old-time writers were seldom critical of the club and its players when the Steelers were one of the worst teams in the NFL. They went over 40 years without winning any kind of championship before Noll and Joe Greene and Franco Harris came along.

"They didn't win shit until Franco came along," said Joe Greene, one fine day at St. Vincent College. Harris was hopping around in the hallway at the Steelers' training complex at Three Rivers Stadium during the holiday season in 1982, like a boxer jumping imaginary rope, when he stuck his handsome face into the screening room, and sensing the subject of the conversation, shouted, "Be careful, Hoakie!"

He need not have cautioned his coach. Hoak has always been cautious about what he says.

He's honest, brutally honest, but he is not a troublemaker. He said his strongest stuff off the record, or "just between you and me."

Hoak told Noll and the other coaches how he felt about the proper use of Harris during staff meetings, but he didn't make waves about the issue. That was not his style. Hoak has always been a team man.

I will have to ask him how he felt about the Le'Veon Bell and Antonio Brown issues. Neither Noll nor Hoak could have handled today's players and their approach to work and play.

The Steelers could not move the ball by passing in the previous Sunday's 13-0 setback by the Buffalo Bills, and they had been shut out twice in the three weeks leading up to the Browns' game in Cleveland. Hoak was hoping the team would run the ball more. Terry Bradshaw and Cliff Stoudt were both shaky, and Harris was rarin' to go.

The Browns always brought out the best in Harris. Maybe it's because he was inspired running against Jimmy Brown's old ballclub, or on the same field as the great runner he's been chasing for years.

Going into this game in Cleveland, Brown was the all-time rushing leader with 12,312 yards. Simpson was second with 11,236 yards and Harris was third with 10,657. The seven games that were erased by a player strike during the 1982 season would haunt Harris forever, but he still had a chance to finish at the top.

Against Cleveland, Harris had more rushing attempts (305), gained more yards rushing (1,649), scored more touchdowns (15) and had more 100-yard games (seven) than against any other team in the NFL. In nine games in Cleveland, Franco had rushed for 777 yards on 163 carries for a 4.8 average, with six TDs and three 100-yard games.

Harris had been critical of the club's offense, and the outcome of recent contests, more than he ever was in the first ten seasons with the Steelers. Like Hoak, however, he didn't want to stir up any controversies. The frown on his forehead said more than his words.

Cleveland figured to be a lot like Buffalo on this Sunday afternoon, with 20 degrees and snow flurries flying in off Lake Erie, but that was of no concern to Harris.

He said in the past that he enjoyed playing in Cleveland Stadium. "It feels good to get some dirt in your ears once in a while," he said.

"I don't care about the weather," he said. "What I care about is how we execute. What kind of enthusiasm do we have? What kind of will to win?"

Following yet another loss in the early days of the Tampa Bay Buccaneers, Coach John McKay was asked about the team's execution. "I'm in favor of it," answered the quick-witted McKay.

That's Harris' careful way—the same way he hunted for openings and danced through them—of saying some of the things that had been missing. Harris preferred to look ahead, and was a positive thinker.

"I dream of long runs—the extinct species. No negative stuff. Most of the time I think about them, anyway."

Three years earlier, on a wet and windy day in Cleveland, Harris carried the ball 19 times for 153 yards. He scored touchdowns from 71 yards and 25 yards out – and helped the Steelers beat the Browns 51-35 en route to their fourth Super Bowl championship season.

I was in the Cleveland Stadium press box on November 25, 1979 when Franco did that. Rocky Bleier rushed for 61 yards on ten carries that same day.

Before he broke off the 71-yarder that day, Harris had gained five yards, then three yards three straight carries. "You never know when he'll get that opening," said Hoak.

Noll did not comment much on Franco's falloff in earlier games. "Franco is still capable of doing what he's done."

Franco played another season with the Steelers then forced a trade to the Seattle Seahawks, who put him on waivers at mid-season. The Steelers never would have done that.

> *"I don't care about the weather. What I care about is how we execute. What kind of enthusiasm do we have? What kind of will to win?"*
> **—Franco Harris, 1982**

Franco disturbed and upset and lost many fans over that contract dispute that sent him to Seattle, but he has gotten back in good graces with the way he has conducted himself since he retired as a player.

As it turned out, Franco was 15th among the all-time greatest running backs. Jim Brown was eventually surpassed in total rushing yards by Emmitt Smith, Walter Payton, Barry Sanders, Frank Gore, Curtis Martin, LaDainian Tomlinson, Jerome Bettis, Adrian Peterson, Eric Dickerson and Tony Dorsett.

MARCH MADNESS—George H. W. Bush, the 41st President of the U.S., and popular singer Dinah Shore stopped in Pittsburgh on March 18, 1982 to promote her TV show and were joined by, left to right, Pitt football coach Foge Fazio, Franco Harris of Steelers, Heisman Trophy winner Marcus Allen of USC, Dan Marino of Pitt, and Lynn Swann of Steelers.

Les Banos

'Immaculate Reception' was a real lifesaver

The Immaculate Reception was a lifesaver for the Steelers in the 1972 AFC playoffs, but it was really a lifesaver for video photographer Les Banos.

The 2019 season marked the 47th anniversary of the amazing catch and run by Franco Harris of a pass from Terry Bradshaw that caromed off the colliding bodies of both Steelers' running back Frenchy Fuqua and Oakland Raiders' defensive back Jack Tatum.

You are going to see that historic sequence – voted the No. 1 play in NFL history even though it was a broken play and then some—from time to time on sports cable outlets. Its anniversary coincides with another iconic incident Pittsburghers of a certain advanced age will long remember. That's the anniversary of the death of Roberto Clemente. He was killed in an air crash on New Year's Eve, 1972, as he was accompanying a cargo of relief goods from his native Puerto Rico to earthquake-ravaged Nicaragua.

Les Banos was supposed to be on that airplane. He had promised his good friend Roberto Clemente that he would accompany him on the flight to photograph the event.

Banos was a video photographer for both WQED and WTAE in his long professional career, and he did stints as a photographer for the Pirates, Steelers, Penguins and the University of Pittsburgh department of athletics. Banos, by the way, means "bathroom" or "toilet" in Spanish, according to my friend Jack Sega, and the locals might have had some fun with Les about that.

He also filmed games of the Pittsburgh Valley Ironmen of the Atlantic Coast Pro Football League, a minor league team that played its home games in Duquesne, Pennsylvania. They were preceded by another semi-pro team known as the Duquesne Ironmen.

I know the latter first-hand because I was the publicity director of the Ironmen during my senior year at the University of Pittsburgh, in 1963, and again the following season before I was drafted into the U.S. Army.

Banos and I used to get together on Sunday afternoons, the day after the Ironmen games, to edit some highlights that would be used on Pittsburgh TV on Sunday evenings. We both liked to talk, so it took us longer than it should have to do that task.

Later, in the mid-80s, I worked again with Banos at Pitt. Les and I and Pat Hanlon, my assistant, joined with Banos and others at WTAE to put together a highlight film on Pitt football. Banos went to pre-season camp with the Panthers at Edinboro University. Hanlon, by the way, is now the vice-president for communications for the New York Giants Football Team, and a real success story.

Hanlon worked with Joe Gordon and Dan Edwards with the Steelers' publicity office. Hanlon had a great time exchanging barbs with Les Banos.

Banos loved to tell stories, and he had some good ones. He told us, of course, how the Immaculate Reception saved his life. He told us about his days in his native Hungary when he was a spy who infiltrated the Nazi regime, and managed to save many Jews from the death camps in Poland.

Pat Hanlon and I used to tell people in jest that Banos had been Adolph Eichmann's chauffeur. Eichmann, of course, was the Nazi general who oversaw the concentration camps and was brought to justice as one of the central figures and criminals by the Nuremberg Trials. It wasn't politically-correct humor, no doubt.

Banos was born in Hungary, but he had some Jewish bloodlines, and he was always an enterprising fellow. He was short in stature, about the same size as Myron Cope, maybe 5-5 or 5-6 at best. Like Cope, he puffed up his chest and came at you like a bantam rooster. He talked with a heavy accent.

Les liked it when I told him I had played for a team called the Hungarians in the Hazelwood Little League, and that there was a Hungarian social club in my hometown. It closed in 2012 and was the only ethnic or service club remaining in the community.

I also told him I remembered that in the mid-50s there were a lot of Hungarians who left their home country, then under siege by the Russians, and relocated in our community. There was a sandlot soccer team in Hazelwood that had all Hungarian players.

A national weekly newspaper called *Magyarsag* was printed a block from my home by a Hungarian ex-patriot named Eugene Zebedinsky. His son was a classmate of mine in high school.

Cope, by the way, was the one who popularized the phrase "The Immaculate Reception." One of the callers on his popular sports talk show suggested the name. Cope checked with his Catholic friends to make sure no one would be offended by the phrase, and went with it.

Cope's other creation, of course, was "The Terrible Towel."

Myron Cope enjoys a "toddy" at Atria's Restaurant & Tavern in Mt. Lebanon.

Like Cope, Banos was fun to be around. I recall being in Montreal with him at a sidewalk café, enjoying some wine and food when we were there in 1967 to chronicle the entry of the Pittsburgh Penguins into the National Hockey League. Banos picked up a check, unusual for any member of the media, and did a double take when he saw the high tariff on the bill.

Banos was the only one in our party who could speak and understand some French, which is always good in the bilingual community of Montreal. It didn't help him to get out of paying the steep bill. His brown eyes bulged at the numbers on that bill. I think the waitress brought us a bottle of champagne by mistake...maybe by mistake.

Banos befriended many of the athletes he covered in his duties as a TV cameraman. Franco Harris was one of them. Roberto Clemente was another.

When Banos died at the age of 86 on April 22, 2012 it brought back memories of this little man with the big heart and such wonderful stories.

"It is significant that he passed our way," said Harris at the Heinz History Center, where Banos had appeared the previous holiday season with a collection of his photos of Clemente. There are 50 of these photos on display in the Roberto Clemente Museum in lower Lawrenceville.

"It is amazing what Les accomplished when you look at his history and have seen his photos," added Harris. "He was a great guy, always enjoyable, a kind and gentle man. You never would have expected what he went through by how kind and gentle he was."

Banos addressed everybody as "Mister," and he liked to get up under your chin like an undersized boxer, again like Myron Cope, and tell you his stories. Banos was a dapper dresser.

Banos was busy filming the Steelers' game against the Oakland Raiders at Three Rivers Stadium on December 23, 1972. When the Steelers won that game, 13-7, on Franco's frantic catch-and-run with a deflected ball he picked off his shoe-tops for the game-winning touchdown.

It meant the Steelers would be playing another game the following weekend, on December 31, 1972, a day that will live in infamy in Pittsburgh and Puerto Rico. The Steelers lost that one, by 21-17, to the Miami Dolphins, victimized by a fake punt by Larry Seiple of the Dolphins that was a game-changer.

So Banos had to stay back in Pittsburgh to work that game for WTAE-TV instead of accompanying Clemente on his mercy mission to Nicaragua. It ended the life of Clemente, all too early, and gave Banos a bonus 40 years.

Pittsburgh sports fans were disappointed, of course, by the defeat suffered at the hands of the Dolphins, but they were far more shocked by Clemente's death. Fans over 50, and some as young as 47 or 48, can tell you where they were that New Year's Day when they heard the news. What a way to start a year.

If you go to a Pirates' game at PNC Park these days you might be surprised to see how many fans still wear Clemente's name and number (21) on their backs to the ballgames. He remains a popular member of the Pirates, even more popular since his heroic death than when he played for the Pirates.

There's a statue and bridge outside PNC Park to memorialize the man from San Juan who came to our city and set new standards for a baseball player, on the field and off the field. Young fans are fascinated by his story and the way he died, trying to help his fellow Latin Americans when they were in trouble.

It's a shame more of them didn't hear those stories as told by Les Banos.

Jim O'Brien

Les Banos shows off some of the vintage work in his collection of Roberto Clemente photos during a show at the Heinz History Center in December of 2011.

ROCKY

Bleier remains a Top Ten performer back home in Wisconsin along with "The Horse" and "Crazy Legs"

I always say that things start falling out of trees or file drawers when I am near the finish line of writing a book. They are people or photos or stories I hadn't thought about when I conceived the idea of writing a book. People suddenly appear, I find something at the bottom of a file drawer, or I bump into them by accident at a service station. I find something while looking for something else.

When I was working on this book on January 27 of 2019, Rocky Bleier forwarded a story that had just appeared in his hometown newspaper *The Appleton Crescent* that a boyhood friend of his sent him that same day.

It was about a Top Ten listing of the greatest athletes to come out of Wisconsin. Rocky Bleier was third on the list, which was in alphabetical order.

I recognized a few of the other names. The list started with Alan "The Horse" Ameche, who came out of Kenosha to win the Heisman Trophy at the University of Wisconsin in 1954. He's best known for scoring the game-winning touchdown for the Johnny Unitas-led Baltimore Colts against the New York Giants in overtime in the 1958 NFL Championship that was hailed as "The Greatest Game Ever" in football lore.

Another running back was Elroy "Crazy Legs" Hirsch of Wausau who also starred at the University of Wisconsin and was an All-Pro end for the Los Angeles Rams who were quarterbacked by Bob Waterfield

Elroy "Crazy Legs"
Hirsh

Alan Ameche
All-America Boy

and Norm Van Brocklin. As an 11-year-old in 1953, I remember seeing the movie "Crazy Legs," with Hirsch playing himself, at the New Hazelwood Theater.

Bleier joined those two in the all-Century backfield for Wisconsin natives. He starred in three sports at Appleton Xavier. He was a two-time all-state back on a team that was undefeated for three straight seasons and all-state in basketball and a standout in track & field. He was an All-America boy, a real-life figure from one of Clair Bee's books for young boys. He was Chip Hilton in the flesh. One of my buddies, Alex Pociask of Wausakee, is of the same mold.

He would later be a member of four Super Bowl championship teams with the Steelers who were quarterbacked by Terry Bradshaw.

I had three files full of Rocky Bleier stuff and I found a full-page tear sheet from the *Appleton Post-Crescent* that had an orange Post-it on it that read: "Jim, It was good talking to you—here's the article you requested. R."

It was the size of a pack of playing cards, wrapped tightly by a rubber band, and was a reminder that Rocky Bleier has always been the most cooperative ballplayer I have come across in my career.

The newspaper was dated February 15. 1999. The tear sheet is in pristine condition. The headline reads: **Rocky's Road** and the story by Mike Woods hails Bleier as Appleton's "most proficient athlete of all time."

John Paustian, the former sports editor of *The Post-Crescent* who put in 35 years there, said of Bleier, "He's once in a blue moon."

Gene "Torchy" Clark, who was Bleier's high school coach and comes in for mention in "The Play" as well as Bleier's books, said, "The Good Lord, he just distributes people like that.

"You know," his coach continued, "I always thought Appleton should put up a sign 'Home of Rocky Bleier.'"

Rocky has told me there is a dead-end alley in Appleton named after him. "If I had played for the Packers, they'd have named the main street in my honor," he said with a bright smile.

And Woods wraps it up by writing: "No Appleton resident, before or since, has ever achieved athletic success like Rocky Bleier. It's not even close."

I recall talking to another Notre Dame back, 1947 Heisman Trophy winner Johnny Lujak of Connellsville when he came home from Davenport, Iowa to be honored with his 1941 Coker teammates.

Lujack said, "Nothing compares with being honored in your hometown."

Lujack led Notre Dame to three consecutive national championships. Bleier was a member of Notre Dame's 1966 national championship team as a junior under Coach Ara Parseghian, and a team captain as a senior.

He was taken on the 16th round of the NFL draft in 1968 by the Steelers, the 417th player chosen. Today there are seven rounds with 32 teams in the draft. Only 224 players are actually drafted.

"He was just a good bowl of chili."

Torchy Clark, his high school coach, said, "I just think Rocky had a little tad bit of insecurity. He always felt he had to prove himself all the time. A little insecurity can be a good thing."

One of Clark's favorite stories, according to sportswriter Mike Woods, was about what occurred after Rocky's final high school game.

"We won 39-13 up at Marinette, and Rocky did everything that night—running for touchdowns, returning punts, intercepting passes," Clark told Woods. "And we're in the locker room afterward and my assistant comes up to me and says, 'The Marinette players are here and they want to see Rocky.'

"So, I go over to the door and the whole team is standing there, like 35 of them. So I go, 'Say, Rock, come on over. They want you to say a few words.'

"So he goes over there, takes off his helmet, and goes, 'Boys, you guys are really a tough team.' He was just a complete bucket of humility. That guy was such a good example for other people. He was just a good bowl of chili."

Clark coached Bleier for exactly 100 games, in football and basketball. His record during that span was 96-4.

"A guy once said to me, 'Boy, you really made Rocky.'" said Clark. "I said if that was the case, I would have made another one."

Vietnam Veteran Rocky Bleier shares his message of strength, attitude and optimism with Doug Larsen during a North Dakota National Guard safety conference on Jan. 24, 2009. Larsen has Rocky's four Super Bowl rings on his fingers.

Rocky

Reliable Rocky, Franco reunited for Chiefs' contest in Kansas City
It would be like old times.

Rocky Bleier would be back in the starting lineup, paired with Franco Harris at the running back slots, when the Steelers were to play the Chiefs in Kansas City on Sunday, November 11, 1979.

Sidney Thornton, who started the first ten games in the offensive backfield, would sit this one out. He sprained an ankle in the 38-7 victory over the Washington Redskins the previous Sunday at Three Rivers Stadium. He had returned there the day before to see trainer Ralph Berlin and I saw him hobbling through a hallway with the aid of a single crutch. He had a date with a dentist later to have a tooth removed. Understandably, he wasn't in the best of moods.

It had to be comforting to Coach Chuck Noll, though, to know when a back who had been having as much success as Thornton gets hurt, he had a replacement like Rocky Bleier to call upon.

Behind Bleier, he had Antony Anderson, who was spectacular in the late going with the Redskins, as he was against the Denver Broncos two weeks earlier. Then there was Rick Moser, who ran well and scored his first NFL touchdown the previous Sunday. Top draft pick Greg Hawthorne was healthier, after being slowed by an ankle injury, and did see some playing time, though he didn't carry the ball. (J.T. Thomas thought Hawthorne had all the physical equipment to be a star.)

"It's just another example of the Steelers' depth," declared Mike Kruczek, who came off the bench when

338

Terry Bradshaw got his bell rung and did some impressive relief pitching.

Bleier had seen only spot duty to this date, but had been useful in many ways and contributed big plays on several occasions. Bleier came off the bench in St. Louis, for instance, when Harris hurt his ankle and the Steelers were struggling, and sparked a second-half comeback that resulted in a victory.

Against the Dallas Cowboys a week earlier, Bleier carried the ball only once, but it was an 8-yard off-tackle slant that put the ball on the Cowboys' one-yard line. Harris scored the first of his two touchdowns on the next play. Bleier carried the ball six times against the Redskins and gained 26 yards and threw a crunching block that enable Moser to score.

Noll expected Bleier to be excited about being back in the starting lineup and would look upon it as a new challenge.

"I think Rocky has always entered into everything eagerly," said Noll, while his assistants screened films in nearby rooms and began the weekly preparation for the next opponent. "That's one of the joys of having Rocky around."

This was Bleier's 11th season with the Steelers and everybody who hasn't been ship-wrecked on a South Seas island the last decade is familiar with his heroic tale. Of the Steelers, only Sam Davis was older than the 33-year-old Bleier. There had been talk that Bleier might retire at the end of the season to devote full time to his extensive business interests.

Being used on a part-time basis by the Steelers, as he had this 1979 season, might have enabled Bleier to continue his playing an extra year or two. The demands on his body had not been what he might have expected at the outset of training camp.

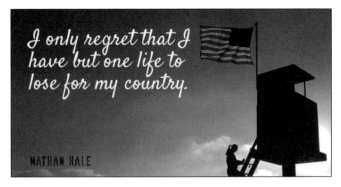

I only regret that I have but one life to lose for my country.

NATHAN HALE

Noll acknowledged this was a possibility. "Yes, it could extend his career," the coach said in reply to a question. "The thing Rocky has going for him is that he's helpful in a lot of areas. You know he'll do the right thing and use good judgment. He's still a demon on special teams, and he's like the quarterback of our punting team."

Bleier could have been the Steelers' designated hitter. "In a sense, yes," said Noll.

Owning a piece of the Rock provided the Steelers with a sense of security.

Kansas City stirs up all kinds of good memories

I'm going to Kansas City, Kansas City here I come.

I always enjoyed going to Kansas City. I had a history there and so much was familiar to me.

I spent 10 months there as an editor at the U.S. Army Hometown News Center from 1965 into 1966, before leaving for another 10-month stint at the Army's Cold Weather Test Center at Fort Greely, Alaska.

Both were a long way from Vietnam and the dangers that were encountered by Rocky Bleier and our good friends, Tony Accamando and George D'Angelo, who both do so much these days to help veterans.

Beano Cook had connections in Kansas City. He was a good friend of Roger Valdiserri, who came out of Belle Vernon, Pennsylvania and was the public relations director of the Chiefs. Valdiserri had a long stint as the sports information director at Notre Dame before that. Cook was the sports information director at Pitt back then.

Jim Schaff, the general manager of the Chiefs, was a lineman at Notre Dame and came from Erie, Pennsylvania.

When I was doing research for this book, and checking facts and dates, I realized how lucky I was to be in Kansas City in 1965. It was the only year that Valdiserri was with the Chiefs. He'd come there from his alma mater where he worked from 1959 to 1964. He returned to Notre Dame after his one year in K.C. and stayed from 1966 to 1988. He's a legend in the business.

It was Schaaf's first year as general manager. He had previously worked for the Kansas City Athletics in Major League Baseball.

The Hometown News was located in a former industrial building at 603 Hardesty Avenue and Municipal Stadium where the Chiefs and Athletics played was within walking distance.

Which was ideal because I didn't have a car with me in Kansas City until Beano Cook had a friend drive mine to me. I had my own room in a partitioned complex. I had a record player I bought on a payment plan with a Columbia Record-of-the-Month Club. My work was easy. I had it made.

In the evenings, on my free time, I helped out in the press box for both pro teams. I was a spotter for Charlie Jones and Paul Christman on Chiefs' telecasts. Best of all, I got to eat for free in both press boxes. I remember meeting Eddie Lopat, a former Yankees' pitcher, who was a coach for the A's, in the baseball press box. Eating for free was critical. I think the Army gave us something like $8 a day to get something to eat at a local restaurant. I remember Charles O. Finley owned the A's and the team mascot, a goat named Charlie O., used to roam a grassy knoll near the leftfield scoreboard, keeping the grass mowed. The A's had Jim Gentile and Dick Green and would soon sign Jim "Catfish" Hunter, a future Hall of Fame pitcher.

The Chiefs' had a great team, starting with quarterback Lenny Dawson, Buck Buchanan, Jim Tyrer, Bobby Bell, Fred Williamson, Johnny Robinson, Curtis McClinton, Mack Lee Hill, Fred Arbanas, Ed Budde and E.J. Holub.

I covered Monday Night Football from the outset in 1970, and I was there when the Steelers were the opposing team. That game is famous for a fumble by Steelers' rookie receiver Dave Smith, who had played his college ball at Indiana University of Pennsylvania.

Smith snared a pass from Terry Bradshaw and just before he entered the end zone for a touchdown he held the ball high in his right hand to signal his achievement and he lost his grip on the ball. A TD became a fumble. On Monday Night Football! That's why it's one of the most famous fumbles in NFL history.

There were a lot of sports media from Pittsburgh in the press box that night and I can still see the look on their faces when that fumble occurred.

There was a typewriter on display in the lobby of the *Kansas City Star* that had been used by Ernest Hemingway when he wrote for the paper. Beano Cook knew Bill Richardson, a sportswriter who covered the Chiefs, and Tom Farrell, a newscaster at KMOX-TV, a proud Duke grad from Mt. Lebanon in Pittsburgh. He also introduced me to Jay Randolph, who had come away from working for a 200-watt radio station in Clarksburg, West Virginia to be a nationally-known, especially in the golf world, broadcaster out of St. Louis.

I was able to do some free-lance pieces for *SPORT* magazine, and saw Jim Ryan run a sub-four-minute mile at Wichita East High School in Kansas, and interviewed Bill Koman, twice a Pro Bowl linebacker for the St. Louis Cardinals, for a story in *SPORT*. Koman came from Hopewell High School where the field house is named after him. He was named the NFL's Father of the Year in 1966. He was so badly injured in a bicycle accident when he was nine years old that doctors considered amputating his leg. He had a stiff leg when he played at the University of North Carolina and during a 12-year pro career. He was bright and had a beautiful wife who was a graduate of Duquesne University. I think her name was Ann. For me, she still looks like she did in 1965. He later owned casino boats (Queen Casino) along the Missouri River and became a rich man and was known for his philanthropic deeds.

I visited with another smart football player in St. Louis, Charley Johnson, the quarterback of the Cardinals, who had a degree in chemical engineering from New Mexico State. This was on assignment from John Lake, the sports editor of *Newsweek*, who also had me file a report on Jim Ryan for them while I was in Kansas City. Johnson later became a professor in the chemical engineering department at his alma mater.

I had a chance to talk to Johnson and Billy Kilmer, another outstanding quarterback, at Andy Russell's Celebrity Golf Outing in the summer of 2017.

I used to spend a lot of time at the Country Club Plaza that was located four miles from downtown Kansas City in one of the better neighborhoods. It was a series of stand-alone buildings and shops done in a Saville Spain architecture.

Jim O'Brien

Charley Johnson and Billy Kilmer appear at Andy Russell's celebrity golf outing at The Club at Nevillwood.

Charley Johnson
NFL QB 12

It was a great getaway, great for window shopping. You felt like you were in Spain. It was built in 1922 and was the first shopping center in the world designed to accommodate shoppers arriving by automobile. It's still there. Buck O'Neil, the late great ambassador for baseball, erected the Negro League Baseball Museum on 18th Street in Kansas City. I highly recommend a book called *The Soul of Baseball*, written by Joe Posnanski with O'Neil.

I met a "crazy little woman" in Kansas City that I used to take to The Plaza. She reminded me of a girl I dated in high school and college. I had her scheduled to come to Pittsburgh to meet my parents. I called it off and never saw or spoke to her again. I came to the conclusion that I was just lonely in Kansas City. The Army will do that to you. There's a country song in there somewhere, but we weren't allowed to play country music on the camp radio station in Alaska because it was so depressing.

I like to listen to oldies from the '50s and '60s on Sirius Radio when I am traveling in my car and I love it when they play Wilbert Harrison's hit song, "I'm Going to Kansas City." It stirs up some great memories.

"Some people see today;
I see history."
—Buck O'Neil
Negro League Star

Cadillac Harris

The father of Franco Harris was called Cad, short for Cadillac. No kidding. Franco resisted any temptation to buy a Cadillac, or some other expensive automobile, when he signed his first contract to play for the Steelers in 1972.

He had a humble apartment in East Liberty, and he took a bus, or walked, or hitch-hiked to work at Three Rivers Stadium.

"I still run into fans who tell me they picked up when I had my thumb out in those days," said Franco.

He got a nice car when he was named the NFL's Rookie of the Year. He was awarded another nice car when he was named the MVP of the Steelers' first Super Bowl victory.

Lou Malkin/Vinard Studios

FOR A GOOD CAUSE—Gracing the dias for American Diabetes Foundation fund-raiser were left right front row, Cliff Stoudt, Jim O'Brien, Randy Grossman, Bennie Cunningham and Theo Bell; second row, Lynn Swann, James Smith, Stan Savran, Calvin Sweeney and John Stallworth.

FRANCO

His family was frugal from necessity

"There were no extras"

From an interview with Franco:

I always thought I was an all-right guy. But there was talk when I was still at Penn State that I might be blackballed from the NFL. I wanted to find out where that was coming from. Joe Paterno was on vacation, out on a boat somewhere. I tracked him down and called him, and asked him if he was saying anything negative about me. He assured me he wasn't.

But it was going around that I might be a problem. I remember wanting to send the Steelers a telegram not to draft me, because I didn't want to go where the fans threw snowballs at the players. But the guy who was my agent told me not to send the telegram because I probably had a bad rap now, and it would just make it worse. I got a call that the Steelers had drafted me, and I was in shock.

I think the Steelers thought I might be lazy, and that image persisted after my first week in training camp. I'm still trying to figure that out. After the first exhibition game, the coaches came up to me saying, "Good game," like they didn't expect it from me. It was hard to believe that they were disappointed in the first week of practice. Maybe it was because I didn't allow people to beat on me.

I always feel that the easiest thing you can do is run into somebody. If it's a matter of winding up in the same place, I'd rather not get hit than get hit; chicken as that may sound.

I was always watching runners run. We'd be studying films, supposed to be watching defenses, and I'd find myself running along with the runner, putting myself in his shoes. Lots of running backs were faster than I was on a straight-ahead run, but not in the first 10 or 15 yards, dodging people and being quick about it. I'd be watching where other backs' feet were, how they moved their hips. I saw a certain move I liked, and I'd run it over and over again in my mind, and I'd try it.

I considered O.J. Simpson the best running back. I liked to look at myself in the same light. He, to me, had so much natural ability. I knew there was no way I could touch him in that respect.

In some ways, I was luckier than he was. Being on a team that wins the Super Bowl, not just once but four times. I had the good fortune to be with a winner, and not have anything bad—injury-wise—happen to me.

I was always interested in doing something that involved kids. I enjoyed going to Children's Hospital and things like that, in many cities.

I liked being able to do nice things for my parents. Football afforded me that opportunity. As a child, we never went to a restaurant. I mean never. We never went on a vacation. I was the third oldest of nine children. We always had what we needed, and we were never without essentials, but there were no extras. It felt good to give them something back.

Coming from a situation where my father didn't have much of a formal education—he really couldn't read or write—and my mother had only an eighth-grade education. Well, when it came to school, they were very strict about it. We had to show them our report card. If we got anything less than a "C" it was whipping time. I remember one time my sister had a bad report card, and my dad tore her up. Man, my dad didn't play.

He was always there, though. He worked two jobs to make ends meet. He worked hard. He had his certain ways. When you have nine kids, I guess you've got to have rules. It's funny, but with all those kids he still controlled the total situation in the home. He controlled everything. He only said something once and you better do it.

I'd have to say that it was because of him and the way he controlled the house that none of us ever went astray in any way. There could have been opportunities when I was young, on being on that thin line when I could have done something bad, and I thought of my dad and the consequences, and I didn't do it.

I really had a happy childhood, relating to other people, other kids. My father was great with people. He didn't care about color. He knew all kinds of people. When I was three or four, we moved into this project area of Mt. Holly. I guess we were like the second black family to move into that area. Soon the street was full of families with mixed marriages, blacks with European wives, Italian and German. There was quite a bit of that.

At the funeral for my dad, I saw a lot of them. I hadn't seen some of them between the time I was five and ten. A lot of the old Italian ladies who had come over with my mom were there. They were all shipped over together, and they had stayed together.

I think it helped, coming from a family like I did. I really do. My mom, she thought European. She was strict and conservative. The children always came first. They would do certain things for us.

One thing they had a dream of doing. They wanted to get out of that project area. When I was nine, my mother went out by herself, bought a piece of land. She had to go by herself. My dad couldn't go; they wouldn't have sold that land to him. It was seven years later before they had the money to build a home on that piece of land. They did it and we moved into the new house. They had accomplished that dream. Maybe that's where I got my patience.

Cadillac Harris, left, and two of his sons, Giuseppe and Franco.

John Banaszak

"I've been lucky."

John Banaszak credits Franco Harris and Czarzina duck blood soup for his success with the Steelers. That requires some explanation so stay with us.

Let's start with a cold night in Waterdam Farms, an attractive senior community along the border of McMurray and North Strabane in Washington County, Western Pennsylvania. After residing in Upper St. Clair for 37 years, we had moved to North Strabane in June of 2016.

The temperature outside around 8 o'clock on March 9, 2019 was 32 degrees, the high for the day. Our doorbell was ringing and my wife Kathie and I paused in our almost-daily Scrabble game on a granite island in our kitchen. She went to answer the door.

"Hi, Kathie," a voice said. "I'm John Banaszak."

Kathie recognized that name and invited him in. It was 66 degrees in our home—that's the standard thermometer setting—and John was happy to get a break from the brisk evening.

He was wearing a Steelers' black and gold stocking cap with STEELERS on the front of it, a Steelers' scarf and one of his Super Bowl rings, in case anyone didn't recognize him by his face. He removed the head covering and his gloves.

Who's going to turn John Banaszak away at the door? He was out soliciting signatures to endorse the political candidacy of his son Jay, who was running for a district judgeship in Washington County.

Before I knew it, Kathie was checking out John's ring. Banaszak was wearing his third Super Bowl ring, from Super Bowl XIV, when the Steelers won their fourth Super Bowl in six years. He is the only member of the Steelers' alumni who can sign his name followed by Super Bowl X, XIII and XIV.

Banaszak missed the first Super Bowl, but he was a rookie in 1975 when they won their second. "I recognize the placement of the four diamond stones," said Kathie. "I have a pendant with the same design that they gave to the wives."

Kathie was in the stands at the Rose Bowl in Pasadena, California where Super Bowl XIV was played and where the Steelers defeated the Los Angeles Rams, 31-19, before a Super Bowl record crowd of 103,985 on January 20, 1980.

Banaszak later told me a story about something a young man said to him at Starbucks in McMurray, one of John's regular morning haunts. "When he saw how big my ring was, he asked me, 'Mister, what high school did you graduate from?'"

* * *

The Banaszak Bunch were the featured guests at my Good Guys Lunch at Atria's Restaurant & Tavern on Thursday, February 21, 2019. They were all big hits. John spoke about his playing and coaching days, Mary about the opioid crisis in this country from her experience in dealing with drug addicts at Greenbriar Rehabilitation Center in Washington, Pennsylvania, and Jay about his judgeship candidacy. He has dealt with many court cases as a liaison for Greenbriar.

"I get recognized quite a bit out this way," said Banaszak when I met him for coffee and an interview on Tuesday, March 26, 2019 at Panera's in McMurray.

"And that's pretty cool. When I am in a community like Waterdam Farms where so many seniors live, I get, 'Yes, I remember you.' Now I'm 76 and I can fit into a neighborhood like that. Those are the people who turn out to vote on election days.

"They know our team. It's different today. There's a whole different locker room with the Steelers. It's not like it was in our day. They don't get together after a game and enjoy each other's company.

"I know for a fact that they rarely have a team party. Jack Ham and his wife Joanne used to hold a party for the team at the beginning of the season and at the end of the season. Franco and Dana held parties at their place, and Franco hosted card games with some of the guys.

"I remember one time after the Steelers had lost a playoff game that we came across Kordell Stewart sitting with his family in a room at Morton's Steak House downtown. We would've never left a teammate by himself in that situation.

"Jerome Bettis was different from most of the guys. He'd have fit in with our team. Rocky Bleier and I had the military bond. I never talked to him about Vietnam. That's something you just don't talk about. I was a non-combatant Marine. Rocky called me the luckiest Marine in the world. Back in January of 1969, there were more Marines in Vietnam than any other branch of the service. Rocky was in the Army, but I tell him he was a wannabe Marine.

"His experience was of a higher level than mine. His story is an amazing story. We share something; we both served our country.

"We both took a lot of hits. I have had my head examined a few times. My doctor told me most of my forgetfulness is just age. You go upstairs and you forget why you went there. I read Merril Hoge's books

354

(*Find a Way* and *Brainwashed*) and they give you a better understanding of what's going on. I'm not a Hall of Fame guy. I'm a teammate. When I was helping to plan a fund-raiser for my son Jay's political campaign, I asked how it could be different. I thought if I could get a teammate to come and appear that would be different. I immediately thought of Franco and Rocky. After two phone calls, it was a done deal. Getting those two to come would attract more people. We just had to find a date—and that's not easy to do with their schedules—and we did. April 4th is going to be a special day.

"Franco is the reason I made the Steelers' football team in the first place.

"I focused on Franco in all my training before I reported to the Steelers' summer training camp. I thought about what it would take for me to make the team. I was a long shot, to say the least.

"The first chance I get to tackle Franco Harris, I'm going to put him on his back. Franco and I still talk about this story. That was my motivation. They had Oklahoma Drills on the first day the veterans reported to camp, a week after the rookies came in.

"The Oklahoma Drill was a one-on-one collision of an offensive lineman and a defensive lineman. They had me do it eight times, and guys told me they didn't recall anyone being told to do it that many times. I won most of the battles. My father used to tell me you only get once chance to make a first impression, and I was hell-bent on doing just that.

"Then we scrimmaged. They don't have Oklahoma Drills these days—too dangerous—and they don't really scrimmage much anymore.

"But they did in those days. It was a big deal. When the offense broke from the huddle, I didn't see Franco. He was sitting on his helmet on the sideline.

"When they broke from the huddle the next time, Franco was still sitting on his helmet on the sideline. Same thing the next time. Franco avoided contact, I would learn. Rocky was just the opposite. He relished running the ball. He'd take a hit and get up and go back in the huddle.

"I had a great day. I won every one of my battles. I later realized I was all charged up to put Franco on his back that first day. That was

George Gojkovich

Franco sitting on his helmet at practice.

going to be my shining star. He's Franco and I'm just a rookie no one knows much about.

"When I did get to see Franco in practice, he didn't look so great. He wasn't the guy I saw in the playoffs the year before. Franco wasn't really running that hard. He and Rocky were both fast when it counted the most.

"I remember the game Rocky scored on a 74-yard touchdown run against the Browns in Cleveland. Franco had a 70-yard touchdown run and they both had 100-yard days.

"I grew up in a Polish home. My grandparents came from Poland and they had it rough there. The Germans and Russians hated the Poles and gave them a tough time.

"There was a Polish dish called duck blood soup. Nothing went to waste in our home, and my mother

356

put all sorts of things in with the duck to improve the broth. Lots of leftovers went into that concoction.

"My mother was a tough woman. She was the one who often put a belt to my butt. She didn't want my dad coming home from a hard day's work and having to discipline me."

* * *

I saved the toughest questions for last. I asked John how difficult it was for him to fail so badly in his final coaching job at Robert Morris. Once again, he got wet-eyed and I hoped I hadn't upset him too much.

"I had the players, talented, smart and disciplined, at Washington & Jefferson," he said. "At Robert Morris, I had a lot of problems with discipline. I'm a disciplined individual, and that hurt me.

"What I did at Robert Morris might have been my best coaching job, but we couldn't win. My record was almost the complete opposite of what I had accomplished at W&J. Our record at W&J was 38-9 and our record at Robert Morris was 8-34.

"After I signed as a free agent with the Steelers, I called my father to tell him. He didn't say anything. I heard a click. He hung up on me without a word. He was such a loyal Cleveland Browns' fan and the Steelers were the enemy. It took him a while to come around, but he did."

When Banszak was leaving Panera's, he ran into a friend and neighbor of mine, Anthony Accamando, a Vietnam veteran who has spent a great deal of his adult life looking out for veteran causes.

"Here's a guy," said Banaszak, "you ought to write a book about."

*　*　*

When the majority of the outstanding players of the Steelers of the '70s were cut from the squad it did not go well. They didn't go quietly into the night. They felt betrayed. They thought they still had something to offer. They complained bitterly to the media about being released. There's no good way to fire somebody.

It was that way with Joe Greene, L.C. Greenwood, Steve Furness and Dwight White, to name a few I recall from covering the Steelers at St. Vincent College in the summers of the early '80s. It was no different for John Banaszak.

I remember visiting the home of Mary and John Banaszak in McMurray back in 1992 and checking out all the family photos and telling John he had a great-looking family. He had a son, Jay, and two daughters, Carrie and Amye.

"I've been lucky," said Banaszak. "I remember how awful I felt when I drove home from St. Vincent College when I was cut from the team (in 1982). I was so upset. But I was listening to the radio in my car and that's when I heard the news about Doug Kotar of the Giants having an inoperable brain tumor."

Kotar had grown up in a community near McMurray called Muse, just outside of Canonsburg, and was a fine running back for the New York Giants. Kotar would die soon after a difficult hospital stay. "I had played in football and in softball games with Doug," said Banaszak. "That helped me realize that getting cut from the Steelers wasn't the worst thing in the world. It helped put things in perspective for me."

Then the USFL came along and Banaszak, who played his college ball at Eastern Michigan University after he came out of the Marines, played in 1983 and 1984 for the Michigan Panthers and in 1985 for the Memphis Showboats.

One of his teammates with the Memphis Showboats was Reggie White and Banaszak, surprisingly, has said that White was even better than Joe Greene.

Banaszak might have thought of Doug Kotar again in April of 2009 when Banaszak was hospitalized after suffering a hemorrhage of the brain. At first, it was thought he had an aneurysm. He recovered at Allegheny General Hospital. Banaszak had had a few close calls with his health. He once was hospitalized with a serious life-threatening staph infection and there was another time when he tipped over a golf cart and was submerged under it in a small pond on the golf course.

Banaszak no longer even includes that incident in his list of close calls.

Banaszak remains a recognizable figure on the Pittsburgh sports scene. He played for the Pittsburgh Steelers from 1976 to 1981, and was the starting right defensive end for the Steelers in Super Bowl XIII and XIV.

He turned 63 in August of 2013 when I saw him as he was overseeing practices of the Robert Morris University football team as the top assistant to veteran coach Joe Walton. Banaszak already had been told he would be succeeding Walton, who was 77, as the head coach the following season when Walton would step back but remain involved in the RMU athletic picture. The football stadium, after all, is named in his honor. Walton, an All-America end at Pitt and a star with the New York Giants and Washington Redskins, and a coach in the NFL, started the football program at Robert Morris in 1993 and the 2013 season would be his 20th at the Moon Township campus.

Banaszak had previously been a top assistant to John Luckhardt at Washington & Jefferson College and succeeded Luckhart as the head coach. Banaszak

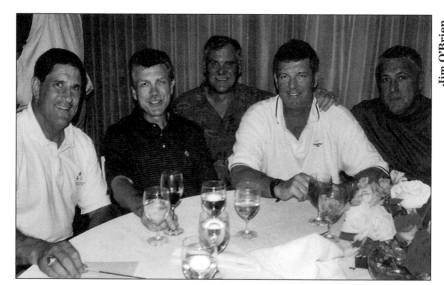

John Banaszak, at left, is joined by former teammates Mike Wagner, Gerry Mullins, Gordon Gravelle and Dave Reavis at Andy Russell's annual fund-raising golf outing at The Club at Nevillewood.

John Banaszak
76
SB X, XIII, XIV

BANASZAK BUNCH – Mary and John Banaszak and family celebrate John being honored by teammate Mel Blount (in rear at left) at his annual Mel Blount Youth Home Celebrity Roast.

was quite successful at W&J, but was fired by the school president because he was publicly checking out other coaching positions.

Banaszak says the college president was out checking out possible jobs for himself when he fired him.

Before Banaszak got into coaching, he operated some auto lubrication centers and worked for the recreation department in Peters Township.

* * *

When John wants to get a point across, he often refers to Jack Lambert, Joe Greene and Chuck Noll.

"They love to hear those old war stories," Banaszak said. "I may embellish it a little bit when I talk about myself. I still remain a student of motivation and two most emotional players I've ever been around are Lambert and Greene.

"Lambert's motivation was to not fail. Greene's motivation was his passion to win. My players here play with an intensity very similar to the intensity we had during my Super Bowl years. My defensive players are as good at this level as the Steelers were at their level.

"Being a former Steeler certainly helps in recruiting."

I have seen Banaszak escorting recruits near the RMU campus. I have also seen him at Andy Russell's golf outing and Mel Blount's roasts to raise money for his boys' ranch in Claysville and Banaszak remains a standup guy. Banaszak has always been easy to talk to and to be around.

I was with Joe Gordon in early June of 2013 when we learned at a luncheon meeting at DeBlasio's Restaurant in Mt. Lebanon that Mike Adams, slotted to start at right tackle for the Steelers for the 2013

Photos by Jim O'Brien

Chuck Noll and John Banaszak recall good times during cocktail hour at Andy Russell's golf outing at The Club at Nevillewood.

John Banaszak is all smiles at Applebee's in Peters Township that was then owned by former teammates Larry Brown and J.T. Thomas.

season, had been stabbed in the stomach on the South Side the night before when he tried to stop three men from stealing his truck. We noted that the incident occurred at 3 a.m.

Adams had a checkered history for off-the-field activity when he was at Ohio State, and he had talked Mike Tomlin into taking him in the draft, promising he would stay out of trouble.

Gordon, who had been the publicist of the Steelers during the glory days of the '70s, offered that the players who had good, solid wives were the ones who stayed out of trouble. John Banaszak has such a wife in Mary. He knows it.

They were high school sweethearts and they have been married more than 47 years. Mary served as director of Greenbriar Rehabilitation Center in Washington, Pennsylvania, and more recently as chief executive officer. It is a rehab facility for those addicted to drugs and alcohol.

I saw her twice at funerals for teammates of John Banaszak, notably Steve Furness and Mike Webster, comforting her husband and holding his hand, and the images remain with me.

John may be a big guy, a Marine forever, but Mary keeps the Banaszaks on course. She's the rock.

When I mentioned about seeing him and Mary at so many funerals, Banaszak got wet-eyed, and I mentioned this observation to him. "I'm an emotional guy and it hurts when you lose teammates, guys like Furness who was my roommate. We used to share a ride to and from practices quite a bit. More recently, we lost Ernie Holmes and Dwight White and L.C. Greenwood and that hurt, too. They were teammates; we lined up together. I had a few close calls of my own, but I came out of them okay. I was lucky."

*　*　*

Cleveland was something John Banaszak had in common with Chuck Noll, his coach with the Pittsburgh Steelers. "We went to rival high schools," said Banaszak. "Chuck went to Benedictine and I went to Holy Name. We'd talk about it the week before we'd play Cleveland. He'd come to me in the locker room before we'd go to Cleveland and say to me, 'We're going home this week.' He'd go and see his sister, who lived near the hotel where we stayed on the west side of Cleveland. I'd go home and have some good Polish cooking."

If his days as a Steeler came to a crushing close, his start with the Steelers was something special as far as NFL training camps were concerned.

"One of the reasons I signed as a free agent with the Steelers was because I had a college relationship with Woody Widenhofer, one of the Steelers' assistant coaches. He told me, 'I'll see to it that you are in camp at least until the College All-Star Game.' That gave me two weeks to make an impression.

"I knew some guys in college who signed as free agents and they were home in two days. I think I had the team made after the 'Oklahoma Drill' the first day, though I didn't know it then. I was ready from Day One."

The "Oklahoma Drill" used to be one of the highlights of the Steelers' training camp. A defensive lineman would go nose-to-nose with an offensive lineman. A running back followed his blocker through a narrow pit—blocking dummies were laid on their sides to provide a channel to contain the activity—and it was always a real collision course.

"I had to beat out two veteran defensive linemen—Jim Wolf and Charlie Davis—and I didn't know how I'd be accepted if that happened. Both of them were black, and the starting defensive linemen were

BANASZAK DANCE—John Banaszak (76) leads a polka dance to celebrate a tackle, followed, left to right, by Joe Greene (75), Ron Johnson (29) and Tom Beasley (65).

all black. This was 1975, and there were still rumors about racial problems in pro football. But there was never a problem. I was accepted from the start.

"They kept putting me in the 'Oklahoma Drill' over and over again. They couldn't believe what I was doing. They had me do it eight times, which I was told never happened before.

"That was against other rookies and free agents. The talk was about how I'd fare against the veterans. I went up against Jon Kolb and Gordon Gravelle and Jim Clack and held my ground. Then it was just a matter of if I could play for the special teams. That's what you had to do in those days to stick with the Steelers.

"Chuck gave me a real opportunity. He told us free agents would be taken care of and looked at just like everyone else, and he was good for his word.

"Chuck and his staff treated free agents like equals on the playing field. Their decisions were not made on how much they had invested in a player. Look how many guys were second or third round draft choices who didn't make the team, and ended up playing for other teams. Noll knew who he wanted on his team."

From an earlier interview:
John Banaszak:

I always thought I had a good relationship with Chuck Noll. Chuck was always interested in my career outside the locker room. Chuck made it very clear that football was only a passing thing. "This is not your future," he'd say. "This is only a stepping stone." He talked a lot about it. We all benefited from his constant reminders.

My first off-season employment came in 1977 when I was working for the Dart Trucking Company out of Canfield, Ohio as a sales rep. I wore a business suit to the stadium one day, and was going to work out after I'd been working at my job all day. Chuck came up to me and said, "What are you doing?" When I told him I was in the trucking business, he beamed.

He said, "Trucking? Hey, when I was with the Browns, I had a job as a sale rep for the entire Cleveland area for a trucking company." He started to tell me about federal trucking regulations and other stuff. I was shocked he knew so much. He was genuinely interested.

Probably the least known asset that Chuck brought to the Steelers was an interest in our lives beyond the football field. The public had no idea that discussions like that ever occurred. It was encouraging that he had an interest in us like that. When I saw him after my playing days were over and he was no longer the coach he still inquired about what I was doing. When I had a string of quick-change motor oil places, he discussed that with me, too. He was fascinated by the operation. And he was one of my customers.

When I think about Chuck, I always go back to my rookie year. We were playing the Baltimore Colts in the first round of the playoffs at Three Rivers. I really thought that was going to be the last game I ever played with the Steelers because of something I did in that game.

The Colts had a good team. They had Bert Jones and Lydell Mitchell and 'The Sack Pack,' and a great defense. We kicked off to them and they drove down to our 35. It was fourth down and three and they're going to punt. Chuck gets everyone on our punt return team together on the sideline and says, "Let's get after this one and block it!" J.T. Thomas and I had worked on a crossing rush to get their blockers mixed up. We crossed just like it was drawn up, and I got in free. I'm in midair in textbook fashion to block the kick, and I get knocked into the kicker.

I'm on the 50-yard line and 50,000 fans are hollering. I look next to me and I see a yellow flag by my face. And I could hear Chuck hollering at me, over the voices of 50,000 fans. I wanted to hide under the carpet.

He's trying to get at me when I come to the sideline and I ran the other way to get away from him. He runs down the sideline at me. He's hollering, "What are you doing? How'd you do that?" I told him, "Chuck, I got knocked into the kicker!" He screams back, "You can't get friggin' bumped into the kicker!" I heard him say that. I feel lower than a curb at this time. I'm saying to myself, "If we lose, it's my fault. I'll be gone by Tuesday. I'm outta here!"

But we won. That's the game where Andy Russell picked up a fumble and ran 94 yards for a touchdown. Yeah, that's the one where they took a commercial break during Andy's run. Isn't that how he tells the story? Russell and Ray Mansfield made a living off that story on the banquet circuit.

I figured I'd get vindicated by watching the game film. I'm thinking he'll apologize to me for he way he hollered at me in the stadium. Chuck was the special teams coach then, and it was the second play we had to watch on the special teams group. They broke down the film for each group to see what they needed to work on.

Well, we see the play and J.T. Thomas was the guy who knocked me into the kicker. He'd come free, too. I'm waiting for an apology, and Noll hollers out in the dark room, "You can't get friggin' blocked into the kicker." He said it again. "Next time, you'll be outta here!" It was like somebody shot ice water up your veins. You just wanted to die.

Sometimes his expressions spoke louder than words. He could look at you and melt you. Or he could look at you and instill confidence. I'll always remember that when we were coming off the field at halftime in Super Bowl XIV and we were losing to the LA Rams, 13-10, Chuck was smiling. Like we had them just where we wanted them. That made such an impression on me. He could just look at you and instill confidence stronger than any motivational speech that Lombardi ever gave.

Chuck never really gave a motivational speech. I'm still waiting for his first motivational speech.

Hey, I'm one of the few guys from our team who still goes to the games. I'm still a fan. I was a fan when

I was eight years old, and my dad was taking me to the ballgames. I'll always be a fan.

When fans think of me, I hope they'll feel the same way I feel about my career. I enjoyed every minute of it. There's nothing I could look back upon and say I had a bad time or that was a disappointment to that it was work. I enjoyed every single practice, every single meeting, every single camp, every single game. I enjoyed the entire seven years in Pittsburgh as a Steeler.

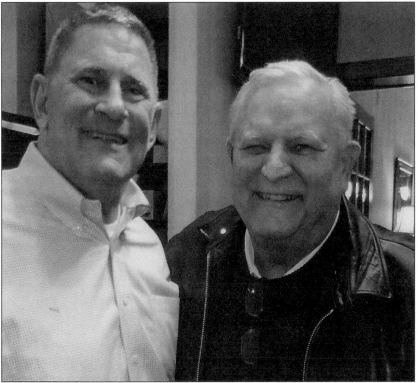

Jim O'Brien

John Banaszak and John Luckhardt at Good Guys Luncheon at Atria's in late February, 2019.

When Franco couldn't find the football

In 1973, I was in my third year on the sports staff of *The New York Post,* covering all the major league teams in town. New York had more pro teams than any other city in America, and it was a sportswriter's paradise.

The previous year, I had done stints on the beat of the New York Giants as well as the New York Jets. One day I'd be talking to Fran Tarkenton of the Giants and the next day it would be Joe Namath of the Jets. Both liked to talk. Both are in the Pro Football Hall of Fame.

One day it was Yankee Stadium and the next day it was Shea Stadium, in the fall and winter for football, and in the spring and summer for baseball, the Yankees and the Mets.

Bobby Murcer and Tom Seaver, Ralph Houk and Gil Hodges and Yogi Berra. Can it be any better?

Yes, there were Old Timers Games where I had an opportunity to meet and talk to Roy Campanella, Sal Maglie, Don Larsen, Hank Bauer, Monte Irvin, Carl Erskine, Duke Snider, Mickey Mantle, Willie Mays, Joe DiMaggio, Casey Stengel, and even the widows of Babe Ruth and Lou Gehrig.

Here's a story I wrote in the fall of 1973, after a game in which the Steelers lost to the New York Giants, 29-24, in a pre-season game that was the flip side of Franco Harris and his "Immaculate Reception."

Footballs really do take funny bounces, and no one knew that any better than Franco Harris of the Steelers. Unless it was John Madden, who still insists that the ball bounced off Frenchy Fuqua and not Jack Tatum before Franco seized it and scored the game-winning touchdown over Madden's Raiders in an AFC playoff game the previous season.

Fans will never forget how Harris scored the game-winning touchdown in the Steelers' 13-7 victory over the Raiders on December 23, 1972. It was the Steelers' first playoff victory in 40 mostly frustrating seasons. It was a sheer case of Christmas coming early to the long-suffering followers of football in the Steel City, back when the city could still honestly claim that tag.

I was covering that game in my hometown of Pittsburgh for *The New York Post*. I still cared about the Steelers, certainly more than the Raiders. I don't think I knew what happened when it happened. Most Steelers' fans were downcast, staring at their shoe tops, swearing S.O.S. for same ol' Steelers. Even Arthur J. Rooney missed it, riding down in an elevator to console his Steelers in the locker room because he thought they would lose this game. That's when Franco found the ball at his shoe tops from a ricocheted pass and ran 42 yards for the game-winning touchdown. It was a 60-yard TD play.

Harris re-enacted that "Immaculate Reception" in February of 2019 while wearing a tuxedo at a party in Atlanta the weekend of Super Bowl 53. It never grows old. Franco found out that things can go the other way in the fall of 1973 at Yankee Stadium. Fortunately, it happened in a pre-season game so it didn't count.

For the second straight Sunday, the Giants' defenders found the ball in their hands often enough to offset what their offense wasn't doing with it, and came up with all the big plays to pull out a 29-24 victory over the Steelers.

One such sequence stands out that happened midway through the second period, and explains something of the crazy character of the game, and why the Giants were 4-0 in pre-season play.

Terry Bradshaw was back to pass on first down at his own 39-yard line, and as he let the ball loose it was tipped by defensive end John Mendenhall. It hung high in the air directly over the head of Franco Harris. Harris had blocked for Bradshaw, then slipped off toward the right sideline, just the opposite direction of what he did during the early stages of the sequence known forever as "The Immaculate Reception."

"My back was to the ball," Harris told us afterward. "I heard the ball get batted, but I didn't know where it was."

Brian Kelley, a rookie linebacker for the Giants from California Lutheran College, knew exactly where it was. "I saw him go up quick," said Harris. "Right then I knew the ball was somewhere in my vicinity. Before I knew it, there he was running down the sideline for a touchdown."

Now Harris knew how Jack Tatum felt.

Kelley went 39 yards for that touchdown. On the first play of that same second period, Spider Lockhart intercepted a pass by Bradshaw and returned it up the left sideline 43 yards for a touchdown. And, on the next-to-last play of that period, Willie Williams picked off another Bradshaw pass to set up the third of five field goals in the game by Pete Gogolak. It gave the Giants a 23-10 halftime lead, and the Steelers simply couldn't overcome Bradshaw's generosity.

This game would've gained its own fame except that it didn't count in the final standings. It may have been Bradshaw's worst outing in his Hall of Fame career.

The week before at Yale Bowl, the Giants returned two interceptions for touchdowns, and set up three more touchdowns in the same manner against the Jets in the annual pre-season New York City clash. I was there to see that game. Chuck Noll, the no-nonsense coach of the Steelers, saw films of that game, won by the Giants, 45-30.

"That's great defense," he said.

Was it really, though? The Jets, after all, racked up nearly 600 yards offensively, and the Steelers gained 99 more yards passing than the Giants, and 13 more yards rushing.

"I don't care," said Noll, not one to agree with any sportswriter's view. "You got to call that good defense. They're making things happen. It's heads-up football. They pay off on points. That's the game. Losers talk about yardage gained and statistics."

As I am typing that paragraph it strikes me that Noll talked the way Hemingway wrote, hard-hitting simple sentences.

Noll kept saying that the Giants had beaten their behinds, or words to that effect. And yet the Giants' offense had never really steamrollered the Steelers in any way.

"No matter," Noll continued in the same vein. "The thing you count is points scored. They had 29 points against us. We had 24. That's how you measure it."

Noll, who had done a super job in building a ball-club, didn't believe that Bradshaw or the Steelers' offense had nearly reached its potential during the pre-season schedule. "We haven't come along offen-sively yet," he said. "Today was especially bad. But maybe their defense had something to do with it."

Bradshaw had a bad day, that's for sure. And he had a lot to do with it himself. He played heads-down football, for the most part. He called a lot of poor plays, confused his own club on occasion, contributing to one of two consecutive penalties that kept the Steelers from scoring when they had a first down inside the

Giants' 10-yard line late in the period, and didn't pass consistently well.

As for the Giants' defense, Bradshaw said, "It's vulnerable. You can run on it, but you can't score on it."

I still retain an image of finding Franco Harris in the visitors' clubhouse after the game, and getting almost nothing from him. He had little to say, and he wasn't interested in talking much. Willie Mays provided a similar disappointing meeting for me in a New York clubhouse. My first impressions were not positive ones. Oh well, even the great ones have bad days.

Terry Bradshaw gets an earful from Coach Chuck Noll.

BIG RED

They were all Giants
for my father-in-law

One day, when my assignment was to cover a practice of the New York Giants at Yankee Stadium, I took my father-in-law, Harvey Churchman, along with me. I knew he'd get a kick out of the insider's experience.

He had a chance to meet Alex "Red" Webster, the former hard-charging running back of the Giants, who was now the head coach, Emlen Tunnell, a Hall of Fame defensive back for the Giants, who was now an assistant coach, and a long-time scout named "Jungle Jim" Trimble.

We stood on the sideline. It was a bit cold and dank, a gray sky over the ballpark where Babe Ruth, Lou Gehrig and Joe DiMaggio had played baseball, and where some great Football Giants had played as well. It was an iconic sports venue.

I spotted Jim Trimble, who scouted for the Giants over 20 years, and called him over. Trimble was from McKeesport, Pennsylvania, where my father-in-law lived in the White Oak section. My father-in-law also remembered that Trimble once played for the McKeesport Olympians, a heavy-weight sandlot football team.

Trimble recalled those days—not many New York writers asked him about that time in his life—so he was an eager and enthusiastic visitor with us.

Trimble was once the head football coach of the Philadelphia Eagles in the National Football League and Hamilton Tiger-Cats and Montreal Alouettes of the Canadian Football League, and one of the few to have a Super Bowl and Gray Cup ring.

He was also primarily responsible for inventing and introducing the sling-shot goal post to pro football, so called because of its Y-shape. Old-time football fans will recall that goal posts once had a post at each end and that football players would often crash into those posts and, sometimes, get hurt in the collision. Trimble's goal post was stationed at the back of the end zone and extended outward to the cross-bar above the goal line.

When you think about it, that was quite a significant contribution to the game, and a safety measure for players.

*   *   *

During the practice, Coach Webster came over to say hello, and I introduced him to my father-in-law. Webster exchanged some pleasantries and made my father-in-law feel more comfortable. Not many coaches would be so kind.

Following the workout, I led my father-in-law across the football field and we entered a dugout on the third base side. I told Harvey Churchman to take a seat there and wait for me. I wouldn't be long.

As I started asking Alex Webster some questions, he hesitated, and asked me about the whereabouts of my father-in-law. I told him he was waiting for me in the dugout. "It's too cold to leave him out there," he said.

"Emlen!" shouted Webster. "Do me a favor and get Jim's father-in-law in the dugout and bring him into our clubhouse!"

So, my father-in-law was being escorted by the great Emlen Tunnell to come into the Giants' clubhouse where Y.A. Tittle, Frank Gifford, Sam Huff, Roosevelt Brown and Andy Robustelli had once had lockers. Tunnell had been inducted into the Pro Football Hall of Fame in 1967. He was the first African-American to play for the Giants and the first to be inducted into the Pro Football Hall of Fame.

It was a random act of kindness I won't soon forget. My father-in-law couldn't wait to get back to McKeesport and tell his friends about his day with the Giants at Yankee Stadium. I wonder how many football coaches today would take the time to be so welcoming to a complete stranger on the sideline.

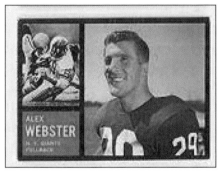

Alex "Red" Webster

Emlen Tunnell

FRANCO

Sleepless in Seattle

You could not see ten feet in front of you when you came out of the Kingdome in Seattle on Sunday night, November 4, 1981. So the Steelers were told they would not be flying back to Pittsburgh, as scheduled, but instead they would have to spend the night in Seattle.

"That wouldn't have been so bad if we had won," offered Franco Harris. "It's always more fun when you win."

They didn't sleep well. Talk about sleepless in Seattle. This game offers insight into how the Steelers dealt with difficult losses, as the glory days of the Steelers started to fade out in the Seattle sky.

But the Steelers had been playing in a fog, even when they were inside the Kingdome, a sports venue in the city's SoDo neighborhood that would be imploded on March 26, 2000, and leave a dust-choked pile on the site.

That's how they managed to blow a 21-3 lead and lose, 24-21, to the Seahawks, who had won only two of their previous nine games in the 1981 schedule.

"They're a good team, not a great team, nothing you'd lose any sleep over," Terry Bradshaw said after the game. You can bet Bradshaw and others associated with the Steelers lost some sleep over this one. It was just as bitter to swallow as the one before that to the San Francisco 49ers.

"Would you look at this fog," asked Harris as he fell wearily into a seat near the front of four chartered buses that returned the Steelers to the hotel where they had stayed for two nights. "This fog is unbelievable."

*　*　*

No, not really. The fog was just as believable as the setback to the Seahawks, a loss that left the Steelers with a 5-5 record, two games back of the Cincinnati Bengals in the AFC Central, and scratching their heads in disbelief.

For Harris, it was especially hard to handle. That's why he hammered his arm rest as he rode the bus. The bus was dark except for a single reading light above him which illuminated Franco's face in a manner befitting his position in pro football history.

This could have been a great day in Franco's life. It should have been a great day, but as Chuck Noll often noted, "could have been" and "should have been" were the words of losers in football and in life.

Harris reached and passed an important milestone, gaining 61 yards on 15 carries to boost his career total to 10,003 yards. Only two players in pro football history had rushed for more than 10,000 yards —Jimmy Brown and O.J. Simpson—and Franco felt honored when they stopped the game to present him with the ball when he twice rushed for three yards to hit the 10,000 mark right on the button.

"They don't stop football games for too many things," said Harris. And he was right on the mark again.

It took ten seasons to achieve what he did, while it took Mark Malone only ten seconds, if that, to get his name into the Steelers' record book with a 90-yard touchdown reception of a Bradshaw pass at the outset of the second quarter, but neither could enjoy their special moments much. Not after a loss like the one they had endured.

Mark Malone, Emil Boures and Rocky Bleier at The Club at Nevillewood.

What hurt Harris were the numbers that would never be inscribed in the record books, an 81-yard touchdown run he reeled off after taking a pass from Bradshaw in the backfield on a third-and-one call midway through the fourth quarter.

Franco was fantastic on that one, but guard Craig Wolfley was human. He made a mistake, tackling Seattle linebacker Keith Butler at his ankles instead of blocking him. Wolfley has been a sideline reporter for Steelers radio broadcasts for 19 years as of 2019, and Keith Butler has been the defensive coordinator during some of that span, so Wolfley is constantly reminded of his wrongdoing in Seattle.

"I still can't shake that," says Wolfley.

Wolfley was in front of Franco as he made his dash through a swarm of Seahawks before breaking into the open, and Coach Noll said there was no doubt about what Wolfley did to draw a penalty flag from the official and erase Harris' heroics.

Craig Wolfley, Casey Hampton and Tunch Ilkin during a radio broadcast at Cupka's Restaurant on East Carson Street on Pittsburgh's South Side.

* * *

"It's no fun losing," said an especially subdued Noll, his voice barely audible in his post-game reflections. "We blew a 21-3 lead and we were not able to muster any offense in the second half. The combination of those two things killed us.

"The mistake by Wolfley cost us the touchdown we needed to win. It would have been a great way to win. It would have been a very dramatic play. Everybody in this locker room would be very enthusiastic and excited and happy as hell. And we'd be making a lot more of Franco's reaching a great milestone in his career. That's a helluva accomplishment."

Harris and Noll were not the only ones talking about what might have been. Bradshaw was doing the same. He spoke about going to Noll the previous Tuesday and asking Noll to call the plays for him in this game. Bradshaw felt it might help him and the team.

"I've been feeling pressure," Bradshaw said. "From within. Everybody here has been backing me all the way. I just want to excel and I haven't been. I thought this would relieve some of the pressure."

Franco could be a difficult interview back then. Terry was always talkative. Seeing the words they spoke that night in Seattle points up why it was such a pleasure to report on that team. There was an honesty about the coach and his players that makes one realize why covering the Steelers was so special.

Writers no longer travel with the team, and I believe they miss out a lot on what's going on.

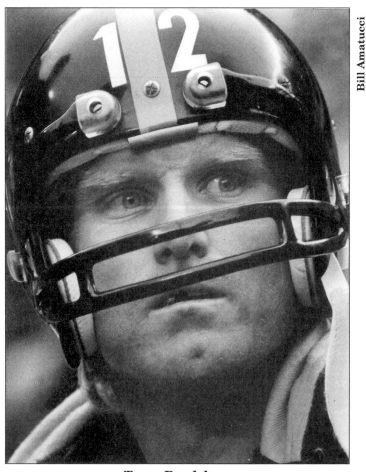

Bill Amatucci

Terry Bradshaw

Perhaps it helped ease the pressure. It didn't, however, succeed in stopping the Steelers' or Bradshaw's backward slide.

Terry fretted over Franco's TD being called back, and even more about the Steelers' failure to get a first down on a third-and-one call at the Seahawks' five-yard line in the last minute of the game. On fourth down, the Steelers turned to Dave Trout and the rookie kicker from Pitt was wide left with a 22-yard field-goal try. A successful kick would have tied the game.

"I always thought we were going to win it," said Bradshaw. "I thought we'd make it on third down and we didn't. We had a good field-goal kicker, so we called on him. I thought we'd tee it up and he'd kick it. Then we'd win the coin toss for the overtime, take the kick and march down the field for the winning points. We'd just go down and beat them."

Terry's thoughts were all positive; he felt no pressure.

He said he didn't want to do any second-guessing, either, but responded to a question by saying that he would have gone for the first down on fourth-and-one at the Seahawks' five with 20 seconds showing on the scoreboard clock.

"What I felt was to go ahead and go for it," said Bradshaw. "I, personally, think we could have made it. If we could have won this, we'd still be very close in the race. Now we've got problems."

Craig Wolfley
73

Steelers' broadcaster brought out best in his friends

Let's observe a moment of silence in memory of Myron Cope. Picture him as you remember him. Have him saying something that sticks in your mind, or have him singing his annual holiday season song. Do your best imitation of his distinctive voice. Are you smiling? You betcha!

I was sitting at a round table with the best of company on the last day of February 2008. On my right was Franco Harris with his wife Dana. To their right were Rocky Bleier and his wife Jan. Across from me were Andy Russell and his wife Cindy. Think about that Steelers' trifecta. They will always be hailed as gridiron giants by Pittsburgh fans.

Franco, Rocky and Andy. Any self-respecting Steelers' fan doesn't need their last names to know these men. They remain three of the most popular Pittsburgh Steelers of all time. I recognize that. They have stood the test of time. They have made significant contributions to our community. They still make us proud. As I sat there, talking with them, swapping stories, reminiscing, it struck me how a Steelers' fan might feel to be sitting in my seat. I always feel that way when I am in the company of an admired sports star, whether it's Arnold Palmer, Bill Mazeroski, Mario Lemieux, Bill Dudley, Joe Greene or Mel Blount. And I didn't have to pay a license fee for my seat. It wasn't business as usual.

This was at a bereavement luncheon that followed a private funeral service to say goodbye to a dear friend and colleague, Myron Cope. We were in a banquet room on the eighth floor of the Best Western Hotel in Green Tree. It was about two miles away from the William Slater II Funeral Home where a funeral service had been held two hours earlier for Myron Cope, the Steelers' celebrated broadcast analyst and color man. His son, Danny, 40 at the time, and his daughter, Elizabeth, who was 38, were seated at a table in the middle of the large room.

I hadn't seen Danny since he was a toddler. He sat in silence the entire luncheon. That's been his life. His father was known for his voice, and Danny doesn't talk. He was in the restroom when I went there and when he came out a woman was waiting for him and helped him fix his slacks properly, and pull up his zipper. I'd seen Liz from time to time. She is an attractive young woman, but she's been challenged to find herself and establish her own identity.

A month later, she would appear, along with her brother, on a TV interview on WPXI-TV with Peggy Finnegan. It was the first time Danny had appeared on television. "He's the man behind the Terrible Towel," allowed Liz. "I wanted people to see who inspired that symbol that represents so much more than the Steelers or sports in this town."

I wondered what Myron would think about all this. The television station had promoted the appearance to great extent. It was an exclusive. Peggy Finnegan was sensitive to the fact that Danny had never appeared on television when his father was alive, and asked Liz, "Why now?"

She spoke of her father's deep interest in his children and how much she was going to miss her Daddy. There was no doubt that Myron Cope cared deeply about his family, to hear Liz speak with such enthusiasm about him and their special relationship.

Cope used to upset many of his female listeners the way he spoke of them, often referring to them as "girlies."

I remember sitting with Liz and her mother, Mildred Cope, at a YMCA Scholar-Athlete Dinner at the Hilton years earlier. Myron was being honored as the Man of the Year. When he was speaking, he pointed to Mildred and said, "She's from the old school where women are mentioned in the newspaper on three occasions: when they're born, when they get married, and when they die."

Mildred just shook her head. She'd heard it before. Anyone who knew her knew she didn't agree with Myron on that note. Like me, he was lucky to have a wife who looked after him. When she died, I remember the sign at the doorway of the funeral home read: MRS. MYRON COPE. A friend of hers told me that's the way Mildred would have wanted it. I wonder about that.

Myron's three sisters, all less than five feet tall, were at the same table as Liz and Danny at the bereavement luncheon. I never knew he had three sisters. I had a chance to talk to Myron's sisters and tell them what a good mentor and model Myron was for anyone who was a writer.

The last time I had seen Cope was a year earlier when he made a surprise appearance to pay tribute to Steelers' owner Dan Rooney at the Dapper Dan Sports Dinner at the Convention Center. I recalled that I was stunned by Cope's physical appearance, how frail and weak he looked. I was impressed that Andy Russell got out of his seat and assisted Cope in crossing the platform when Russell recognized that Cope was having some difficulty. The lighting was poor and Myron was walking unsteadily with the aid of a cane. I spoke to him as he was leaving and wished him well. He smiled. It was the last time I saw him.

Danny Cope was always thought to suffer from autism, and Myron raised much money through the years for the Pittsburgh Chapter of Autism Society of America, only to learn later that Danny had suffered brain damage at birth and was not autistic as originally diagnosed. Danny lived at the Allegheny Valley Complex in Coraopolis that cared for youngsters and adults with mental and physical challenges. I first saw Danny when he was an infant in a playpen and Myron and his wife, Mildred, were living in Scott Township. They had suffered the loss of an infant daughter early in their marriage.

Myron Cope had succeeded Bob Prince as the prime fund-raiser for Allegheny Valley School, turning over the profits from the sale of the Terrible Towel to the school. Ironically enough, Cope suffered from the same ailment as the Pirates' esteemed broadcaster, dealing with throat and neck cancer in recent years. The cancer had spread to his brain, the same affliction that caused the death of Mayor Bob O'Connor two years earlier. Cope succumbed in the end to respiratory problems resulting from the effects of earlier surgery on his throat. A doctor had accidentally nicked his vocal chords on one of the early operations and it resulted in a lawsuit and a suspension of the doctor's privileges in the hospital. He had botched it, you betcha. How he hurt Myron's vocal chords had to be difficult to determine. How could you ruin that voice?

Franco and Andy had been among the six pallbearers at the funeral. They had accompanied Myron to the Chartiers Cemetery for burial. They had been wearing dark blue yarmulkes at the service, but had put them away. Franco's yarmulke had sat up high on his head.

Cope's casket—in the Jewish tradition—was closed. It had been draped with several Terrible Towels and a Steelers' jacket. I spotted several former Steelers at the service. It was a private service and there were only about 150 people present to offer their respects. I saw Mike Wagner, Mel Blount, Randy Grossman, Lynn Swann, Tunch Ilkin and Craig Wolfley at the service.

Dan Rooney and his wife, Pat, were present, along with Art Rooney II and his wife Greta. Art Rooney Jr. was across the aisle from where I was sitting with my friend Bill Priatko, who had played football at Pitt and with the Steelers and was a pen pal of Myron's. They both had a son with a disability. Mary Regan and Joan Regan were across the aisle. Mary had been the secretary for Art Rooney Sr. for many years. Bill Nunn, one of the team's most valuable scouts, was nearby. There were many people who had worked with Myron during his WTAE Radio days, including John Conomikes, an executive with the Hearst Corporation, who had supported the idea of having Myron Cope doing commentaries and such on the radio, despite having a raspy voice that took some getting used to, and was certainly different from most radio broadcasters.

A friend, Frank Haller, was one of the pallbearers. Haller had been a creative writer in the advertising game in Pittsburgh when I first met him. He had written a column for the newspaper, *Pittsburgh Weekly Sports*, that Beano Cook and I started in 1963. Haller had been a neighbor of Cope when Cope was first living in Scott Township. Cope had come back to the neighborhood in recent years when he moved into The Covenant of South Hills, where he had assisted care in his last months. Haller had driven Myron to many of his doctors' appointments and other meetings on his busy calendar. When Cope's driving privileges were suspended for DUI charges, it was Haller who came to the rescue and served as his loyal chauffeur for a few months. Haller had been a faithful friend. Haller also had a son who was mentally challenged so he and Myron had a common bond from the beginning of their special relationship. Haller helped him and Foge Fazio coordinate their annual golf outing to raise funds for the local chapter of the Autism Society.

Cope had been involved in a fender-bender on the west side of the Fort Pitt Tunnels that led to his last driving suspension. I was driving into the city that day, and saw some cars in a grassy strip between the merging lanes. I thought I saw Cope standing in the midst of the mess—looking like that Budweiser-sponsored painting of General Custer at Little Big Horn—as I shot by. He looked a little frazzled and bewildered. He'd been taking medication for his back ailments, and he didn't have feeling in his feet. He didn't press the brake pedal hard enough and that caused him to bang into the car in front of him.

I called Joe Gordon later to find out if that had been Cope, indeed, that I thought I saw, and Gordon told me it was our buddy. He said he was okay. Cope wasn't perfect, but no one enjoyed life more than he did. And he made it more fun for the rest of us.

I think everyone who was at his funeral felt special. They were all going to miss Myron.

Jim O'Brien

Myron Cope calling out to his "Copanut" fans following a Steelers' football game in 1995.

FRANCO

"How do you explain Myron Cope to anyone?"
—Franco Harris

Myron's close friend, Joe Gordon, the former public relations director of the Steelers, had made all the arrangements for the funeral. And he did this over the telephone from Florida, where he was wintering with his wife, Babe. If Gordon missed anyone, forgive him the oversight. I was honored that Gordon made sure I was invited to the funeral and accompanying events.

Gordon was good at seeing that things were done right. That's why he was respected and regarded as the best p.r. man in the National Football League during the glory days of the '70s. I remembered that he had looked after arrangements in a similar manner when Mike Webster died of a heart attack.

Franco had offered one of the eulogies at the funeral service. He drew some smiles when he asked those in attendance, "How do you explain Myron Cope to anyone?"

It was Cope, after all, who took a cue from one of his faithful callers on his WTAE Radio talk show and referred to Franco's game-winning heroics in the 1972 AFC playoff game with the Oakland Raiders as "The Immaculate Reception." Cope was reluctant to do so at first lest he offend his Catholic listeners. One of them told him it would be okay and that was good enough for Cope. And it wasn't Bishop Wuerl.

This memory prompted Franco to say, "From my rookie season on, Myron and I were joined at the hip. Well, let's say, hip and shoulder."

Franco's observation lightened up the mood of the room.

It was a reference to Myron's diminutive size. But Franco always knew that Myron was a giant in his own game, and that he was nearly as much a part of the Steelers' story as the Rooneys.

Art Rooney II, the team president and the grandson of Art Rooney Sr., said that Myron made football more fun. He didn't always take it as seriously as some of the Steelers' hierarchy did. "He helped keep things in perspective," related Rooney. He credited Cope for creating the kind of incredible following for the team that became known as the Steeler Nation.

"You're always working."

Sitting with Franco, Rocky and Andy was a special way to spend an otherwise difficult morning. Randy Grossman was sitting behind me.

A heavy snowstorm had hit Pittsburgh just before the funeral service got underway and it made traveling a challenge for everyone in attendance. Some thought it was Myron's final joke on everyone, or that it was simply Steelers' weather and appropriate for the occasion.

There had been a tribute to Myron in midtown at noontime, with hundreds of fans waving their Terrible Towels in front of the City-County Building with Mayor Luke Ravenstahl and County Executive Dan Onorato presiding over the gathering. Dan Rooney had been delayed getting to the funeral service because he attended the downtown event and because traffic had been slowed by the snowstorm.

It's been too many years since Franco, Rocky and Andy starred for the Steelers. There is gray in the hair that remains on their heads. Once they were reluctant to examine their lives and offer commentary about what they were doing on the football field. Now they need to know more about just what that experience was all about.

Now they are asking most of the questions. Franco was an especially difficult interview during his playing days. He had a dressing stall in the far corner of the team's locker room at Three Rivers Stadium, and he was there by choice. Whenever I'd come over to talk to him, notebook and pen in hand, he'd smile and wag his head. Like why do you insist on torturing me with your questions? You'd have thought I was bringing him a dose of castor oil to swallow. He'd talk, but in short sentences, most of which began, "You know." I think Franco was the first Pittsburgher to pepper his thoughts with "you know" pauses and it became fashionable. I'd ask him, for example, about his feelings about passing Joe "The Jet" Perry of the 49ers in the career rushing stats and he'd say something like, "I hear he was a great one. I gotta read up on him, you know. If it happens it happens. I'll reflect, you know, on those sorts of things when I'm old and retired."

He was always pleasant, mind you. He just didn't like to talk about himself. He was somewhat shy in that respect. He never wanted anyone to write a book about him. Rocky and Andy were always more comfortable in a crowd, masking their insecurities perhaps with great grins and firm handshakes, and familiar bromides. They had their own hang-ups, I have since learned. Franco didn't feel right comparing himself to Jim Brown or Joe Perry or O.J. Simpson, that's all.

Years later, sometimes I'd be signing books at Ross Park Mall and Franco Harris would happen by. He'd stop by, covertly, popping his handsome head out from the wall to where I could see him, then smile and extend a hand, and put a finger to his lips so I wouldn't identify him to anyone around me. He just wanted to say hello. He didn't want any fuss. But he didn't want to pass without a word either.

When I was covering the Steelers in the early '80s for *The Pittsburgh Press* , I was trying to recruit some players to appear at a father-son sports dinner at The Press Club downtown. Franco came into Joe Gordon's office one day and spotted me. "Jim, I will come to your dinner," he said. "I don't want to eat. I'll be there at 7 and stay for an hour and sign anything anyone wants me to sign. Is that okay?"

It was just peachy, as Myron might say. There were 40 Pittsburgh-based sports celebrities who came that evening, but none of them was as big a hit as Franco Harris. He arrived on schedule and departed exactly an hour later. He never stopped signing autographs— or smiling that bemused smile of his—the entire time he was there. That hour was what his friend Rocky Bleier calls "Franco's time."

I've gotten to know Franco better and on a more personal level in the past five years. Harris chaired a "championship committee" that I served on to establish a sports museum at the John Heinz History Center in The Strip. He always came to the meetings with a prepared agenda and got things accomplished. He was impressive. Gordon was on that committee as well.

I usually took advantage of Franco's presence by pulling out a notebook and pen, or to take a picture of him with my camera. He'd just grin. "Jim, you're always working," he'd say, scolding me in his own way. "Is this going to be in your next book?"

Franco Harris had come a long way from Mt. Holly, New Jersey and the Fort Dix military installation nearby where he once lived. He had confessed to Rocky Bleier that he'd been so fortunate for what his football career had provided him. He told Rocky that his dad had been a career military man, and that's all he knew. He thought that someday he'd be a soldier too. He had no idea he'd be doing that soldiering for the Pittsburgh Steelers.

Now Franco, Rocky and Andy were all more comfortable with themselves and their thoughts. They were more willing to share their stories, talk about their accomplishments, and ask about things they weren't sure about. What amazing careers they had all enjoyed. They knew I would be selective about what I would write. I wasn't out to undermine anyone.

Sam Zaccharias, a long-time friend and business associate of Russell, was seated at the same table, to my left. He was with his wife, Anne. They had just gotten married a few months earlier. Sam had been in my class at the University of Pittsburgh. His first wife, Sophia, had been in my English classes. She had died, suddenly, during the holiday season a few years earlier. I had seen her a few weeks before she died. She looked lovely, as usual, vibrant and in good spirits. She came over to where I was sitting and offered a holiday greeting and a kiss on the cheek. She always made a fuss over me. We had a bond besides that English writing class we'd shared. She was from Braddock and I was from Hazelwood, so our backgrounds were similar. She was pleased that I had become the writer I wanted to be when I was a student in her class at Pitt.

Her death was difficult for Sam and Andy to accept. They missed her dearly. She was a great gal.

Sitting next to Zaccharias was Chuck Puskar. He was in the seat to my immediate left. Puskar had been a partner with Ray Mansfield in the insurance business, operating out of an office in Canonsburg. Mansfield had been Russell's closest friend among his teammates on the Steelers. They traveled the world together searching for new adventures and challenges.

Puskar still talked about Mansfield a lot, and seemed lost without him.

Russell reminded us of how he used to question Cope's football knowledge. He knew Cope knew his football history and had all his stories, but he'd say, "You don't know what a Cover Two defense is."

Cope would come back strong and tell Russell, rightfully so, that no one cared about a Cover Two defense. He didn't want to bore his listeners to death. He wanted to entertain them, inform them, and keep them interested in the action. Cope was colorful. He was never an analyst. Andy tends to over-analyze everything, the way Merril Hoge and Ron Jaworski often do on network television. Tony Romo is the best.

Bleier was just listening and smiling during most of this conversation. He didn't stay as long as the others. But Bleier is always easy company. "I just want everyone to like me," he says. "I'm not sure what's behind that."

Rocky shared a story with me a few weeks earlier that had stayed with me. He said a friend of his told him, "You know I always wondered what people thought about me. Now I realize that they're not thinking about me."

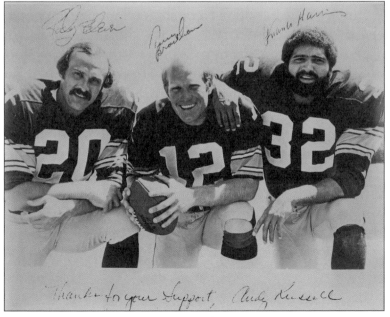

Dick Goetz

Whistling through a cemetery

Dick Goetz is the son of the late owner of the Pittsburgh Sports Shop, Joe Goetz, who was a dear friend of Art Rooney, and supplied sports equipment to the Steelers for many years. Dick often visits a cemetery on the North Side—Holy Redeemer Cemetery—where Mr. Rooney and his wife, Kathleen, are buried, as are Dan Rooney and Chuck Noll. Former Pirates owner Barney Dreyfuss is buried in nearby West View Cemetery.

I had Goetz take me to Holy Redeemer Cemetery for a tour in April of 2019. I figured Bernard "Baldy" Regan, the renowned "mayor of the North Side" had to be buried there, but I learned that he is buried at Arlington National Cemetery.

Why was I not surprised? There was never a club Baldy couldn't get into.

Goetz is a good guy, and he lives alone now that his brother and two sisters have passed. He calls me from time to time.

"Rocky and Franco are both good guys in my book," he said. "I can remember vividly the first time I met Rocky Bleier, even though I didn't know it was Rocky Bleier. I was delivering some sports equipment to Tony Parisi and Ralph Berlin, the equipment manager and the team trainer, in the early '70s.

"I am coming down a hallway and I see this guy wearing a white T-shirt, white shorts, and high white socks and white sneakers. He looked preppy to me; whenever I'd see him after that he always looked preppy to me. He had been lifting weights. He said hi, and asked me if I needed any help. I said I didn't, but he said, 'Sure you do,' and he helped me. After that, every time I'd deliver something and saw him, he'd say hi to me, and ask if I needed any help.

"One day, I asked Ralph Berlin, 'Who is that?' He said, 'That's Rocky Bleier.' I said, 'He seems to be a pleasant guy.'"

At the mention of Franco Harris, Goetz goes on to say, "I love Sewickley, such an attractive little town. I used to see Franco at the Sewickley Hotel. It's not really a hotel, just a restaurant and tavern. Franco goes there a lot, I'm told.

"I've seen him there, and I'd say hello as I passed. He'd say hello back and smile. I never stopped to talk to him. My mother taught me not to bother people like that; they get enough of that. So, I feel like I know Rocky better, but I think they are both good guys."

Robert Pavruchak

Art Rooney and his wife Kathleen

Val Jasante & Ray Kemp

Faded memories...
Do the names Ray Kemp and Val Jansante ring a bell?

If they don't this will be a history lesson for you and most of the Steelers' alumni and current players. They should know about these former Steelers who distinguished themselves as players and as coaches.

Fans are always sending me scrapbooks with faded newspaper clippings and photos of players from the past. Kemp and Jansante are in some of those scrapbooks.

Ray Kemp came out of the coal mining community of Cecil, Pennsylvania, in Washington County where he worked in the mines for a year before entering Duquesne University. When the Steelers came into being in 1933 as the Pittsburgh Pirates, Kemp was a two-way end and was the first African-American to play for the Pittsburgh pro team and one of two black players in the National Football League.

Joe Lillard of the St. Louis Cardinals was the other African-American player in the NFL. I firmly believe the Steelers had another black player on the team. If you would check out the team photo of the 1933 Pirates of the NFL, I think you would find him as well. But more about that later.

Kemp was turned away from a New York hotel where the Pirates were staying while playing the Football Giants. The NAACP urged Kemp to file a law suit for discrimination, but he didn't because he didn't want to cause any uproar. There would be no blacks in the NFL for the next 13 years, until 1946, and it is believed that Art Rooney went along with the other NFL owners in an informal ban of black ballplayers.

I had a chance sometime in the '80s to introduce myself and talk to Ray Kemp in Joe Costanza's popular restaurant in McKees Rocks. Kemp coached at Duquesne University and at Bluefield State.

I first met Valerio R. Vansante in my freshman year (1956) at Central Catholic High School in Oakland. He was the head football coach at Central. He cut me after the first day of practice, after we ran in circles around the field in the rear of the school. Jansante recognized a sportswriter when he saw one.

As a kid, I collected football cards and always loved the name Val Jansante. The Steelers had some players with some great names in those days, short hard-hitting names such as Joe Geri, Bill McPeak, Bobby Gage, Jim Finks, Pat Brady, Dale Dodrill, Ernie Stautner, Ray Mathews, George Tarasovic, Bill Walsh, Elbie Nickel, Jack Butler, Jack O'Brien, Lou Tepe, Fran Rogel, Willie McClung, Bill Priatko, Gary Glick, Richie McCabe John Nisby, Jerry Nuzum and Jack "Goose" McClairen. Another name I loved was Lynn Chandnois.

Jansante was a good one. He was a two-way end and he led the Steelers in receiving five straight years, a team record until Hines Ward came along and led the Steelers in receiving for six straight years. Ward eclipsed Jansante's record in 2007.

I introduced Ward to Jansante one night when

Val Jansante

the Steelers' basketball team was playing a game in the off-season at the Bethel Park High School gym. Jansante's son, Zeb, was the principal of the high school and had brought his dad to see the Steelers in action as basketball players.

Jansante lived his entire life in Bentleyville, Washington County. When the Steelers traded him to the Green Bay Packers midway through his seventh season. Jansante turned down an offer to stay another year with the Packers because he was "homesick" for Bentleyville.

Kemp and Jansante both played in the days of leather helmets, no logos, no face masks. When Kemp was at Duquesne, his coach was Elmer Layden, once a member of the famed "Four Horsemen of Notre Dame." Layden later hired Kemp as an assistant coach at Duquesne, before Layden became the commissioner of the National Football League. Kemp was always referred to in those newspaper clippings as "a class act," just like Joe Louis and Jackie Robinson.

Kemp came to mind in early spring of 2019 when I attended a fund-raiser for Judge Traci McDonald Kemp at the Pepsi Cola Roadhouse in Burgettstown, not far from Bentleyville and Cecil.

When I said hello to Judge Kemp, I asked her if her husband was related by chance to Ray Kemp. She smiled and said he was, indeed, that Ray Kemp was her husband's late uncle. "And he was the first African-American to play for the Steelers, who were then called the Pirates," said Judge Kemp.

I had met Judge Kemp a month earlier at another fund-raiser, this one for challenged women, at Bella Sera's Banquet Hall in Canonsburg.

Her proud father, Jim "Cookie" McDonald, a man of stature in Washington County, had invited my wife

Kathie and I to attend a "fun evening to support his daughter's campaign for Court of Common Pleas Judge."

I was impressed with the straight-forward message she delivered that night as to what everyone in attendance should tell their family and friends about her, and why they should vote for her. It was refreshing in this day of cut-throat campaigning for political positions on every level.

A ticket for a family cost only $25, there was free beer and soda drinks, plus a fine buffet dinner. The real draw might have been Mel Blount & Friends from his Steelers' days. Blount is a most recognizable figure in Western Pennsylvania. He operates a boys' home for challenged at-risk kids in Claysville, Washington County. He stands out above the crowd with his signature white cowboy hat. He rides horses every day at his ranch so he is a real cowboy.

His friends included John Banaszak, Craig Bingham, Mike Wagner, Robin Cole and Louis Lipps. Banaszak's son, Jay, who was running for a district judgeship, was also present. A shiny Steelers helmet, with all their autographs plus that of Mel's close friend, Joe Greene, went for $2,000 at an auction where four footballs signed by the Steelers in attendance went for about $400 apiece.

Kemp and Jansante both stood on the sideline as honorary captains at Heinz Field for the Steelers' home opener in 2001. It was a proud moment for both. The couple that was sitting across the table from us said they were from Bentleyville. I asked them if they knew Val Jansante. They did not. They remembered a Steelers' defensive back—Ike Taylor—speaking once at their church.

I asked Blount & Friends if they were familiar with the names Ray Kemp and Val Jansante, but none of them did. They had blank looks in their respective eyes. Shame on them.

401

* * *

Earlier that same day, I had hosted a Good Guys luncheon at Atria's Restaurant & Tavern in McMurray, less than an hour's drive from the Pepsi-Cola Roadhouse, and Andy Russell was present. Russell played in seven Pro Bowls and was the captain of the Steelers during a similar span. He has been a big success in business ever since his playing days.

He had just been on a cruise with his wife Cindy and many members of the current Steelers' team along with Steelers' fans who paid to be part of the event. "Most of the current players don't know me, and they asked me what I did for the Steelers' organization to be on such a cruise," said Russell.

"They looked at me, at 76, and figured I couldn't have been a ballplayer."

Jim O'Brien

Mel Blount, John Banaszak, Mike Wagner and Judge Traci McDonald-Kemp at Pepsi Cola Road House.

Wes Lyons, a 6-7 tight end for the Steelers in 2010 and 2011, first as a player and then as a member of the reserve squad, was at the same luncheon. Lyons continues to play on the Steelers' basketball team, naturally, and he directs a program to assist at-risk kids in conducting themselves properly, and operates Cakery Square at the Waterfront in Homestead.

Lyons grew up in North Braddock and starred in football for George Novak at Woodland Hills High School and at West Virginia University. He signed a two-year contract to play for the Steelers upon graduation from WVU.

"I had two parents and I had the guidance many of my friends didn't have, and that many of these kids that I am dealing with don't have today," allowed Lyons, one of the nicest young men, at 30, I have ever met in my travels.

"My dad kept me busy, running up and down hills when I was a kid, and my parents provided me with a stable and safe environment. The kids who chose to follow the wrong models in our community always liked me and supported what I was doing, even though they didn't do what I was doing.

"I want to help kids get jobs and live good lives."

Lyons credited Coach Novak for giving him good guidance and a supportive family at school.

Lyons said he often visits with Franco Harris, who has been in the bakery business for over a decade and draws upon Franco's experience and knowledge to improve his own business. "I was with the Steelers only a short time," allows Lyons, "but I get invited to a lot of their events because I maintained contact with the guys. They all have helped my growth.

"I had a vision of what I wanted to be when I was young and I moved in that direction."

Mel Blount & Friends continue to lend a helping hand to worthwhile causes when asked to do so.

Mike Wagner always had an enlightening perspective on things and when I told him I thought he and Randy Grossman were two of the most intelligent players on the team, he said, "We had a lot of smart guys. Jack Lambert was smart and Jack Ham had an unreal memory. Andy Russell, John Stallworth, Lynn Swann, Larry Brown and J.T. Thomas were all smart. Donnie Shell was smart and spiritual. There were others."

Ray Kemp. The pride of Cecil, Pa. and the first black to play for Steelers when they were known as the Pittsburgh Pirates in 1933.

Red might have been black *see page 93*

Christian "Red" Kelsch was a charter member of the Pittsburgh Pirates in 1933, before they were renamed the Steelers. He had grown up as an orphan on Troy Hill, the highest point on the city's North Side, and played sandlot baseball and football. He was also called Mose. He was 36 years old in 1933, the oldest player in the National Football League. He was a placekicker and running back for the Pirates. Before that, he had played for several sandlot football teams sponsored by Art Rooney, namely the Hope-Harveys, James P. Rooneys, and Majestic Radio. Many people have been asked to check out the team photo of the 1933 Pirates and asked if they could find a second black ballplayer besides Ray Kemp. Everyone pointed quickly to Red Kelsch. They included Louis Lipps, J.T. Thomas, Dwayne Woodruff, Robin Cole and Randy Grossman. I received a phone call from a woman who said she was related to Red Kelsch and that he was an African-American. He died in an auto crash near West View Park on July 13, 1935 at the age of 38. Art Rooney served as a pallbearer at his funeral in the home of Red's sister.

Aaron Smith

"I slept with a baseball bat under my pillow."

Aaron Smith was among the former Steelers who roasted Casey Hampton at the 21st Mel Blount Celebrity Roast at Heinz Field on Friday evening, April 5, 2019. Smith was a surprise in his comedic efforts because he had been the strong, silent type when he was a defensive end for the team. But he was so funny in the way he tortured his teammate.

He told a few fat jokes and added some personal reflections on the man known as "Big Snack."

I had not seen Smith in a long time. When I was writing *Steeler Stuff* in 2007, I had not planned on interviewing Smith. One day he said hello to me in the locker room and struck me by how friendly he was, and I asked him if I could interview him for my book.

"How big is your book?" he asked me. That was the first time anyone has asked me that question.

"Why do you ask?" I replied with a question of my own.

"Because I have a long story."

It turned out to be one of the best, shockingly candid chapters in any of my books about the Steelers. It's worth revisiting.

Seeing Smith at the Blount dinner reminded me of seeing him in the same room at Heinz Field 13 years earlier.

I saw Aaron Smith signing autographs at a fund-raising luncheon in early October of 2006 and I had to smile. Smith was one of several Steelers, past and present, who was lending his support for a fund-raising luncheon to benefit Holy Family Institute at the Heinz Field East Club Lounge.

Holy Family Institute looks after children who are neglected or abused. It's been a pet project for many years of the Rooney family that owns the Steelers. This was the 14th annual Arthur J. Rooney Sr. Courage House Luncheon. Greta Rooney, the wife of Steelers' president Art Rooney II, chairs the event.

Smith knows just what it's like for many of the children who benefit from the programs and support offered by Holy Family Institute. A few weeks earlier, Smith appeared at a fund-raising event for the Auberle Foundation in McKeesport, which looks after the same kind of challenged children. Smith was the starting defensive end for the Steelers, and one of the stalwarts of the squad.

I would later see him participating along with other Steelers, including Ike Taylor and Charlie Batch, at a fund-raising affair for Every Child, Inc., at Dave & Buster's at The Waterfront in Homestead. Every Child, Inc. is an East Liberty-based organization that assists hard-to-place children to find foster and adoptive homes.

Smith has a passion for helping such institutions and the kids they care for. "We lived in a trailer park," Smith said, sitting with me in a one-on-one session at the cafeteria at the Steelers' complex at the UPMC Sports campus. He told me some stories that raised the hair on the back of my neck because they were so candid and revealing. "We were the family that got the Christmas turkeys, the government cheese, welfare coupons. Things were often tough."

I have spoken to many Steelers about some of the challenges they encountered as kids. It's the theme in my book, *Steeler Stuff*. Such stories are a passion of mine. I am interested in knowing where pro athletes come from, what their family life was like, and how they got from there to here. How did they succeed?

Who helped them along the way? I have always been more interested in these stories, about these people who play sports, than I was in the games themselves.

When I was in high school, I loved to read books about athletes who had overcome one kind of adversity or another to succeed. Now I write those comeback stories. At the Blount dinner, I realized that the Steelers who won two Super Bowls—XL and XLIII— might have been just as special as the Steelers of the '70s. They, too, share a special bond and genuinely still care about one another.

Alan Faneca, for instance, found out he had epilepsy when he was 14. Kendall Simmons has to poke himself with needles every day to deal with his diabetes. Troy Polamalu had to move from his parents' home to relatives' home in another state as a child because he was getting into serious trouble in the mean streets of Los Angeles.

Aaron Smith had a father who stood 6-4, and weighed about 250 pounds, and was having a tough time dealing with diabetes. It turned him into a menacing and difficult dad. He was a mean drunk and Aaron and the family feared him.

None of the Steelers have stories as horrific as Aaron Smith's story. "I can't remember when my father wasn't swearing at us. I thought it was the American way," said Smith, now in his eighth NFL season.

Smith has a long, often stoic face, like one of those carved stone faces on Easter Island. He is even more chiseled today because he has dropped the weight he needed to play defensive end in the National Football League. He played 11 seasons (1999-2011) for the Steelers and was good enough to be on the *Sports Illustrated* team of the decade (2000s). As a kid, his face was even longer because he was often sad. His home was hardly a haven. In truth, it was a dangerous place.

"I was 12 when my mother divorced my dad," said Smith as a starter for his compelling story. "I remember that my mom called my oldest brother, David, and had him get all the firearms out of the house before she told my dad what she was doing. She was worried about what he might do. He scared all of us.

"When I was eight, nine and ten, I was so angry with my father. I told him every night I loved him because I was afraid he'd kill us, and I thought maybe he'd spare me if I told him I loved him. I slept with a baseball bat in my bed in case I had to protect myself.

"My dad's name was Harold Smith. He died when I was 16. He had a heart attack and died in bed. He died alone. I saw him four to six months before he died. I went to my grandmother's house for some family function, and he was there. He stood up to hug me, and I walked right past him. Talk about guilt. I thought about that a long time after he died."

Aaron and his wife, Jaimie, live year-round in Pittsburgh's North Hills. Smith has served in recent years as an assistant coach for basketball—his first love—and football at North Allegheny High School. He and his wife Jaimie have five children.

When the kids were little, Aaron's mother moved in with them to help out with her grandchildren.

"It's good to have her here," said Smith back then. "She's been a big help, and I just want to help her have a better life. She didn't deserve the life we led in that trailer camp out in Colorado. Things are fine now. I think anyone who has ever accomplished anything had to overcome some kind of adversity"

I thought I was hearing a confession instead of conducting an interview when I spoke with Smith. I couldn't believe how candid he was, how trusting with his heartfelt disclosure. I'm not sure I'd have shared such stories with anyone. My dad drank too much and smoked too much, and he was not home as much as he should have been. But he loved us and he was never in my face. He didn't hit anyone in our home. He had a good sense of humor. I realized how lucky I was by comparison to Smith's experience.

When I later ran into Smith when he was out supporting one of the charity fund-raisers close to his heart, he came over to say hello. I extended my hand to shake his, but he brushed that aside. "Hey, give me a hug," he said with a bright smile. "Hugs are good." I could not have agreed more with Smith's observation.

I thought about that hug later. Maybe Aaron Smith appreciates anybody who likes him and anybody he truly can trust.

Aaron Smith at St. Vincent of Latrobe training camp.

Aaron Smith rushes passer against Cleveland Browns.

Antonio Brown

Never enough attention to satisfy star receiver

Here is a story about Antonio Brown, the former Steelers' sensational and controversial star receiver who is now with the Raiders. It is one you have not heard or read before because I was the only writer aware of what he did this one day during his second season with the Steelers.

I was charmed by Brown the moment I met him, just inside the entry to Hometowne Sports at Station Square, a must-stop for visiting Steelers' fans to refresh their black and gold game uniforms, not complete without Myron Cope's iconic Terrible Towel on the hip.

For starters, Brown is a shade under 5-10, so at 5-8½, I could look him in the eyes without craning my neck. He was in the midst of a break-out season, as a receiver and kick-returner, the first in NFL history to top 1,000 yards in each category. He was a fan favorite. I prefer players my size. Makes my job easier.

You had to love Antonio Brown. But I soon grew tired of his histrionics, both on and off the field. It's hard to admire a man who fathered five children to three different women, none of whom he married. It's hard to learn about integrity if you grew up in the Liberty City community of Miami.

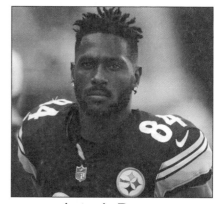

Antonio Brown

His behavior, as well as that of Le'Veon Bell and Roethlisberger, prompted Nancy Cardiello, who has been cutting my hair for nearly 40 years, to ask me, "Do the Rooneys still own the Steelers?"

The Steelers had set the bar high, but players were no longer held to it.

Speaking of haircuts, how about that Antonio Brown look? I'll bet he pays either $500 for that haircut or gets it for free. With his sports coats he could fill in with the Five Satins. His hair looked like it had been cut by hedge clippers before they cleaned up his act for his press conference in Oakland.

* * *

Brown showed up on a cold and dreary Saturday afternoon in the winter of 2011 to sign autographs, his first appearance at the store often referred to as "Steelers' Heaven," which has since relocated on East Carson Street in the heart of the city's South Side. The Steelers share a UPMC training complex nearby, along the Monongahela River, with the University of Pittsburgh football team.

Antonio was admired there for his work ethic. He was said to be one of the hardest-working players on his team. He was already making big money and would soon sign contracts that made him a multi-millionaire. He had it made. Only he didn't know that. That handsome smiling face and gleaming eyes landed him TV gigs and commercials for giants such as Pepsi.

You didn't see him or the Steelers in the 2018 NFL playoffs, but you did see him in a Pepsi commercial, sitting in a hot tub, smiling away, while taking a "selfie" with his Smartphone. It's an image that will stay with us. It's not Mean Joe Greene tossing his jersey to an adoring young fan in a stadium hallway, but it's pretty good.

Antonio Brown signed 135 autographs that afternoon for $35 per autograph. My friend Gene Musial kept count. All that money went to Brown. The store's owner Frank Meyer sold ballcaps and towels and photos, and took his share from that pot. So, Brown's share amounted to $4,725, income I am sure—sure—he reported to the IRS on his 2011 income tax filing.

I sat at a table on the other side of the store entrance, signing copies of my books about the Steelers. Brown, by far, had the longer line.

He showed up with a personal parade of about five or six friends, all football-playing sized friends, many of whom nodded when customers asked them if they played for the Steelers. For the record, none of them played for the Steelers.

They were the Great Pretenders.

They were all bigger than Brown, and an imposing sight. He had to feel safer in their company then he did when he was returning punts and kickoffs and catching passes from Ben Roethlisberger. They might have been in the early stages of being the best pass-and-catch combination in the league.

I go back to collecting bubble gum cards of the Steelers in the late 1940s, and I have seen them all, from Elbie Nickel, Jack Butler and Val Jansante to John Stallworth and Lynn Swann, Louis Lipps, Hines Ward and Santonio Holmes, and I can say unequivocally that Brown is the best catch-and-run receiver in Steelers' history. He can catch the ball as well as any of them, but it's what he does after he grabs the ball that sets him apart from the pack. The NFL changed the rules relating to defensive play and what was permitted and they freed receivers like Brown to make more catches than ever.

I don't know how he split shares of that money he got for signing autographs that Saturday afternoon, but he had to come away with at least $4,500 for himself. All cash.

He grew up in the Liberty City section of Miami and I went there a few times when I was writing for *The Miami News* and covering the Miami Dolphins. Larry Little, an offensive lineman who would one day be honored in the Pro Football Hall of Fame, took me to Liberty City, not far from his boyhood neighborhood. His younger brother David would play linebacker for the Steelers when they were my beat at *The Pittsburgh Press.*

Let's just say neither of the Littles nor Brown came from money. That might explain when Brown called back the next morning to a staffer at Hometown Sports and asked if he could stop by later in the day to sign more autographs.

The Steelers had a 4 o'clock game that afternoon at Heinz Field, and Brown figured he could kill some down time by picking up $35 per autograph, just a short boat ride from Heinz Field.

Meyer told Brown he didn't think his coach, Mike Tomlin, would be in favor of that, signing autographs before he played football that afternoon.

Brown was disappointed to say the least. Not many have shinier dark eyes than Antonio Brown, and I saw a gleam in those eyes when Frank Meyer counted out his money the day before. I know the feeling. When you didn't have much money as a youngster it's exciting to feel real money. He might have signed a contract calling for millions each season, but this money—in his hand—was real money.

He liked the feeling.

Brown has gone on to make a lot more money. He is one of the best paid receivers in the game. As long as there are other receivers who make more money than he does, Brown will not be satisfied. It's the same way with Le'Veon Bell. Plus, he will find a way to spend all his money before he is 60. He came to camp in 2017 in a custom-made black and gold Rolls Royce and in 2018 in a helicopter. The Steelers had a stellar receiver named Plaxico Burris who had five luxury cars in his Coraopolis driveway. He banged up one of them in an accident and learned he had not kept up the insurance on the car. You have to be responsible to take care of stuff like that. Burris ended up in prison after shooting himself in the leg with a hidden pistol he was carrying. One year, when Jack Lambert was holding out over salary, Chuck Noll said, "Excess will kill the NFL!"

* * *

Brown was not voted to playing in the Pro Bowl in 2018. It would have been his eighth Pro Bowl. The panel that picks the teams punished Brown for abandoning the Steelers and skipping practice prior to a must-win 16th game against the Cincinnati Bengals.

Tomlin benched Brown for that season finale. He could have suspended him and taken away his final game paycheck.

Brown was upset because his teammates bypassed him in favor of Ju Ju Smith-Schuster in the voting for team MVP. Brown had caught 104 passes for 1,297 yards and an NFL-high 15 touchdowns, yet he did not make the All-Pro team. Brown was replaced in the Pro Bowl by Ju Ju.

Bell and Brown both sabotaged the team's chances of playing in the AFC championship and the Super Bowl two weeks after that. The team had the talent with those two to go all the way. They became "The Killer Bs" in the worst way. Brown got into it with Ben—the other B—in the clubhouse the week before the Bengals' game. Brown also got into trouble with the law in Florida when he threw furniture off his condo porch and nearly killed a child. He also claimed that someone stole $80,000 from his room. Who in their right mind travels with that kind of money? I'll bet it was an inside job, if it happened at all.

There will be a day when fans won't be willing to shell out $35 for Brown's autograph, and I know the price has gone up in more recent years. I sat with Santonio Holmes, the hero of the Steelers' Super Bowl victory against the Arizona Cardinals in 2010, and we both went largely ignored at the Vintage Grand Prix event at Schenley Park.

My granddaughters, Margaret, 14, and Susannah, ten, surprised me in 2018 when I asked them what they wanted for Christmas. Keep in mind they live in Columbus, Ohio.

They told me they both wanted the Steelers' jersey of Ju Ju Smith-Schuster. When I told a friend about this, he said, "My grandson lives in Ohio and he asked me for the same thing."

I was able to buy both jerseys at Hometowne Sports.

Antonio Brown can't stand sharing the spotlight, or losing it, with Ju Ju Smith-Schuster. As John Banaszak, one of the Steelers' old guard, put it, "Antonio Brown is a spoiled brat."

Ju Ju Smith-Schuster

FRANCO

Linda the librarian finds Franco
At the Heinz History Center

Through the years, I have met many people who have shared stories about finding themselves on an elevator with famous individuals, all by chance, but meetings they will forever remember.

Linda Raub Esposito is such a person. She is a children's librarian at the Peters Township Library, with whom I conduct writing workshops for children who enjoy reading books.

"What children's librarian—especially one from Pittsburgh—would miss the opportunity to attend the 'launching' of the book *The Good Neighbor: The Life and Work of Fred Rogers* by Maxwell King," asked Linda.

"This event was taking place at the Heinz History Center on Tuesday evening, September 4, 2018. Pumped up to see the Mr. Rogers display before attending the program, my husband, Tim Silbagh, and I spent some time exploring. We were on the second floor and decided to go back to see what we missed on the first floor.

"The door of the elevator opened and I gasped. Franco Harris, one of my sports heroes, was on the elevator. 'You are Franco Harris,' I said hesitantly. He said he was, indeed, Franco Harris and he smiled brightly and said hello. For a gabby person, I was lost for words. Franco couldn't have been more patient and kinder during an elevator ride. It felt like the elevator ride lasted hours instead of two minutes.

"You have to realize I have been a Steelers' fan since high school in the '70s. I have season tickets, watch every game and even take the Terrible Towel with me on all of my trips.

"When we reached the first floor and the elevator emptied, Franco didn't go running away from me like he was chasing that football for 'The Immaculate Reception.' He was not annoyed when I asked if we could take a picture. We got a few pictures, a handshake, a big hug, a smile.

"I remained frozen on the first floor with thoughts of just meeting a Steelers' superstar and my football hero, Franco Harris. I shouted it out to my family and friends. What a wonderful and memorable experience."

Linda, Franco and Tim

Troy Polamalu

A different breed of cat

*"He seems too nice
to be a pro football player."*

Let me tell you my story about Troy Polamalu. You already know what kind of a ballplayer he was, a defensive demon, something of a Tazmanian Devil on the football field, racing here, there and everywhere. Torpedoing people left and right. That long black hair flowing out from under his helmet and draping his shoulder pads like a black cape. He's a Polynesian version of Darth Vader.

There were times you wanted him to cut that hair—you hated that look on opposing players—but you got used to it, and it became part of Polamalu's persona. He was from another world, or so it seemed.

Polamalu is a deeply private man, yet he commands your attention. He does so in the best way, not the way Terrel Owens and Chad Johnson do, not with a big mouth and look-at-me theatrics. He's no jerk, just the opposite. It would be nice if the National Football League had more like him. Opposing quarterbacks can't keep their eyes off Troy Polamalu, and Pittsburgh football fans learned fast that he was the catalyst for much of what happened in a positive way when the other team had the ball. He was the Steelers' strong safety, but there were times you might think he was a linebacker, an end, and a nose tackle.

There are times when he appeared to be a running back in the other team's backfield. He seemed to know just when the ball would be snapped. And boy could he run whenever he got his hands on the football.

Polamalu became one of the most popular sports figures in Pittsburgh, and his jersey one of the best-selling ones around the country.

*　*　*

He was the Steelers' No. 1 draft choice out of Southern Cal in 2003. He didn't do much for the Steelers in his rookie season, playing mostly as a nickel-back in obvious passing situations, Long-time fans might have suspected the Steelers had selected another stiff from USC, recalling an offensive tackle named Mike Taylor they took on the first round back in 1968, in Bill Austin's last season as head coach. Austin, a Vince Lombardi protégé in Green Bay, gave way the next year to Chuck Noll, and long-suffering fans were finally rewarded with a coach who knew what he was doing, and would, in time, deliver solid contenders and, eventually, championship teams.

It was difficult to assess Polamalu at his first Steelers' training camp at St. Vincent College that summer of 2003. The following summer, there were stories coming out of the camp that Polamalu was impressive in drills, and looked like the real deal. Polamalu was a promising prospect after all. I paid a visit toward the end of that summer session, and I traveled to Latrobe hoping I might be able to interview Troy Polamalu. He sounded like an intriguing individual.

*　*　*

When I covered the Steelers for *The Pittsburgh Press* from 1979 through 1983 it was easy to interview whomever you wanted to talk to at the Steelers' training camp. You'd catch a player coming off the practice field and ask him if you could come up to his dorm room at Bonaventure Hall during the break. You could sit at his bedside while he relaxed and stretched his legs, and talk to him for a half-hour or so, just a casual conversation. You could get a better read on a guy, checking out his simple surroundings, maybe spotting a book or two, or some music tapes, a clue to his interests, something to start a conversation. No rush.

The rules had changed, however, during the days after Chuck Noll gave way to Bill Cowher, and now it is like moving around a concentration camp. You had to have a media badge. You were constantly checked for your credentials by an army of security guards, and there were barriers wherever you went. You had to check with the team's public relations staff to see if it was all right to see one of the Steelers, and you might get ten minutes of his time, stopping him on a sidewalk as he was going to lunch in one of the campus cafeterias. Sound bites don't work when you're writing a book.

Let's just say it was different. The same can be said for Troy Polamalu. He's just different, that's all, different from most football players you've met through the years, different from the Dolphins, the Jets and the Giants you'd met and interviewed while covering teams in Miami, New York and then back home in Pittsburgh through the years. I was used to traveling on airplanes and buses with the ballclubs I covered. You could get to know the guys better, and you could sort out what to write and what not to write. You didn't want to rock the boat or the bus—though I did at times—and kill off news sources or willing subjects.

*   *   *

It was Tuesday, August 10, 2004, two days before my 37th wedding anniversary, when I was walking across the campus at St. Vincent College, heading for lunch with the Steelers. As I was walking by myself, I was suddenly aware of someone at my left side. I glanced over, and lo and behold, it was Troy Polamalu. Was this a chance meeting, or had my prayers been answered? We'd never met, so I introduced myself, told him I was working on a book, and wanted to do an interview. Perhaps after lunch.

"Let's do it now," said Polamalu. He pointed to a bench where we might sit and talk. It was perfect. It was off the beaten path. There was lots of shrubbery and it was like a grotto. We sat on a wooden bench where I'd seen the Benedictine priests who teach and work at St. Vincent sit and relax, and perhaps say some prayers. I liked the privacy. I didn't want any of the other writers to see me talking to Troy Polamalu. I didn't want to share him. I prefer one-on-one interviews to the mob scene where one guy asks all the questions and the rest get the answers on their tape recorders or communication devices. Besides, I hadn't cleared the interview with the p.r. staff. Shame on me.

Jason Gildon, a veteran linebacker, drove by on his bicycle and waved to Troy. Squirrels scurried under the surrounding shrubbery and raced up tree trunks. We were in the shade on a warm, sunny day.

Polamalu was so pleasant. At one point, trying not to keep him from eating, I asked him if he wanted to continue our interview after lunch. He said it was okay to continue. He had time. He even met me after lunch and accompanied me to a site where I thought I could take some good photographs of him. Polamalu posed for me. He couldn't have been more obliging. Yet he seemed shy, and not one seeking the spotlight. I'd watched him doing television interviews and he had seemed uncomfortable with a camera pointed his way, and microphone pushed toward his handsome face.

At one point, when we were talking about the Rooney family that owned and operated the Steelers, I explained that Dan Rooney, the team's president at

Troy all smiles.

Troy Palamalu at St. Vincent.

the time, was the oldest of five sons of team founder Art Rooney. That's how the leadership baton had been passed on to him.

"That's how they do it in Samoa," said Polamalu, who was born to Samoan parents in Garden Grove, California on August 19, 1981. I celebrated my 39th birthday the next day, more than likely when I was covering the Steelers' training camp at St. Vincent College. I had one other meeting with Polamalu at the camp a few days later. I gave him a copy of the new University of Southern California football guide I had received in the mail. Polamalu was pictured in the thick guide, and mentioned in several places. He seemed pleased to get this gift.

I watched him during warm-up drills, when the assistant coaches were leading the players through their exercises, to limber them up. Polamalu never seemed to be doing what everyone else was doing. He had his own routine. Normally, this wouldn't be permitted. Jock Sutherland, who coached at Pitt in the '30s and then with the Steelers, must have been spinning in his grave. With Jock Sutherland, a stern, dour disciplinarian, there was only one way, and it was his way.

Bill Cowher made concessions for Polamalu. It took him awhile to get with it, but Cowher came to the same conclusion about Polamalu as most people who've met him. He's just different, that's all.

Polamalu was so pleasant and soft-spoken, and deeper in his ideas and reflections than most players. There was a strong spiritual side to him. He seemed almost too sweet. I remember coming home that night and sharing my day with my wife Kathie. I told her about Troy Polamalu. I said he didn't seem tough enough to be a pro football player. "He seems too nice to be a pro football player," I said. I was wrong. He was a different breed of cat.

John Stallworth was that way, deeply spiritual, such a pleasant fellow, but offering his thoughts with a squeaky voice. You should hear Terry Bradshaw imitate Stallworth's speech. Stallworth was certainly tough enough to play pro ball. He stayed 14 seasons (1974-1987). I'd gone to Canton in the summer of 2002 to see Stallworth inducted into the Pro Football Hall of Fame.

Sometime in December 2004, at the height of the Christmas season, I was doing a book signing at Waldenbooks in the center of the first floor at Monroeville Mall when Troy Polamalu approached me with a big smile and said hello. There was a beautiful woman at his side, and he introduced her. Her name was Isadora, and she was his fiancée. She looked like one of those native beauties from the South Seas you've seen in movies, or an animated Disney production.

Troy Polamalu had met me twice. I wasn't a regular on the Steelers' beat. It was so surprising that he remembered me and more surprising that he stopped to say hello. Then he introduced his girl friend. Polamalu seemed proud to do so. This seems like common social behavior, but it's not, not for football players, not for professional athletes.

About ten minutes later, I looked up and caught sight of Polamalu across the way, and he waved to me. About a half-hour later, Polamalu approached my table once more and placed a steaming hot Cinnabun on my table. He didn't say a word this time. He just put the treat there, an early Christmas gift, and smiled and walked away. Polamalu was a real prince in my eyes, a handsome Samoan prince.

> *"The offspring of birds are fed with flower nectar, but the children of men are nurtured with words."*
> —Samoan saying

Troy Polamalu:

"I'm a sunshine kind of guy."

Who am I? I'm still hoping to figure that out. What do I want to be known as? There have been a lot of great players here, like Terry Bradshaw. I hear a lot about Carnell Lake, and what a class guy he was. I hear about those big names. I would love to be known along with those great people.

The spiritual side of me is important too. My own Christian beliefs. Some people are good at sports. Like Frank Thomas is good. M.J. or Michael Jordan is good. And Terry Bradshaw. I'm aware of their personal lives and they all had struggles of different sorts. They made a commitment to be great. I want to be great like that. But I don't want to sacrifice my personal life. I want to be able to move around and enjoy myself without attracting a crowd. I want to have my own life. It doesn't matter whether you're a baseball player, a basketball player or a football player...you lose some of your own life. Sometimes you lose your way, like what happened to O.J. Simpson. He went to Southern Cal and he was so great, and so many people loved him. He had it all. And he lost it just as fast. What happened to O.J. Simpson? No one can make any sense of that.

For me, when I was growing up, I gave up plenty of things. I had hard discipline rules. I grew up with my own family till age 8. I lived in a Samoan community. There are more Samoans in Southern California than there are in Samoa. Some families have lost the Samoan culture. I moved from Southern California to Oregon. I was there from 9 till I graduated from high school. I lived with my aunt and uncle all that time. He was very hard on me. The head of a Samoan family has a title. He is the head of all the siblings. There is a Samoan word for it. He is the *Matai* of our family. I am the son of Suila Polamalu. I was the next oldest of her 12 children.

Religion was important. Jesus Christ is my savior. I'm very family-oriented.

I looked up to Junior Seau when I was coming along as a ballplayer. He had played at UCLA and he was outstanding with the San Diego Chargers. He said some things that were pretty much true about his strict upbringing, and people in Samoa didn't like him for it. You have to be careful about what you say. I really look up to him for what he's done and what he's accomplished. Another famous Samoan in pro football was Jack Thompson—the "Throwin' Samoan"—who came out of Washington State to play in the NFL.

I got into trouble when I was real young. I was hanging out with the wrong guys in Santa Ana. That's when I was sent to Oregon to live with relatives. My father's name was Troy Aumua. He's still alive, but he's not a part of my life. That was a struggle for me also. I tried to reestablish that relationship. My Christian values are such that I would like to forgive and forget.

You mentioned Carnell Lake. He went to UCLA, too. I never heard of him when I was a kid. I never paid much attention to college or pro football. I never liked football. The last thing I'm going to do is sit down and watch ESPN sports highlights. So I have a lack of knowledge in that respect. Some people say I have the opportunities and abilities and attitude to be the next Carnell Lake. From what I know, that's pretty good.

I had a hard time making the adjustment from college to the pros. The longer schedule is tough on your body. It's no secret that NFL players make a lot of money. I never had as much money as I have now. The problem now is I want to do something for God, but I don't know what. I'm not advertising it, but I am sure I will find the right way to do something.

I grew up in a ghetto and was fine with that. God has completely taken me away from my comfort zone. Pittsburgh is not like where I grew up. It's raining here, it's snowing here. I'm a sunshine kind of guy. Football is important here, though, and we have great support.

I am getting a lot of attention but I want to stay humble. I want to sit like an animal alone out in the field. When I am with people I want to be polite and maintain my principles. You want to please God and show him you are grateful for what he has given you. He made so many sacrifices for us, even sacrificing his life.

People say I am like two different people, the nice guy off the field and a hard-hitting guy on the field. I'm a little ill at ease about that. I don't see two different people when I see myself in the mirror. I'm going to be fully committed to something.

USC was my favorite school growing up. My uncle played football there and I grew up as a USC fan. I'm trying to learn to be a Pittsburgh Steelers fan, and what that's all about.

I'm a guy who goes in the back door up here. I'm not seeking attention. I've walked through some of these buildings. They're very spiritual. I'm very comfortable here. It usually takes me a while to get comfortable. By nature, I'm a loner.

I'm not the type who is comfortable in most social settings. I sit back and watch. I have fun watching people have fun. I'm a stay-at-home-and-watch-TV kind of guy. I don't have a dark side.

The Pittsburgh Steelers are not going to put any more pressure on me to succeed than I'm going to put on myself. Most of the reading I do is Scripture. I like to read my Bible. It's hard to be away from home. So I read, and lose myself, trying to learn. Jesus preaches peace. I don't understand why there is so much killing in the name of religion. People think they have to kill somebody to defend their own beliefs. If you really know the Bible you'll know that's not right. That's not God's plan.

The Eucharist is the symbol of Jesus. I believe that. I'm just worshiping Jesus. I went to a Catholic school and I've gone to Mass. I've been around Mormons much of my life. Many Samoans are Mormons. I'm learning slowly who I am and what I want to be, God willing. I know I'm a Christian. It was good talking to you. God bless you.

Troy with basketball team in locker room.

Troy reading at St. Vincent.

I like to talk to judges when I am not the plaintiff. Judge Jeffery A. Deller is one of my favorites and he tells good stories. He is a huge sports fan and he had great admiration for both Rocky Bleier and Franco Harris.

"They both support a lot of great causes in our city," says Judge Deller, of the U.S. Bankruptcy Court, with offices on the 54th floor of the U.S. Steel Tower. He comes to see me each holiday season when I am signing books for gifts in the lower lobby of the building, next to the YMCA.

"They are not afraid to stand up for what they believe, even when it's not always in their best interest," said Judge Deller. "Franco is out front on a lot of issues, social injustice and when he came to the support of his college coach, Joe Paterno. Rocky is involved in so many causes to support veterans in need, and I have seen him at many meetings that I have attended as well. You can always count on Rocky when it comes to veterans.

"He's overcome a lot in his lifetime, the wounds he suffered in Vietnam, his challenging comeback story, the bankruptcy he went through, a divorce, but he persevered. Franco had the same right stuff.

"One morning when I was coming to work, I was coming up the steps of the City-County Building for an early hearing, and I saw this man sitting on the steps near the statue of Mayor Richard Caliguiri.

"He had a sign with him, but I forget what it said. He looked like a homeless man.

"I approached him, to see if I might help him in some way, and I thought it was Franco Harris, much to my surprise. I asked him if he was Franco and he nodded, and explained his presence.

"Everything OK?" I said to him.

"Yeah, I'm OK," he said.

"He was there as part of a protest over the murder of Jonny Gammage, a cousin of the Steelers' Ray Seals, and there was a Ku Klux Klan demonstration going on at the same time on Grant Street. It was a perfect storm."

Jonny Gammage had been visiting Seals from his home in Syracuse, and Seals loaned his dark blue Jaguar to Gammage to get around the city. They were business partners and cousins. Gammage was stopped for driving erratically by police on Rt. 51 in the early hours of the morning, October 12, 1995. Police responded from Baldwin, Brentwood and Overbrook, and five policemen got into a skirmish with Gammage and pinned him to the ground. They brutally beat him and suffocated him. Within seven minutes, Gammage lay dead on the ground.

His last words were, "Keith, I'm 31. I'm only 31!"

I did not learn the identity of Keith, or what that was all about. "He was killed because he was a black man in a fancy car in a white neighborhood," said a spokesman for the Coalition for African-American Justice.

The coroner's report said he died from asphyxiation, from pressure on his chest and neck. The police were charged with manslaughter rather than murder and they were exonerated. This caused an uproar in the black community, similar to the protest that followed the shooting and killing of Antwon Rose of Rankin in 2018 by a police officer, Michael Rosfeld, of the since-disbanded East Pittsburgh police force. A not guilty verdict came in on this incident as well.

Harris was also upset by the Squirrel Hill Massacre in which 11 Jewish members of Tree of Life Synagogue were slain by an angry anti-Semite from Baldwin. "Hate will not prevail in Pittsburgh," he said at a luncheon I hosted in the aftermath.

Franco stands up for American Flag and NFL

Back in September of 2017, Colin Kaepernick and his disciples were causing controversy by taking a knee during the playing of the National Anthem that precedes all NFL games. Harris believed that Kaepernick should have chosen a different venue to make his protest and not involve the NFL.

Harris conceded that the U.S. has some unresolved social issues and they should be addressed. "A person has a right to express his thoughts about issues," he said. "When he puts that uniform on, it's not just about him, and the things he wants to back, and wants to believe in, because the team has to come first.

"I don't think Kaepernick would have been allowed to do what he did on our football team. Joe Greene and Jack Lambert would have put a stop to what he was doing."

J. T. Thomas

He became a football player
for a scary reason

J.T. Thomas told me something in February of 2019 that he had never mentioned to me in many interviews I have had with him over the years. It was a sensational revelation.

This is one you're going to share with family and friends, especially long-standing Steelers' fans.

"My mother used to ask me all the time why I was playing football," said J.T. Thomas. "'You don't really like playing football,' she'd say. 'You prefer to play the piano. So why do you keep doing it?'"

J.T. Thomas couldn't tell his mother what was behind his need to continue playing football.

"I wanted to take out my father," he said. "I was so mad at him for hitting me, for punishing me, and, even more so, for hitting my mother. I was so pissed off at him."

He recalled one exchange he had with his father. "You hit my momma again," he had said, "and I'm going to kill you."

Then something happened to his father.

"He got religion," said J.T. "He started going to church. He stopped drinking so much. He quit misbehaving. He stopped hitting my mother.

"I was so mad at him for this turnabout in his behavior. I was mad at God. I didn't want to go to church anymore. I didn't want to forgive and forget."

In writing this book I came across an aspect of the Steelers I was not looking for, but it gave me cause for reflection. So many of the Steelers were abused by their fathers when they were young. This might merit a serious study. Did this abusive upbringing help develop their instincts for such a violent game?

It made me stop and think about my own upbringing. My father was a pleasant drunk. There were many mean drunks on our street, men, mostly much bigger than my dad, who hit their wives and kids when they were drinking and upset about something.

I gained new appreciation for my dad. He not only didn't hit me, but he never got in my face. He never gave me a hard time.

I must confess that there was a day when he wouldn't stop talking, though I asked him several times to stop talking. He was upsetting me. I called the police and they came to our house and took him to a jail station in The Strip.

When my mom found out what I had done, she had my older brother come home and drive us to the police station jail to retrieve my dad. He didn't hold it against me. Maybe I should be as ashamed as J.T. Thomas to tell you that, but I want to be honest about my own stories. My wife Kathie still can't believe I did this to my dad.

I have had many luncheon meetings with Art Rooney Jr. at the St. Clair Country Club, not far from his office, and I have gotten the impression that his father had been a strict disciplinarian with Art Jr. and his four brothers, Dan, Tim, Pat and John.

* * *

Thomas told me he wanted to write a book about his experiences and the people he'd met along the way during his nine years of service to the Steelers (1973-1981). He worked for the team as a pro scout, checking out future opponents, during that 1979 season when he had to sit out a season because of a rare illness. That was the year before I came on the Steelers' beat after moving from New York to Pittsburgh.

"That was the best season of my stay with the Steelers," he said, somewhat surprisingly. "People ask me if it was bad to miss out on being on a Super Bowl team, but I learned a lot about myself and my team that year.

"The Steelers were a great organization," he said. "They told me I'd have a job with them in the front office if I couldn't resume playing. They looked after me."

"They're living in a roach hotel"

Thomas thinks today's players are in for a shock when their playing days are over. "It will be more difficult for them to make the transition to their post-playing days," he said. "They make so much money now and there's no way they can continue to make that kind of money. They're millionaires at 22 and they get trophy wives and trophy cars and expensive homes, and they're too young to make those kinds of decisions. They're supporting their family and friends and they spend money like there's no tomorrow.

"They're living in a roach hotel."

I told Thomas I wasn't familiar with that phrase. It turns out that it covers a couple of different situations. It can refer to a seedy hotel or dump to stay in, or a roach trap, a device by that name that gives off an alluring aroma and then kills the roach when it enters the little box trap.

"Pro athletes today get drawn in the same way," he said.

He said he wanted to write a book about his days with the Steelers and in the restaurant business. He

J.T. Thomas

was an owner, along with teammate Larry Brown of a regional chain of Applebee's Neighborhood Grill & Restaurants, and later on his own with Red Hot & Blue Southern Grill at the Waterfront in Homestead. Like other restaurants in the latter chain, it has since closed. Thomas has been doing some consulting in the food industry, including marketing frozen desserts. He's into sales and distribution.

He has a title for his book. It's to be called "From the Balcony," and that's a different view on most things. Thomas thinks that different people have different views about things. Many of his teammates saw things differently than he did, and it's that way about politics, sports and religion.

I assured Thomas that he had a good book in him. He just had to write it. He had the most meaningful insights, stories and the ability to tell them well and share his experiences and wisdom with others. He often speaks at church assemblies and school sessions and always has something to offer.

"There used to be cameras focused on us from the end zones, the sidelines and from up above," he explained where he was coming from with his book title. "It's the eye in the sky. It told you what happened on every play in the game. But it looked different sometimes from every angle."

Joe Greene, Chuck Noll and Jerry Olsavsky on sideline at St. Vincent College.

He still has great respect for Chuck Noll. "He was a great communicator," said Thomas, "even though he doesn't get credit much in that category. He communicated differently with every player.

"I think that was Chuck's greatest asset, his ability to communicate. With me, he'd just give me a nod or a shake of the head. With Joe Greene, he'd hold longer conversations. He'd talk to the guys who needed it, pat the ones on the back who needed it, and in Terry Bradshaw's case, even give him a little hug to help him with his confidence. I saw that, but Terry has forgotten that. I think Terry needed reassurance and kudos more than most of us. He needed more love.

"What Chuck gave us that had the most value was to look beyond football. He talked about your life and purpose and your life's work. Football was a slippery stone. He always had you look beyond the game."

"The boy never dies."

Thomas believes too many young people today lack a two-parent family and the proper guidance and role models to set them on the right course. His parents were James and Annie Ruth Thomas. J.T.'s real name is James Thomas Jr.

"My father was physically present," he went on to say, "but he was emotionally absent. He put food on the table, and he made sure you're safe. My father was there; emotionally he wasn't there. I had an older brother, Ken, and he showed me the way in sports and in school.

"Kids need good role models in their own homes. Otherwise, the boy never dies. He never really matures into a man and assumes the responsibilities that go with that, as a father, husband and citizen of the community. We need to learn what path or action to take. What's going on?

"You need to tell stories and show the way. You need to explain what people are talking about, and what it really means. That's one of the biggest problems today. We all need a Chuck Noll in our lives, but it's better if you have that at home and don't have to look for it from the coach of your local sports team, or high school and college teams. Otherwise, the boy never dies."

As a child, J.T. transferred from a Catholic grade school to a public school with that school's first integrated class. He must have liked challenges. He was the first African-American football player at Florida State University.

He was a big fan of the boxer Cassius Clay who became Muhamad Ali, and dared to stand up for himself when he refused to answer the draft call during Vietnam War. Ali wanted no parts of that, like a lot of young men in America at that time, and he lost several years of his prime boxing years. Many Americans were upset with Clay/Ali for doing that, but not J.T. Thomas.

Thomas told Jim Lachimia of *Pittsburgh Magazine* about that experience:

"At the time, segregation was still paramount in the South. So, I knew I wasn't going there just for me. I knew I was paving the way for a lot of people. I was being watched by a lot of people, and I got a lot of support from people in the states of Florida, Georgia and Alabama. It was breaking down a barrier, and people looked at it and said, 'He has to succeed.' We were being told we couldn't compete on the field or academically in the classroom. So failing wasn't an option. That was my mindset. I had to succeed. I was very much aware of my responsibility."

I'm sure Lachimia liked his interview with J.T. Thomas as much as I always have. He always has something worthwhile to say.

"There was a commitment to excellence," Thomas told him. "Conditioning was important to Chuck. If you weren't in good shape, he didn't want you around. Even the defensive backs had to trim down after we got to camp. If you had a 33" to 34" waistline when you came to camp, you were down to 31" by the time you broke camp.

"Chuck had a sense of his team. I think Chuck's greatest asset was as a communicator. Verbally and non-verbally. He could play with your mind. He could motivate you with a few words, or with a look. He could look at you with a certain look in his eyes and you knew what he wanted.

"Look at the characters he had to deal with. Yet he could communicate with them. I liked him. The guys who didn't, well, I don't think they understood him. From my rookie year in camp, he knew what buttons to push. I was the L3 guy on the kickoff team. I was supposed to go down and break the blocking wedge. I'd be working my way to the ballcarrier… I'm picking and choosing my way. He'd look at me and holler, 'Where is that 4.4 speed?' He knew I was a church person, and he'd add, 'T., you know what they say about the meek shall inherit the earth…?' He just stabbed me. He knew I knew the Bible. He knew how to get to me.

"I was on the punt return and speed team when I was starting at the corner. Chuck took a personal interest in the special teams—he was the special teams' coach, really—and made sure the best people were out there.

"To us, we were all in it together. If our offense was struggling, Chuck would say, "C'mon, defense, you gotta score! We're struggling; we need some help!"

"I think, mentally, there's a level you go to in the playoffs and Super Bowl. It starts at the top. There's an old saying that where a snake's head goes so goes his body. There's a certain mind set you have to have. That comes from the top. It's not emotions; it's not rah rah.

"I know where that zone is. Chuck had us thinking we had already won the game. We were gonna win, no mistake about that. We didn't take the game for granted, but we were going to win. We never thought about losing.

"I remember Super Bowl X, when we were playing the Dallas Cowboys in Miami. Both teams were in the tunnels, waiting to be introduced. We could see some of the Cowboys from where we were standing. Our defense was going to be introduced. We could see Roger Staubach and Drew Pearson. Dwight White starts hollering. He said their eyes were glazed. 'Lookit their eyes!' White is screaming. 'We got their ass!' He was right; they looked petrified. They looked like the

Children of the Damned. Pine Edwards was on them, too, before we even took the field! We beat them better than the final score (21-17) would indicate.

"Athletes are very insecure. They're always comparing themselves with the other guy. 'Am I as good as you?' There's a lot of "if I coulda, woulda, shoulda..." When their athletic careers are over it's like a death. A lot of them can't handle it. They're constantly trying to regain the spotlight. That's all they know.

"I was scared for my life."

"They used to call me "Rev" because I always carried my Bible on the airplane. When there was some air turbulence they wanted to come and sit with me. Most of the guys grew up in church-oriented families, and some of them got away from it for awhile. The Catholic nuns scared me so much about hell when they taught me in grade school, and then I was at Baptist services all day Sunday, so I was scared for my life.

"I was superstitious, too. So I always sat in the last seat on the left hand side of the airplane. When I was in college, I used to see pictures of airplane wrecks and the tail of the plane was always visible. So I figured that was a good place to be. I always sat by the window and Lynn Swann sat in the aisle seat and we kept one open between us so we'd have more room. When anyone asked if the seat was open we made up the name of somebody who was going to be sitting there. The only exception was Art Rooney. We'd let The Chief sit there when he came back looking for a place to sit. I liked The Chief.

"He knew I went to a parochial school. I went back to my old school, St. Peter Cleaver School, after we won our first Super Bowl. They ran a picture of that in a national Catholic newspaper, and The Chief saw that.

He thought I was a Catholic. He and Tom Foerster (the County Commissioner who came from the North Side and once coached the Perry Atoms sandlot football team) went around on Tuesday nights and visited Catholic schools, and they had me come with them and speak. I learned a lot from The Chief as a person. His church on the North Side was also St. Peter's.

"For two years, he always called me T.J. Finally, I said to him, 'Mr. Rooney, my name is not T.J.' He said, 'I called you that because I had a friend named T.J. Tell me, what's the name on your paycheck?' I said it was J.T. He said, 'OK, then you don't have a problem.' I will say this: After I brought it up, he never called me T.J. after that.

"I think Mr. Rooney was important to the success of our team. He set a tone for treating people the right way. You'd see him at practices standing in the middle of the ground crew, talking to them. He took them on road trips, even to the Super Bowl. He had time for everybody. He treated everyone the same. I learned a lot from him. I learned from a lot of people. Dr. J, the great basketball player, taught me about the benefits of skipping rope in my conditioning program.

"I've been in the restaurant business and we tried to create a culture that would enable us to be successful. We stressed teamwork. We were in the people business. I didn't want to manage people; I wanted to lead people. I could manage you with a .38 or a whip. I wanted to be a mentor. I wanted to inspire people to give their best, and to give the customers the best meal and the best experience possible. I wanted our restaurants to be a place of comfort for our customers in every respect. We were into casual dining and we wanted it to be better than the next guy.

"Life is a dash or a blank."
—J.T. Thomas

"When I got sick between the 1978 and 1979 seasons, they said it was a blood disorder at first. It wasn't cancer or leukemia, as was first feared. It was a rare disease called Boeck's Sarcoidosis. It first showed up in chest x-rays. I went in for a check-up because I had no speed or stamina. My lungs were all messed up. I know the value of good health now. Life has no meaning if you're not healthy. That was a big wake-up call.

"When you go to a cemetery, you realize that life is a dash or a blank. They have your birth date and your death date and there's a dash or blank in between. That's what your life is. How you fill that dash or blank is what it's all about. You come into life with a beginning date and you wind up with an end date. I value life.

"What's the purpose of life? It's not about J.T. It's very little about me. One time I didn't think that way. You have to help others. It's more residual. Initially, everything was centered on me.

I came out of a poor background in Macon, Georgia. I had the opportunity to go to a parochial school, and was taught by the Sisters of Blessed Sacrament. They provided me with tutelage and guidance. We wore uniforms and there was a lot of structure in our school. I was with all my friends, mostly black students. When it was time to go to junior high school, Mother Josepha, I remember her name, told my mother I should go to one of the white schools when they were integrated. So I was thrown right into the heat of integration at the age of 13.

"I was escorted to school by state troopers and dogs. They used the same dogs they had used earlier to control us during (civil rights) demonstrations. Now these dogs were protecting us. That's a bit of irony. There were 17 other African-American students. One of them was my friend Ken Nixon, who was the brother of Norm Nixon, who played here at Duquesne University and later with the Los Angeles Lakers.

"Hey, if I wanted to get something at our Burger King in Macon, I had to go to the back door to pick it up. I remember when I couldn't sit in the front of the bus, and I remember when we were allowed, and a lot of blacks still didn't do it. I did. I wanted to sit up front. If you did, you got looked at. I sat right behind the bus driver. And that wasn't so long ago. I shined shoes at a stand at the Burger King. That's how I made some extra money. I could spit shine shoes with the best of them. My shoes always looked good. They still do.

"I was a piano player, and I played at several churches. Otis Redding Sr. had his own Baptist church. His son, the famous singer, sang there at times when he was in town. I used to go to a talent show at our local movie theatre and Otis Redding and James Brown would be performing. Ma Rainey, Bessie Smith and Little Richard all sang there. That was, mind you, before the "Tarzan" movie.

"That was the Douglass Theatre. It's still there. It's a national landmark. It's on Rev. Martin Luther King Jr. Boulevard in the heart of Macon. I went to watch Tarzan beat up on all the black natives. I'd be wearing my PF Flyers tennis shoes, white T-shirt and black pants. I was dressed up. I was 13 years old and thinking I was real liberal in my thinking. And there I was rooting for Tarzan. I was definitely a work in progress.

"I was fighting for liberation. I didn't realize the whole psychology of what I was watching. Tarzan could talk to all the elephants, lions and apes and get them to do things, and the Africans, who'd been there all along, are afraid of the animals. Tarzan can talk these animals into helping him kick the asses of the natives. What was I thinking?

"There were efforts made at one time in this country to get blacks not to trust one another. There was some real brainwashing. It was different with the guys who were on those great Steelers teams. Most of the guys had come from backgrounds where they were principled and value-based. The African-Americans had come out of situations where they'd seen the transition from segregation to integration. We were playing for our manhood and dignity. We were playing to belong.

"We were saying, 'Hey, we are equal.' A lot of our players came from the South, and they had a spiritual background, even the white players like Terry Bradshaw from Louisiana and Jon Kolb from Oklahoma, had been raised in Christian homes. Those two often hosted and led Bible study sessions for the rest of us at their apartments and homes.

"That helped bring our team together. Another thing that helped us that doesn't get a lot of attention is something I think really brought us together. In the early '70s, Dr. Vaughn Nixon had parties for the team, and he invited everyone. The guys brought their families. There was not a lot of integrating of the players otherwise, but we all came. Dr. Nixon's parties had as much to do with our coming together as anything. That's where we got to know each other. The bonding began there."

"I believe that God doesn't really give a damn about football games."

"I know a lot about praying and about celebrating, but I am puzzled and disappointed by what I see going on during NFL games these days. I have a deep knowledge

444

of religion. I went to a Catholic grade school in Macon even though we were Baptists. I went to Mass on Sunday morning with my class, and then I was at a Baptist church the rest of the day. With the Baptists in the South, Sunday was an all-day deal at church. You even ate there.

"My religion is Baptist, but my faith is Christianity. My faith means a lot to me. It's been the backbone of my life. At the same time, I believe that God doesn't really give a damn about football games. I never prayed at pre-game prayer when I was playing for the Steelers. I thought it was dumb. There were 28 NFL teams praying to God that day, asking him to help them do well, to stay well, and to help them win the game. I thought they were all putting God on the spot. He couldn't answer everybody's prayers.

"I used to pray to God at mid-week. So I was already in by Sunday. I never asked him to help my team win, or me to do super things. I just prayed for his blessing. Now I see these guys making the sign of the cross in the end zone after they score a touchdown. Or, I see them gathering at mid-field, from both teams, to say a prayer after the game. I don't understand it. To me, there's a proper time and place to do one's praying. It should be more of a private thing. It shouldn't be for show.

"I love to go to church. It's just something that's in me. I play the piano and the organ, and I have been involved with church choirs since I was a kid.

"I don't understand the constant celebrations on the field. They celebrate like they were surprised they just did what they did. It's like a little kid trying to impress his father. Chuck Noll used to say, 'Look like you've been there before.' He didn't want us showing anyone up, or carrying on after we made a tackle or scored a touchdown or intercepted a pass. These guys are celebrating on every play anymore: a routine tackle or a routine catch, a five-yard run. It's crazy.

"They run down the field 20 or 30 yards after they've done something, and they're losing the game! It's a waste of time in many ways. You have to invest some time into choreographing some of these dances and celebrations. A football game is like a chess game. You've got to keep your head about you. You should be in the huddle, getting the call for the next play. You can't get fouled up psychologically. You lose focus if you're more concerned about how you're going to celebrate the next play. My talking was done in the huddle."

"Chuck Noll and his staff had their work cut out for them."

"Hey, we were crazy in our own way when I was playing left cornerback for the Steelers when we had those great teams in the '70s. Our first Super Bowl teams had some real personalities on both sides of the ball, but especially on our defensive side.

"Chuck Noll and his staff had their work cut out for them managing this crew of disparate personalities.

"On our defensive line, left to right, we had L.C. Greenwood, Joe Greene, Ernie Holmes and Dwight White. Behind them, we had Jack Ham, Jack Lambert and Andy Russell. Then we had Mel Blount and me at the corners, and Mike Wagner and Pine Edwards at the safeties. Donnie Shell was back there later.

"That was some group; that was a great group. But what went on in those defensive huddles was so funny people don't believe me when I tell them about it. I still have to laugh when I reflect on what went on in the huddle.

"Greene was getting on them. He was so nasty in those days. He really was Mean Joe Greene in the beginning. He mellowed out when he got that Coke commercial (in 1979), tossing his jersey to that kid in the hallway when he was coming off the field. He started living up to his new TV image.

"Then you had Lambert. He was nasty, too. If you're going down a dark alley at night you want to have Greene and Lambert with you.

"Ernie wouldn't even come into the huddle half the time. He'd be up there standing over the ball like he wasn't going to let them touch it, telling his man what he was going to do to him on the next snap. Lambert would be hollering at him, 'Fats, get your ass in the huddle!' And Ernie, or Fats, whatever he was going by that day, didn't pay Lambert no mind. Ernie didn't get the play half the time. He didn't give a damn what the play was anyhow. He did what he wanted to do. That upset Dwight. He said you couldn't trust Ernie to do what he was supposed to be doing. He'd leave you out there on an island sometimes.

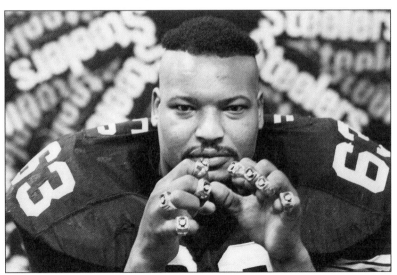

Ernie Holmes with rings

"White and I were roommates for a long time. He'd say, 'Home, I can't trust Fats. *("Home" is short for Homeboy, an affectionate term.)* No matter what we call, he might change his mind.' Fats had a psychological reason for why he changed his mind when he'd get called on it. He never did anything wrong.

"Edwards was from the old school. He and Fats always wanted to take out people, cold-cock them and leave them for dead. He raised a whole lot of hell if somebody let a running back get through the line and he had to make the tackle. He was always praising the line when they did well. 'Hey, you make me look good!' he'd holler. He would say something on every play.

"White was always hollering in the huddle about how he was being held, and how he was getting cut at the knees. He was going to get back at his guy. He was always talking. He'd tell the guy across from him. 'Do your Momma know you're out here?' These guys were always talking about somebody's momma. White was always talking non-stop. I told White I knew what was going on in the trenches. Because I watched them and I knew when things weren't right, when they let some 250-pound back slip past them and I'd have to take him on head-on. So I knew.

"Andy Russell always seemed out of place on that right side of the field. He was more sophisticated than the rest of the guys. He was quieter and more reserved. He was caught in the middle. Sandwiched between some mad characters. Sometimes, Andy was the mediator out there.

"Mike Wagner and L.C. Greenwood—they were both great guys—but they were on the quiet side, too. So they stayed on the outside of the huddle, talking to each other, and laughing at the scene.

"Mel felt he could go bump and run on any receiver in the league, and that's what he wanted to do, no matter what coverage was called. We had a lot of calls and checks, but sometimes we did our own thing within the concept of a call.

"We weren't always on the same page, and Chuck Noll knew it. Bud Carson, our defensive backfield coach, really knew his stuff. But sometimes we didn't like his call, and we'd do something else and say we were confused if he called us over and asked us what the hell we were doing. Carson would go crazy at times when we'd make our own adjustments. We knew what we could do because we knew each other's strengths and habits.

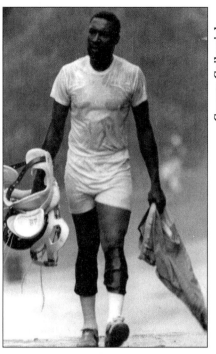

George Gojkovich

L.C. Greenwood takes a walk after practice at St.Vincent

"The other team knew what Mel was going to do. He didn't care. I'm trying to disguise our defensive setup so the other team isn't sure. Mel didn't care what they thought. He was going to bump and run. They knew exactly where he was going to be when the ball was snapped. By the way, and I knew they didn't keep track of those things, but Mel got beat for more TDs than I did. I've got to stay ahead of him some way.

"When they'd hand out the playbook at training camp, Mel would stick it in his car trunk, next to the spare tire, so he could find it, because they fined you $500 if you lost the playbook. Mel would tell the coaches, 'I don't have to read this playbook. Why are you passing out those books? I wrote the playbook!'

"We had more check-offs and audibles. We had good athletes and we were versatile. We didn't like zone. We wanted to go man-on-man. The rules were different then than they are now. We could jam those receivers and stay in their face. Mel liked to hit them in the face before they even got off the line.

"Ham is in the middle of all that, and he didn't know the set we were in half the time. He'd be hollering at L.C. or me, asking what the call was. 'What are we in?' he'd be hollering. 'What's the check?'

"I told him my name should be on his plaque at the Pro Football Hall of Fame as his sponsor or something. He'd be waving his fingers at me, trying to get the number we were in. He was such a good athlete, and had a nose for the ball, and had L.C. and Joe doing the dirty work in front of him. So Jack did the right thing more often than not. At the snap of the ball, Ham knew where to go. How he got it, or how he learned what to do, was a mystery sometime. He would make the play. He had such great instincts. He could size up what he was seeing in a hurry and know how to respond.

"That whole defense was like that. We did some things instinctively. After years of playing with each other, we knew what the other guy was going to do in a certain situation. Carson was a genius. He knew how to coach us. We had a lot of improvisation, and he learned to live with it.

"Chuck Noll was a defensive coach himself, but he let Carson carry the day.

"Bud Carson had you thinking that guy doesn't belong on the field with you. He wanted you to bump them into the ground.

"We all relished the idea."

John Stallworth

Big success back home in Alabama

John Stallworth is an American success story, says former teammate Mel Blount. "He came from a small black college in the South and became a Hall of Fame receiver for the Steelers," said Blount "and then he became an even bigger success in business, and now he's one of the minority owners of the Steelers."

As I made my way through a mob of men in tuxedos and women in their finest outfits at a VIP reception at the Mel Blount Celebrity Roast on Friday night, April 5, 2019, someone reached out and touched my left shoulder. I turned and looked into the smiling face of John Stallworth. He was sitting next to Donnie Shell. They were close as Steelers in the '70s and they stay in touch with each other today.

They were the heart and soul of the Steelers during the team's glory-to-God days. There was a window behind them and I could see the green surface of Heinz Field.

*   *   *

He was Johnny Lee Stallworth when he was an all-conference receiver at Alabama A&M in his hometown of Tuscaloosa in 1972 and 1973. Bear Bryant was not recruiting blacks to play at the University of Alabama back then, so Stallworth went to the predominantly black school in town. Shame on Bear.

Chuck Noll was recruiting black ballplayers at the time, starting with Joe Greene of North Texas State as his first choice in 1969, relying a great deal on the

George Goikovich

JOHN STALLWORTH

judgment of one of the team's scouts, Bill Nunn Jr., who had been the sports editor of *The Pittsburgh Courier* and had chosen an all-black All-American team for the weekly newspaper that served the African-American community. Nunn and Art Rooney Jr. were known by the football coaches at the predominantly black schools in the South.

"John always wanted to go back home to Alabama," said Lynn Swann, another Hall of Fame receiver on those same Steelers' teams of the '70s. "And he's doing well there. You can use him as a yardstick of success among the Steelers of our day."

Stallworth was quite successful in his "life's work." He earned a Bachelor of Science degree in business administration and an MBA with a concentration in finance from Alabama A&M University.

In 1986, he founded Madison Research Corporation (MRC) which specialized in providing engineering and information technology services to government and commercial clients.

Bill Amatucci

John Stallworth and Lynn Swann

Stallworth started out looking after a staff of 15 employees and MRC grew to more than 650 employees and $70 million in revenues, with six regional offices. Stallworth sold his share in the company to Wireless Facilities Inc. in 2006.

He is currently the president and CEO of a family-based investment group Genesis II. When the Rooneys had to restructure the team's ownership in March of 2009, Stallworth became a part owner of his former team.

*　*　*

He played 14 seasons in the NFL, including six AFC championships and four Super Bowl victories. His reception total was a team record until it was surpassed by Hines Ward in 2005. Stallworth played in four Pro Bowls and was the Steelers' MVP twice.

Stallworth had been a fourth-round pick in the 1974 draft class. The Steelers selected Lynn Swann and Jack Lambert with their first two choices. The Steelers had traded their third-round pick to the Oakland Raiders. They got Mike Webster on the fifth round.

Stallworth was inducted into the Pro Football Hall of Fame in August of 2002. Stallworth always had a smile and was an easy interview. He was pleasant and had a squeaky voice that always had a trace of the South. His teammates liked to make fun of the way he talked when they get a chance to roast him at a Blount dinner. He has a strong spiritual bent and was among the twenty-some Steelers who met regularly for Bible study sessions.

When the Hall of Fame honored him in his home-town of Tuscaloosa in October of 2012 he said, "I never dreamt at Tuscaloosa High School that life would lead me to where I am today."

Jim O'Brien

KDKA-TV sports broadcaster Robin Cole was emcee for Mel Blount Celebrity Roast, and is flanked here by Blount and John Stallworth.

Stallworth has attended several celebrity dinners here to raise funds for the Mel Blount Youth Home in Claysville, Pa., out in Washington County. Stallworth looks splendid in a black tuxedo and has the same winning smile. "I have a very special relationship back home with family and friends," said Stallworth. "Not that I don't have some of that in Pittsburgh. But what is near and dear to me is in Alabama. When I was growing up in Tuscaloosa, we had all kinds of cousins right in the neighborhood, and I like that. Having a close-knit family is a sign of success, too.

"One of the things I learned along the way was that no one was going to give you anything. But if you worked real hard, you can attain something.

"One of the things I want for my children is for them to excel at something. You can carry that with you for the rest of your life. I learned a great work ethic from my mom and dad. The players who were on the Steelers came away from that as better people, whatever they choose to get into. They have the right stuff, they know what it takes to win and be successful."

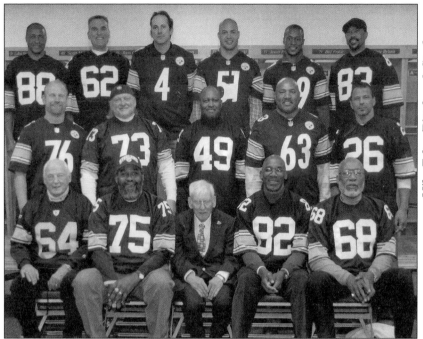

OLD-TIMERS—Front row, left to right, Bill Priatko (64), Joe Greene (75), Dan Rooney, John Stallworth (82), L.C. Greenwood (68). Second row, Chris Hoke (76), Craig Wolfley (73), Dwayne Woodruff (49), Dermontti Dawson (63) and Rod Woodson (26), Third row, Lynn Swann (88). Tunch Ilkin (62), Josh Miller (4), James Farrior (51), Willie Parker (39) and Louis Lipps (83).

KDKA's Bob Pompeani stands between Mel Blount and John Stallworth.

Jim Baker

A famous football

Jim Baker of West Mifflin still treasures a football he found and seized at the bottom of a fans' scrum in the end zone at Three Rivers Stadium on the point-after kick that followed one of the most famous plays in pro football history.

Yes, Baker has the ball that Roy Gerela kicked for an extra point that gave the Steelers an unreal 13-7 victory over the Oakland Raiders in the opening round of the 1972 American Football Conference playoffs.

That was on December 23, 1972 and Baker had the ball that rookie Franco Harris had run with to score a 60-yard touchdown with 22 seconds remaining in the game. I was present, covering the game for *The New York Post*, so it's a special memory.

There was no mention of any "Immaculate Reception" in my story because Myron Cope hadn't yet captured the moment with a label suggested by one of his callers on his post-game show on WTAE Radio. It was a label that has lasted a lifetime and gave it legs that still carry the day.

Dave Crawley of KDKA-TV, who did such fine features for so many years, interviewed Baker before an "Immaculate Receptions Memories" program at the Heinz History Center on the 40th anniversary of that famous play. Jack Sega, a friend of mine from West Mifflin who now lives in Oxnard, California and was one of the proofreaders for this book, called Baker's involvement to my attention. Baker was with his nephew in the lower stands at Three Rivers Stadium that day.

Baker told Crawley—a confession of sorts—that he didn't actually see the play unfold. "I'm only 5-feet-5," said Baker, "so, like everyone else, I had to jump up, get up as high as I could, to watch what was going on."

The ball Gerela kicked bounced off the concrete floor. "A lot of fans went for it," Baker recounted what happened to Crawley. "I'm sure they remember who they are. I come off the bottom of the pile with the football. And, of course, I come out looking for my nephew, instantly focused and shouted, 'Let's run!'"

* * *

Baker brought the ball and his memories to the Heinz History Center on December 21, 2012, two days before the 40th anniversary of "The Immaculate Reception." Franco Harris was the star attraction at the weekend celebration. Harris has been the director of the Champions Committee that continues its efforts to improve the exhibition in the Center's sports history museum. I am a charter member of that group and have been impressed by how Harris has shown up for all but one meeting and came with an agenda for each program. He was no honorary chairman such as Arnold Palmer and Bill Mazeroski. The only one he missed was when he went to Penn State to support his college coach Joe Paterno.

That game had a thrilling climax, as good as it gets for both teams. The Raiders' left-handed quarterback, Ken "The Snake" Stabler ran left for a 30-yard touchdown with 1:17 left in the game to give the visitors, along with an extra-point, a 7-6 lead. It looked like the Steelers were doomed.

This was their first playoff game of this consequence in the 40-year history of the franchise. They had finished with a losing record in 31 of the previous 39 years. Art Rooney had grown used to disappointment, and he left his suite next to the press box early in order to get to the dressing room before the players got there. He went to console his Steelers.

He was on an elevator going down when Franco found the ball just before it hit the turf—some still insist the ball hit the ground—but Myron Cope, who checked the film one frame at a time, insists it was legal. Raiders' coach John Madden doesn't share Cope's findings.

The Steelers had the ball for the final time on the 40-yard line with ten yards to go for a first down with 1:17 to play. They had no timeouts. They failed to gain a yard on three plays and only 22 seconds remaining.

Terry Bradshaw was flushed out of the pocket and tried to throw the ball down the center of the field to Frenchy Fuqua. The ball and Raiders' demon defensive back Jack "The Assassin" Tatum arrived at the same time, and the ball was deflected back toward Bradshaw.

Franco Harris had come downfield to see if he could help and he caught the rebound and the rest is history. It put Franco at the Pittsburgh Airport alongside General George Washington, a hero of an earlier event in Pittsburgh history.

* * *

Sam Baker has been challenged by health issues, and his family has experienced some serious setbacks in recent years, so the football reminds him of better days. He still embraces it the way wounded warriors from recent wars embrace their service dogs to calm them down.

"My four-day-old son came home from the hospital that same day," recalled Baker.

"So, it was a great day in so many ways. I'm the father of a new-born son, my second son. The following few days were special. The baby Jesus is born. I've got the 'Immaculate Reception' football. You put it all together, it's a time of happiness. I'm one of the luckiest persons in the world."

459

Jim Baker holds "Immaculate Reception" football and photograph of his late son, Sam Baker, at Heinz History Center on December 21, 2012.

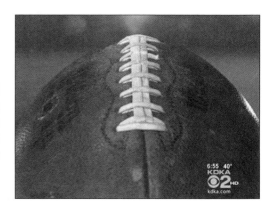

The football remains a treasure. Photos from Heinz History Center

The euphoria in Pittsburgh didn't last long. On New Year's Eve, December 31, the great Roberto Clemente was killed in an airplane crash as the Pirates' star player is leading a relief effort to Nicaragua after an earthquake has devastated the Latin American country. As Myron Cope said of Clemente in a commentary I still have in my files, "He was no honorary chairman. Honorary chairmen don't get killed in plane crashes."

Sam Baker, the little boy who came home from the hospital on December 23, 1972, died of cancer 33 years later. And Jim Baker has a football to ease his pain, and remind him of better days.

He called me on the phone the morning of Wednesday, April 1, 2019, and I could tell he was still hurting. "I hear you have been having a rough time of it," I said, and he started sobbing.

He told me his wife, Mary, had died on July 18, 2018. "She had colon cancer," he said. "We had been married for 49 years and she stuck with me through thick and thin. I was an insurance agent and there were some difficult days.

"The bank once threatened to put us out on the street if we didn't make good on a $2,000 loan. She didn't flinch."

He said they had met at a Terry Lee Dance in Glassport. She was born in McKeesport and raised in Clairton. "I had her for nearly 50 years and I was a lucky man. But I miss her dearly."

Jim Baker said that Peyton Manning, the great quarterback, had been to his house recently to film a feature for ESPN's "Peyton's Place" about him and the football. "He's like Franco," said Baker, "such a great guy. We got the football out of the vault where we keep it."

Jon Kolb

When I was covering the Steelers for *The Pittsburgh Press* from 1979 to 1983, Jon Kolb was one of my greatest challenges in the clubhouse. Conversation was beyond Kolb's skill set.

He was a terrific offensive lineman, guard or tackle, and one of the leaders of the team's Christian ministry, eager to share the Bible and its lessons with his teammates.

He was not eager to be interviewed by sports writers. One day, I asked his roommate, guard Sam Davis, what I had done to turn off Jon Kolb. Davis, a delightful individual at the time, told me not to take it personally. He said that Kolb got into a mental zone the week of a game and had tunnel vision. "He doesn't even talk to me," declared Davis.

Davis doesn't talk much these days, since he's been in a personal care home in McKeesport with mental issues from a beating he took relating to an unsettled debt in his business after football. And you can't keep Kolb from talking.

I have caught up with Kolb on several occasions at Andy Russell's Celebrity Golf Outing and at Mel Blount's Celebrity Dinner for the benefit of his youth home for challenged kids out in Claysville, Pa.

He'll come over with a big smile, like I was a long-lost cousin and start sharing stories. He's a good story-teller. On the last meeting, he told me a story I had read in *Steelers' Digest*. It was written by Teresa Varley, who had been an intern of mine for four years (1984-1988) when I was the assistant athletic director for public relations at the University of Pittsburgh. I am proud to call her a protégé of mine.

I listened to Kolb's story, but I relied on Varley's version of the story to get it right. It's about the time Kolb was not respectful of Art Rooney Sr. when he called him at Oklahoma State University to tell him the Steelers had drafted him on the third round in 1979. He was one of those under-sized linemen, such as Sam Davis, Moon Mullins, Mike Webster, and Larry Brown that the Steelers (with the help of steroids, not outlawed at the time) built into bigger and better and agile performers who were great at trap-blocking and at pulling out to lead end sweeps.

There was no NFL Network and no round-by-round ESPN coverage of the NFL draft in 1969, Chuck Noll's first year as Steelers' coach. Kolb said he had heard and been worked out by every team in the NFL except the Steelers. He said he received a letter from the Steelers the day before the draft. It was addressed to Dear Player and the signature at the bottom was stamped on the stationery.

Kolb didn't keep it. "They didn't ever know my name," he thought. Makes you wonder what the Steelers did right to build a four-time Super Bowl winner that way.

Whenever anyone asked Kolb who he thought might draft him, he had a patent reply: "The one thing I know is it won't be the Pittsburgh Steelers."

He didn't know how the draft actually worked so he went to class and worked out afterward. When he entered the locker room, his teammates were gathered around a phone and told Kolb it was a Mr. Rooney from Pittsburgh on the line.

"Mr. Rooney told me the Steelers were excited about drafting me, and asked me if I was excited," recalled Kolb. "I told him I was not. I didn't know Mr. Rooney and I thought it was a terrible trick."

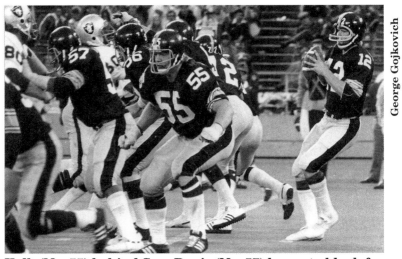

Kolb (No. 55) behind Sam Davis (No. 57) brace to block for Terry Bradshaw.

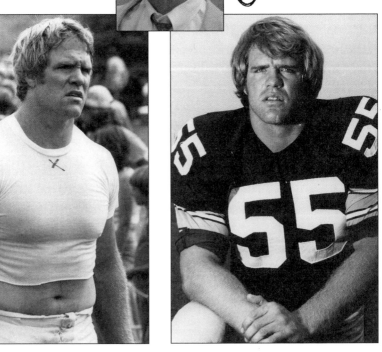

When Kolb learned it was true that he had been drafted by the Steelers, he telephoned their offices and asked for Mr. Rooney. He apologized for being so rude the day before. When he got to the Steelers' training camp, Mr. Rooney was outside Bonaventure Hall at St. Vincent College waiting to greet the players.

"I apologized to him again. I never stopped apologizing to him. When I was hired as the defensive line coach and later the strength and conditioning coach, Mr. Rooney and I would talk about my gaffe and he'd laugh about it.

Kolb represented the U.S. in the World's Strongest Man competition and finished fourth twice. He had a strong spiritual side as well, and contributed to the specialness of the Steelers in many ways. He later worked at Grove City College and Youngstown State and in physical therapy, and stayed in touch with the Steelers. He's a friend and a good guy.

* * *

Ms. Teresa Varley was a surprise visitor to my office at Pitt in my first year as sports information director. She stayed for four years, quickly earned a scholarship with her work efforts, and I treated her as if she were a full-time member of the staff. She was that good.

When I was offered the job by Steelers' publicist Joe Gordon to be the editor of the new publication, *Steelers Digest,*

I hired Varley to be my assistant. I turned the job down two weeks later, not wanting to go on the road with the Steelers again. I recommended Bob Labriola to take my place. He and Varley celebrated their 30th anniversary—imagine that—with *Steelers Digest* during the 2019 season.

Praise for Pittsburgh Proud series

"Author Jim O'Brien has done it again! Each time I read one of his books, I think he can't possibly write another book that will be as good as the last one I read. Somehow, he does it. A down-to-earth guy, O'Brien tells the story of these famous people in such a way that you actually feel as if you are in the room when they are talking."
—Chuck Greenwood, *Sports Collectors Digest*

"His book really hits the human side of those who came to Pittsburgh as football players and remained there after they got on with what Coach Chuck Noll called "their life's work." I have enjoyed reading all of Jim O'Brien's books, but *Always A Steeler* could be the one I like most. Maybe because it's so human."
—Jim Kriek, *Uniontown Herald-Standard*

Praise for Doing It Right

"It's not a sports book per se—not full of boring statistics and rehashing of games, but instead it is a book which zeroes in on the players', coaches', owners' and sportswriters' lives—both personally and professionally. It is rich in anecdotes, and full of a strong sense of the city of Pittsburgh and its people."
—University of Pittsburgh Press

"This book (*Doing It Right*) will do for the Pittsburgh Steelers what *The Boys of Summer* did for the Brooklyn Dodgers."
—Joe Gilmartin, *The Phoenix Gazette*

"Jim O'Brien is Pittsburgh's premier sports historian."
—Myron Cope, *WTAE Radio*

"When you read a Jim O'Brien book, you swear you've been there with him."
—Bob Pompeani, *KDKA-TV*

"The claim that one is separated by any person in the world by only six persons is hard to believe. Knowing and talking with someone like Jim O'Brien makes the six degrees of separation theory more believable."
—Julia Cavallo, *Latrobe Bulletin*

From Matt Marsom in *The Football News*
"This (*Doing It Right*) is the best football book on the market today. It's a unique behind-the-scenes story of what sets the Steelers apart from the pack, yesterday and today. Football fans and non-football fans alike are bound to benefit from the insight into how these men strived for excellence on and off the playing field. Jerry Kramer's "Instant Replay" by Dick Schaap, which chronicled Vince Lombardi's great Packers' teams of the 1960s, has always been my favorite football book. Until now."

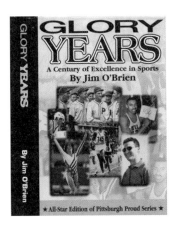

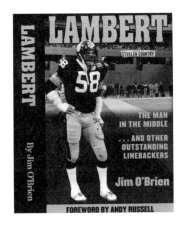

"In more than 500 pages and 200 photos, *Doing It Right* tells these players' stories, anecdotes, histories and where-are-they-nows. It was a sweet time, a time of excellence, of victory and O'Brien captured it, as well as the bittersweet times since. Like David Halberstam's first-rate *Summer of '49*, this book is less a recounting of thrice-told tales than a study of how men came together for a group purpose, driving them to the peak of their abilities.

Over the years, no one's been a better, more committed sports chronicler than O'Brien. Some may have burned more incandescently, some have remained longer in the trenches, but no one's produced a higher volume of solid reporting. *Doing It Right* brought O'Brien back to the players, interviewing them in their homes and offices, bringing himself into the story as Roger Kahn did in the brilliant, elegiac *The Boys of Summer*."

—Abby Mendelson,
Author of *The Pittsburgh Steelers*

From Leonard Shapiro, *The Washington Post*:
"The other recommendation is for 'The Chief,' a biography of the late and much beloved Pittsburgh Steelers founder and owner, Art Rooney. Written by longtime sportswriter Jim O'Brien, a Pittsburgh native, it's a labor of love for the author, who once described Rooney as "the grandfather I never had... the nicest person I ever met in the business.

"The book coincides with the 100th anniversary of Rooney's birth in Coultersville, Pa., on January 27, 1901, and the opening of Heinz Field, the Steelers' new stadium. Heinz Field sits near the former site of Three Rivers Stadium and in the area where Art Rooney's father did a brisk business with his saloon, while the family lived upstairs."

From Gerald Eskenazi, *The New York Times:*

"The first thing a good sportswriter does in the morning is to check the other papers to see whether he's missed anything. And the first paper I would go to was Jim O'Brien's (*The New York Post*). Too often, I picked up his story and said, 'Nuts, why didn't I have that?' He was an indefatigable worker and a talented craftsman. I enjoyed having him as a colleague as well as competitor."

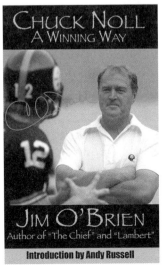

"I have read your books, *Doing It Right* and *Whatever It T*akes, about the Steelers of the—70s. I have always considered myself a loyal fan, but after reading your books, I almost feel as though I've known these players all my life. You've given them a depth and humanity all too rare in sports histories.

"You have helped me understand something of their backgrounds and core beliefs, which in turn creates a greater understanding of what drives these men in their pursuit of excellence. It also helps explain how such a seemingly disparate group can come together for a common purpose.

"I have always sensed that there is something special about the Pittsburgh Steelers, and now I know I was correct. Thank you for a splendid history of the greatest football team of all time."

—Sean Duffy, Program Coordinator
Author/Lunch Programs, Ohio County
Library, Wheeling, West Virginia

"Thank you for writing such superb books on the Pittsburgh Steelers glory years. Your insights and appreciation of those teams—the players, the coaches and the management/ownership—is truly remarkable. I appreciate your effort and the quality of your writing."

—Andy Russell, Former Captain
Pittsburgh Steelers, Presto, Pennsylvania

"Jim O'Brien is the poet laureate of Pittsburgh sports. He knows the streets and the stars and he is passionate about both. I have great respect for him and cherish our long friendship. Have a few laughs."

—Dick Schaap, ESPN, ABC News
June 5, 2001

"If there is a Steeler connection to a Hall of Fame Weekend, it's for sure Jim O'Brien is somewhere in the crowd. O'Brien is the Pittsburgh native who has, over the years, chronicled his pride in the Pennsylvania city with prose, the last three decades of which have been his books."
—Bob Stewart, *The Canton Repository*

"I was given a wonderful book for Christmas entitled, *The Chief: Art Rooney and His Pittsburgh Steelers*. I've been reading it, bits and pieces, and find it fascinating and delightful. As I wend my way through this grand work, I find many old friends and places that are recounted in an endearing style."
—Msgr. Charles O. Rice, *Pittsburgh Catholic*

"Jim O'Brien has, by dint of a keen eye for detail and tenacious reporting, carved himself a nifty niche as Boswell to sporting Pittsburgh."
—Phil Musick, *USA Today*

"Jim O'Brien is uniquely qualified to bring you these stories about the Steelers, whom he lived with and died with during the breath-taking '70s, the unforgettable decade that belonged to the Steelers, creating a heyday of excellence in Pittsburgh. And O'Brien, in his soft, inimitable style, puts flesh and bone onto his characters with a penetrating insight into his subjects. He brings these men alive as to what they what and what they are, which is a damn fine crew from Coach Chuck Noll on down."
—Pat Livingston, Former sports editor
The Pittsburgh Press

"As the precocious editor and publisher of *Pittsburgh Weekly Sports* in the early 1960s, Jim O'Brien was a trend setter. He provided a forum in Pittsburgh for a new breed of literate, humorous, hard-hitting sports writers. Subsequently, during his years with *The Miami News* and *The New York Post*, O'Brien clung to his roots. Pittsburgh was always in his blood, and since returning here in 1979 he has been a knowledgeable observer of the scene. His books are valuable additions to the archives. Part history and part memoir, they follow the Pittsburgh Steelers of the Super Bowl decade into the 1980s and their post-football lives, enriching the folklore."

—Roy McHugh
Columnist, Sports Editor
The Pittsburgh Press

"What *Doing It Right* gives us is not so much the concrete and beams of the dynasty; rather, we get the flesh and blood. O'Brien has not put on paper X's and O's, much as a coach or quarterback chalk up winning plays. Instead, he chose to dip his pen into the heart of the team and its city. Couched within a 'sports book' is a 'feel' for Pittsburgh – its people, its traditions, its pride, its heart. It's a feel provided by one of its sons. You come away liking that feeling."

—Taylor Scott, *Point Magazine*

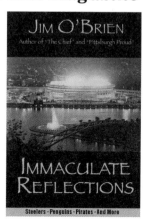

"Jim O'Brien, the prolific author, has another book on the market, *Remember Roberto*. The strength of O'Brien's work—another in a series about the city's proudest sports moments and the athletes who created them—is its scope. He interviewed hundreds of Clemente's teammates, opposing players and Joe Fan." O'Brien skillfully wrapped that package in an interesting read."

—Dave Ailes
Pittsburgh Tribune-Review

"Jim O'Brien's first person writing places him in the room with me, as I read his stories. It's as if he's talking to me over a cup of coffee. His knowledge of sports in general, and particularly of our local teams, is phenomenal. What appeals to me most is his ability to humanize his writing. I really like the way he is able to intersperse personal anecdotes and human interest into his writing." **—Jack Sega, Oxnard, Calif.**

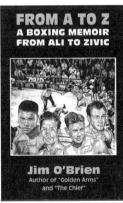

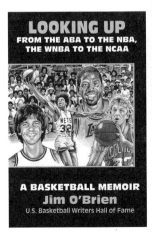

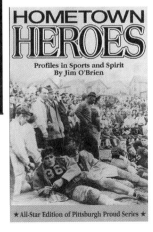

George Gojkovich

I have used George Gojkovich's photographs for nearly 50 years, going back to my days in New York (1970-1978) when I was the founding editor of *Street & Smith's Basketball Yearbook*, the No. 1 selling annual of its kind.

Our art director, the late Herb Stoltz, said his favorite photographer of the dozens whose work we used, was George Gojkovich. Most of the photographs in this book are by George. He's my favorite photographer, too, by George.

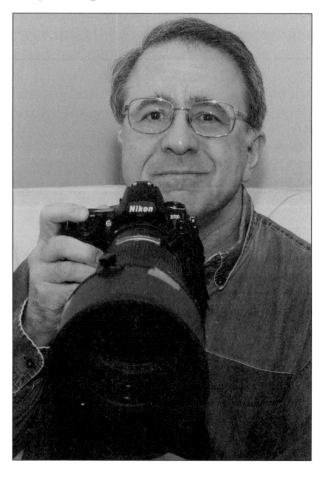

Author's Page

J im O'Brien is the author of 30 books on Pittsburgh sports achievement, with "From A to Z" and "Looking Up" his latest. He has also authored "The Chief" and "Remember Roberto."

He is a contributing columnist to *The Valley Mirror* and magazines in Mt. Lebanon and Upper St. Clair. He wrote a column for 18 years for *The Almanac*, the South Hills weekly, and was a columnist for *The Pittsburgh Business Times*.

He was a sportswriter with *The Philadelphia Evening Bulletin, The Miami News, The New York Post* and *The Pittsburgh Press*, and the founding editor of *Street & Smith's Basketball Yearbook* (1970-1992), and editor emeritus beyond that.

He has been teaching a class on "Pittsburgh's Rich Sports History" in recent years in the Osher Institute program at the University of Pittsburgh. Myron Cope called him "Pittsburgh's premier sports historian." He appears frequently on Pittsburgh radio and TV, and nationally-televised sports documentaries.

He was the first Pittsburgher to be named to the U.S. Basketball Writers Association Hall of Fame, and was given a Lifetime Achievement Award by the Pittsburgh Basketball Hall of Fame. In 2019, he was nominated by NBA officials for the writers' wing of the Basketball Hall of Fame. He is a member of the Western Chapter of the Pennsylvania Sports Hall of Fame, and was awarded the Bob Prince Memorial Award for his contributions to journalism, the David L. Lawrence Award by the Vectors of Pittsburgh for promoting the city through his writing efforts, and was named a Legend by the Pittsburgh chapter of the Italian-American Sports Hall of Fame

"When it comes to writing sports books, Jim O'Brien is No. 1 in Pittsburgh," said Mark Whited, who authored a book on the Pittsburgh Pipers in 2019.

He is a graduate of the University of Pittsburgh (1964) with a degree in English and graduate study classes in English Literature.

He has been married for 52 years to Kathleen Churchman O'Brien and they have two daughters, Dr. Sarah O'Brien and Rebecca O'Brien, and four grandchildren, Margaret, Susannah, Jeffrey and Madeline.

Check Jim's website at www.jimobriensports author.com for information about his latest books in the Pittsburgh Proud series.

Kathleen Churchman O'Brien

Frank Deford, award-winning sports author, and Jim O'Brien meet at Chicago Book Festival.

Acknowledgments

David McCullough, a Pulitzer Prize-winning author and historian with western Pennsylvania roots, was asked what we can learn from the past. He replied, "That there is no such thing as a 'self-made man or woman' —we all are influenced by people around us. And that integrity and character do count in the long run."

I have been fortunate to have met and interviewed and learned from so many outstanding individuals, most of whom have been associated with and excelled in the world of sports. I am grateful for those who were generous with their time and thoughts, stories and insights.

Significant financial support has been offered through the years by the following: Armand Dellovade of A.C. Dellovade, Asbury Heights, Atria's Retaurant & Tavern, Bill Baierl, Rich Barcelona of Bailey-PVS Oxides LLC, Miles Bryan of Bryan Mechanical, Don Carlucci of Carlucci Construction, Tom Sweeney of Compucom, Eat'n Park Restaurants, Bill Tillotson of Hefren-Tillotson, Dick Swanson, Elsie Hillman, James S. Hamilton of Federated Securities, Inc., Frank B. Fuhrer Wholesale Company, David J. Malone of Gateway Financial, H. J. Heinz Company, Hoddy Hanna of Hanna Real Estate Services, Thomas B. Grealish of Henderson Brothers, Steve Fedell of Ikon Office Solutions, William V. Campbell of Intuit, Andy Russell, Jack Mascaro of Mascaro Construction, Joseph A. Massaro Jr. of the Massaro Company, Robert Santillo and Danny Rains of McCarl's, Dave Jancisin and Derek Jancisin of Merrill Lynch, Angela Longo of National City Bank, Lou Grippo of the Original Oyster House, Dan R. Lackner of Paper Products Company, Inc., PPG Industries, Tom O'Brien, James Rohr and Sy Holzer of PNC Bank, Pittsburgh Brewing Company, Robert J. Taylor of Taylor & Hladio Law Offiices, Jim, Barbara and Ted Frantz of TEDCO Inc., Bob Randall of TRACO, Inc., Thomas J. Usher and John Surma of U.S. Steel Corporation, Clark Nicklas of Vista Resources, Inc., Kenneth Codeluppi of Wall-Firma,

Inc., Western Pennsylvania Caring Foundation, Jack McGinley of Wilson-McGinley Co., Rudy Zupancic of Giant Eagle, Jack McGinley Jr. of Eckert Seamans Law Firm.

Others who have worked with me: Ron Livingston of Babb, Inc., Chuck Belliotti, Dale Blaha of Altany, Loynd & Lindquist, Inc., Don DeBlasio of DeBlasio's Restaurant, Dan Bartow of Legends of the North Shore, Art Cipriani, Dave and Frank Clements, Joseph Costanzo Jr., Ralph Cindrich, Todd Cover, Dr. Patrick J. DeMeo, Herb Douglas, Kim Geyer, Zeb Jansante, Kevin Joyce of The Carlton, Gregory L. Manesiotis, Robert F. McClurg, Dennis Meteny, George Morris, Andy Ondrey, John Paul, Jim Render, Jim Roddey, George Schoeppner, Len Stidle, Barbara Stull and Don Yannessa, Jack McKay, Mark Whited, Bill Neal.

I want to thank the following individuals for their loyal support: Tony Accamando, Aldo Bartolotta, Howell Breedlove, Suzy and Jim Broadhurst, R. Everett Burns of E-Z Overhead Door Co., Susie Campbell, Renny Clark, Ray Conaway, Gayland Cook, Judge Jeffrey A. Deller, Tony Ferraro, Gregory W. Fink, Dick Goetz, Marshall Goldstein, Bob and Frank W. Gustine Jr., Mike Hagan, F. Edwin Harmon, Donald J. Hastings, Karen Horvath, Jeff James, George Jordan, Bob Keaney, Daniel Koller Jr., Andy Komer, Robert Lovett, Jim McCarl, Mac McIlrath, Nancy and Pat McDonnell, Carl R. Moulton, Pitt Chancellor Mark Nordenberg, Jim Droney of Mt. Lebanon Office Equipment, Ron Parfitt, Joseph Piccirilli, Alex Pociask, Charlie and Steve Previs, Pro Football Hall of Fame, Joe Reljac, Arthur J. Rooney Jr., John Rooney, Patrick J. Rooney, Ed Ryan, Patrick J. Santelli, Fred Sargent, Vince Sarni, Vince R. Scorsone, Rich Snebold, Tom Snyder, Stanley M. Stein, Joyce Stump, Dick Swanson of Swanson Group, Ltd., W. Harrison Vail, Larry Werner, John Williams, WQED Multimedia, John Zanardelli, Tom Anderson, Tom Averill.

Special assistance has been given to me by Debbie Keener of Reed Smith Shaw & McClay, Joe Gordon, Beano Cook, Sally O'Leary, Dan Hart, Jim Trdinich, Doug Huff, Kevin Evanto, Gigi Saladna, Mark Fisher, Celeste M. Welch, Dave Lockett, E.J. Borghetti, David Arrigo, Beth Ann

Conway, Burt Lauten and Rodgers Freyvogel of Pittsburgh Steelers, and Bill Keenist of Detroit Lions.

Special thanks goes to my friends Joan and Tom Bigley, Kelly Bird, Rocky Bleier, Rudy Celigoi, Jack Chivers, Rich Corson, Carl A. Dozzi, Jim Duratz, Dan Frank, Terrence G. Hammons, Jr., Dr. Haywood A. Haser, Harvey, Darrell Hess, Bill Haines, Baldo Iorio, Joe Landolina, Dick LeBeau, Joseph Lohman, Glenna and Pete Mervosh, Maureen and Bob Milie, Valierie Milie, David O'Connor and John D. O'Connor & Son Funeral Home, Tom O'Malley, Jr., John Pelusi, Alex Pociask, Bill Priatko, Bob Shearer, Al Tarquinio, Albert Elovitz and Rudy Celigoi.

I was able to get started in self-publishing thanks to the interest and cooperation of Stanley Goldman of Geyer Printing and Ed Lutz of Cold-Comp Typesetting. Now my books are printed by RR Donnelley, with assistance from Jake Zoller, Bob Goodrick, Tom Frank and Trudy Simpson. The transition has been seamless.

This is the first book I have done without the assistance of Bruce McGough of Geyer Printing and then RR Donnelley Printing. He died in 2018.

I owe a debt of gratitude to Cathy Pawlowski and Denise Maiden of Cold-Comp Typographers, and Keith Maiden of Heeter Printing.

Proofreading was handled by Roberta Sarraf, Dallas Frey, Tom McGuire, George Morris, Pat Santelli, Ed Lyness and Jack Sega. They were outstanding.

Outstanding photography was provided by George Gojkovich, Bill Amatucci, Bill Fabus and the late Harry Homa of the Pittsburgh Steelers, and Al Herrmann Jr. and Robert Pavuchak of *The Pittsburgh Press*.

Writing this book reaffirmed my regard and respect for Franco Harris and Rocky Bleier and so many of their teammates and friends. Mel Blount, Mike Wagner, Randy Grossman, J.T. Thomas, John Banaszak and John Stallworth were especially helpful.

My basic support team is my wife of 52 years, Kathleen, and our daughters, Sarah and Rebecca. They make it all worthwhile.

479

Epilogue

D r. Joseph C. Maroon, one of the team doctors for the Pittsburgh Steelers, is an internationally-respected neurosurgeon and professor and vice-chairman of the Neurological Surgery Department at the University of Pittsburgh Medical Center (UPMC), an author and iron-man triathlete. He is familiar with Franco Harris and Rocky Bleier and offers these thoughts on them:

"Both rate the title of Good Guys. I was young and green when I first met them but they both showed me great respect. They were humble and quiet in their demeanor. They were never boastful or just about themselves.

"They were the ultimate in team players, a quality as important with a medical team during surgery as with sports. I'm pleased to call them friends. I respect them for all they do for our community.

"It's too bad we don't have more like them in today's environment. We have shared some special moments in our lives."

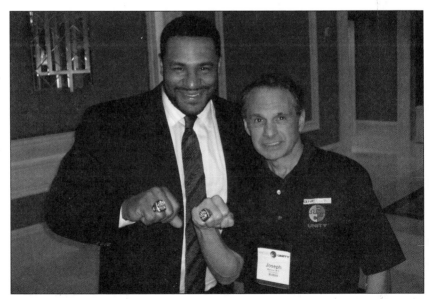

Jerome Bettis and Dr. Joseph C. Maroon. Two Steelers' stars.